Teamster
Rank
and
File

Teamster Rank and File

Power, Bureaucracy, and Rebellion at Work and in a Union

Samuel R. Friedman

COLUMBIA UNIVERSITY PRESS
New York   1982

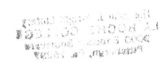

Library of Congress Cataloging in Publication Data

Friedman, Samuel R., 1942–
  Teamster rank and file.

  Bibliography: p.
  Includes index.
  1. Teamsters Local 208. 2. Teamsters for a
Democratic Union. 3. International Brotherhood
of Teamsters, Chauffeurs, Warehousemen, and
Helpers of America. I. Title.
HD6515.T32L735   1982 331.88′11388324′0979493
ISBN 0-231-05372-X   82-9510
ISBN 0-231-05373-8 (pbk.)   AACR2

Columbia University Press
New York   Guildford, Surrey

To Teamsters and other rank and file activists, in the hope that this book can help them in their struggles
and
To Judy, Cathy, Paula, and Joey, whose help and patience made it possible for me to write this book

Contents

Foreword by Douglas J. Allan and Peter J. Camarata   ix

Acknowledgments   xiii

Introduction   1

Part One: Background

Chapter 1: Bureaucratic Unionism   13

Chapter 2: Teamsters Local 208   34

Chapter 3: Drivers and Driving   45

Part Two: History of Struggle

Chapter 4: Rank-and-File Rebellion in the Late Fifties   59

Chapter 5: Rank and Filers in Office   92

Chapter 6: Changes in the Trucking Industry and
the Teamsters Union   116

Chapter 7: Apolitical Activism Ambushed: The 1970 Wildcat   136

Chapter 8: Trusteeship   169

Chapter 9: Militants Enchained   189

Chapter 10: Teamster Rank-and-File Organizes Nationwide   209

Chapter 11: Conclusion: The Many Meanings of Local 208   244

Appendix: Dates in Local 208 History   277

Notes   279

Bibliography   285

Index   291

Foreword

VIRTUALLY EVERY book coming out that talks about the Teamsters Union focuses almost exclusively on the gangsterism, the corruption, and misdeeds of the upper levels of the union bureaucracy. The two million rank and file drivers, dockworkers, warehousemen, production workers and public employees who make up the union are hardly mentioned at all or are viewed as poor, pathetic, powerless victims. (In the less academic mass media the view of the Teamsters is the even less sympathetic beer drinking, ignorant redneck.) Sam Friedman's new book, *Teamster Rank and File*, is a welcome departure from that total misconception of the Teamsters. His book focuses on how ordinary working Teamsters, in this case mostly truck drivers from Local 208 in Los Angeles, had the drive, the intelligence, and the courage to make substantial changes in their local union and in their relations with their employers. The book talks about how consistent rank and file activity changed one Local from an ineffective petty dictatorship that rolled over and played dead when confronted by the employers, to a democratic union that improved the conditions of its working members and forced the employers to respect the Teamsters' right to a safe and decent job.

This book focuses on a small but significant rebellion that took place in one Teamster Local in Los Angeles starting in the late 1950s. What makes that rebellion so significant is that it foreshadowed another larger and growing rebellion in the Teamster ranks that had its roots in the Teamster wildcat of 1970. Since 1970 we have seen a series of growing rank and file rebellions and organizations form and take hold on a national level, culminating in the development of Teamsters for a Democratic Union as a coherent and disciplined national movement. In this book, Sam Friedman gives an accurate and detailed history of these events both locally and nationally.

The Teamster's Union is now in its most serious crisis in history. But it is important to understand that it is *not* a crisis for the Roy Williams, the Provenzanos, the Pressers or the thousands of lower full-time union officials who make their living off the Teamsters Union. The union is not on the verge of bankruptcy from losing much of its membership nor is it in any serious danger from government attacks centering around corruption. The crisis in the Teamsters is among the working members, because never in the history of the union have the real wages and working conditions of the members gone downhill so rapidly. And from the rank and file's point of view preserving and upgrading conditions at work is what the union is all about.

The Freight Industry (i.e., the common carrier trucking companies) used to be the heart of the union and of the transportation system in this country. In 1976 450,000 workers were employed in this section of the industry and they moved 70 percent of the industrial products of the U.S. These workers had the best contracts and conditions in the union and their contracts were the model for the rest of the trucking industry, and a pattern agreement that even other unions followed. But all this is no longer true. Now, despite a greater percentage of total goods moving by truck, fewer than 200,000 Teamsters work under the Freight Agreement. And even this figure is continuing to drop sharply. Now most of these 250,000 "lost" jobs still exist and most are still Teamsters, but they are increasingly covered by local sweetheart agreements with the workers sometimes making as little as half as much as before this crisis. But this battle over working conditions is not yet finished: who will win, the employers or the rank and file, rests in the hands of the rank and file. Their collective effort could make the difference.

The 1981 IBT Convention proves that the officials of the union aren't going to challenge the employers. They didn't even care to address the issues at hand. This includes "reformers" who have won office on a reform program across North America. The defense of the rank and file thus depends on our own actions.

It should be made clear that we reserve the right to disagree with some of the conclusions Sam draws from the analysis of the crisis in the Union. However, as stated above, his historical account is well worth reading and the method of analysis is useful. We both agree that analyzing our actions has been key to the limited success we have had at building the rank and file movement in the Teamsters.

We also suggest that rank and filers save till the end Chapter 1. They are important but may make more sense after the historical accounts are read.

Sam, we thank you for your efforts and are grateful that you found our struggles worth writing about.

For the Rank and File

Douglas J. Allan
Teamsters Local #208
Co-Chair International T.D.U.

Peter J. Camarata
Teamsters Local #299
Co-Chair International T.D.U.

Acknowledgments

IN WRITING this book, I piled up hundreds of debts. Sam Farber and Judy Friedman were constant advisers, critics, and friends whose support was totally essential to my being able to understand the matters discussed in this book and to my being able to write it intelligently.

My greatest debts go to the many Teamsters whose assistance made the book possible. It is impossible to list them all—in part because being listed might expose some of them to reprisals. Among those I can name, my greatest debts are owed to George Alexander, Doug Allan, John Franklin, Alex Maheras, Archie Murrietta, Pat Patton, Ray Smith, and John T. Williams of Local 208; and to Peter Camarata, Sharon Cotrell, Frank Greco, Steven Kindred, Joe Naback, Lou Nikolaides, and Duncan West of TDU. Other TDU members whose help was essential included Howard Cohen, Rob Fram, Mary Ann Meany, and David Wolfinsohn. Among 208 members past and present, Bob Amy, Ed Blackmarr, Charlie Brenner, Benny Brown, John Butler, Pete Carrillo, Ples Clark, Eddie Dietrich, Peter Graves, Jim Henderson, Jack Higham, David Kamins, Mannie Labastida, Bob Lopez, Eddie McKiernan, George Minnehan, Pat Sabriuski, Bob San Soucie, Felix Santoro, Harrell Schultz, Vance Scott, Andy Soto, James Speceiro, Mauricio Terrazas, Lyle Tingler, Carlos Valdez, and Bill Weber were of great assistance. There were several other 208 and TDU members who were extremely helpful whose names I have omitted at their request or because I thought mention might embarrass them. Jerry Scott was kind enough to let me accompany him while he did his duty as a Business Agent of Local 235. Paul Blinco, a higher Teamster official, was also helpful. Jerry Lundberg and John Manser were helpful in giving me managerial viewpoints on 208 and on trucking. The New Jersey Motor Truck Association made documents available to me.

Rank-and-file activists in other unions or industries helped me to understand these struggles. These include Carl, a steelworker; Kathy; Donna; Frances, Stewart, Susan, and Jack, all in auto; and Larry and Artie, in warehouse.

Many other people helped me whose fields are in academics or politics. Unfortunately, I did not keep good records, so I apologize to those I leave out. However, I gratefully acknowledge the aid of Daniel Anker, Stanley Aronowitz, Sandy Boyer, Johanna Brenner, Robert Brenner, Muriel Cantor, Barbara Chasin, Norma Chinchilla, Nancy DiTomaso, Robert Emerson, David Epstein, Lynda Ann Ewen, Richard Franke, Oscar Grusky, John Horton, Jan Houbolt, Wells Keddie, William Kornblum, Kenneth Kusterer, Dick Logan, Bonnie McCay, John McDermott, George Martin, Paul Nyden, Phil Nyden, Martin Oppenheimer, Mel Pollner, Roberta Spalter-Roth, Warren Ten Houten, Stan Weir, Robert Windrem, Julia Wrigley, Michael Yarrow, Craig Zabala, Barbara Zeluck, and Steve Zeluck.

The editorial assistance and organizational advice of Paula Friedman was absolutely invaluable.

My editors at Columbia University Press, John Moore, Charles Webel, and Leslie Bialler have helped me greatly.

The University of California at Los Angeles aided me with a Faculty Research grant. Montclair State College gave me a Released Time for Research Award.

The manuscript went through several drafts. A number of different typists thus worked on it. These included Deanna S. London, Doris Mier, and Ida White. Florence Dinerstein helped proofread the galleys.

Teamster
Rank
and
File

Introduction

FOR THE modern American intellectual—from television screenwriter to university professor—workers often serve as objects for the creation of myths. Fears, hopes, and pities are projected onto workers, and embodied in stereotypes that reflect more the personalities of the myth-makers than the realities of workers.

In the 1970s, two such myths prevailed: The Archie Bunker myth, which portrays at least white male workers as bigots, reactionaries, and dolts, and the "eternal victim" myth, which sees workers as helpless victims of implacable forces that damage their lives. Examples of this view are the U.S. Department of HEW Report on *Work in America* (1973) and Harry Braverman's *Labor and Monopoly Capital* (1974).*

A less widespread myth was the vision held by some—but not all—Marxists. For them, workers were indeed victims—but so angry that they would revolt the moment the proper leadership could be given.

For the intellectual, unions, too, are a focus for myth-making. On the one hand, you have the view expressed in the films *On the Waterfront* and *Blue Collar*—unions are corrupt, and are a major problem rather than in any way the solution for workers. On the other, there is the view found in official union histories of any of the unions, or in the writings of their spokespersons, such as Patricia Cayo Sexton and Brendan Sexton, who in *Blue Collars and Hard Hats* (1971) depict unions as the workers' saviors, doing their best to defend them in a hard and never-ending battle. Marxists differ widely in their views of unions:

---

* Citations of other published work will usually give the author's name, the date of publication and, where relevant, the page numbers. The full citation appears in the Bibliography. Source notes appear, in numerical order, at the back of the book; substantive footnotes appear at the bottom of the relevant page.

some see them as "the enemy," some see them as heroic warriors, and some share the views expressed in chapter 1 of this book.

I shall look at the realities of workers and unions. I shall not do this by searching for the "average"—a meaningless concept since workers, at least, are extraordinarily diverse at this time. Nor do I try to describe some range of types of workers. Instead, I have examined one, unusually successful, group of workers—those of Teamsters Local 208—as they have tried over the last generation to make a decent union and a decent life for themselves. My book, then, by eschewing myths, aims to discover workers' actual *potential,* and the obstacles to its realization. I look at a group of ordinary truck drivers as they developed new capabilities, transformed themselves from victims to heroes, and created one of the most democratic and militant locals in any union in the country.

Thus, I draw out the universal aspects of a particular experience—and develop ideas about what workers *can* do, and *can* become—if they choose to do so. It discusses opposition workers face, from both employers and union leaders. Since this opposition leads to lasting conflict, it also discusses the power dynamics involved in building a rank-and-file movement against such opposition, and the strategies and tactics developed by the various actors in the battles around Local 208. The book also deals with a developing national opposition group—Teamsters for a Democratic Union—and how this has affected 208.

The Teamsters Union as Context

It is startling that the members of 208 could build an extraordinary Local in the very same union that has been the focus of nationwide scandal as the most corrupt, most gangster-ridden, and most undemocratic large union in the United States and Canada. The International Brotherhood of Teamsters, Chauffeurs, Warehousemen, and Helpers of America (IBT, or Teamsters, for short) was the major target of Congressional hearings into union corruption in the 1950s. As a result, its President at that time, Dave Beck, and his successor, Jimmy Hoffa, both went to prison. IBT pension funds are notorious bankrollers of organized crime. Numerous opposition candidates in local Teamster union elections have been beaten, or even murdered. Further, when Jimmy Hoffa was released from prison and started organizing support to regain the Presidency of the IBT from Frank Fitzsimmons, Hoffa disappeared, and is universally considered to have been murdered. On another level, the IBT added to its notoriety in the early 1970s by siding with California growers in their attempts to crush the United Farmworkers Union, led by Cesar Chavez. However, the Teamsters Union is not just a gangland mob. It is a union, and the shape of this union affected what happened in 208.

The IBT is huge, with over 2 million members. Local 208 is only one of about 800 Teamster locals. Trucking and warehousing are the core jurisdictions of the union, but it has also organized cannery workers, teachers, police, airline attendants, and a host of workers in other occupations. The Teamsters are therefore powerful, and could use their power to transform the social and political climate of America. Business depends on the movement of freight, and it is precisely freight which is the core jurisdiction of the IBT. After all, a commodity is of no profit if it cannot get to market, and, indeed, most commodities cannot even be produced unless supplies are trucked into the factory. While some freight moves by ship or train, in most cases it then needs a truck to move to its final destination from the port or station. Further, when other workers strike, support by the Teamsters often brings victory, but if the Teamsters cross the picket line, the strike is prolonged and often defeated.

This economic power has been the basis for the growth of the IBT into the largest union in the United States. Even though IBT officials have seldom made full use of the drivers' bargaining power, the union has changed truck drivers from a low-paid group of workers to a relatively highly paid group. Used in behalf of rank-and-file power and in behalf of the interests of workers, the Teamsters' potential power could turn the tide against bureaucratization in other unions and could make possible the successful unionization of millions of workers. Used in behalf of struggles for social liberation, Teamster power could also win enormous victories—how long could a racist employer hold out against the Teamsters' refusal to deliver or pick up goods?

Unfortunately, the IBT rarely uses its power in behalf of workers. Instead, Teamster officials attempt to crush the organization and activity of any rank and filers who try to defend themselves against their employers. Further, the union officialdom denies the right of the rank and file to a voice in union affairs. Since 1961, for example, the IBT Constitution has stated that almost all delegates to the conventions that make Teamster policy and elect officers of the International must be the regular officers and business agents of the local unions, rather than elected delegates. This makes it very rare for a working Teamster to become a delegate, since most officers are salaried and hold no other jobs.

Many instances of pro-employer actions by Teamster officials will be discussed in the context of Local 208. For example, we shall look in detail at how the IBT bureaucracy has bargained away key clauses in the national labor contract in freight—the Master Freight Agreement (MFA). The MFA once gave drivers the right to strike every nine months to protect themselves, and the right to take employers' warning letters to grievance proceedings so the workers would not have these threats hanging over their heads; but the IBT officials gave these rights away in negotiations. Now, the MFA even lets companies transfer operations from terminal to terminal in order to "whipsaw"' tough Locals into complying with management demands and to get high-seniority, high-benefits workers off the payrolls. This is done by threatening to transfer work into terminals where the local unions agree to employers' wishes, with resultant job loss for workers in the tough Locals. The IBT officialdom, as we shall see, frequently uses trusteeships to keep the membership in line by taking over direct rule of Locals that do not go along with its policies. And we shall see that, even in freight, the officials have failed to protect the membership against speedup, surveillance, inflation, injury, and layoff; members who are not in freight get even less.

There are exceptions to Teamster failures, of course. Some locals are democratic; some are effective in defending their members' interests; some are both. But such locals are always under the threat of trusteeship. In most cases, they also have to cope with contracts negotiated by the International.

One result of the failure of the IBT officials is reported in an official Teamster newspaper, the *Southern California Teamster,* on July 23, 1975. It cites California Division of Industrial Relations data that show employees in the California trucking industry "are injured more often, sustain more serious injuries and spend more time recuperating than all other workers."

Indeed, the members of the most powerful union in California have *not* been protected against unsafe working conditions. One in ten of them "suffered job injuries or illnesses severe enough to cause days away from work or days of restricted activity" in 1973. "Lost-time injuries in the industry have been rising, up 30 percent between 1964 and 1973, while employment grew by only 24 percent." Nationally, over 1,000 truck drivers died in accidents involving heavy-duty trucks in 1979—an increase of 52 percent since 1975 (*Convoy Dispatch,* "Washington Wire," March 1981, p. 3).

This, then, is the International Brotherhood of Teamsters, in which 208 tried to build decent and effective unionism.

A Brief History of Local 208

At any given time, Local 208 has from 5,000 to 6,000 members, mostly truck drivers involved in moving freight around the Los Angeles region. Its members have had a stormy history during the last thirty years. In the midst of the Great American Celebration of the 1950s, they organized a small-scale social movement to overturn their corrupt and ineffective local union officers in order to be able to bring their united power to bear on their employers through militant actions. They succeeded—which in itself is highly unusual—and then broke from the usual union pattern by not drifting back into routinized ineffectuality. Instead, they increased the democracy of the local, actively involved more and more drivers in its affairs, and used the resulting power to force the trucking companies to provide better working conditions, more job security, and above all, more respect. Some of the activists in the local became activists in, and leaders of, the social movements of the 1960s.

The employers—and the higher officials of the Teamsters Union—were not at all happy with the direction 208 was taking. On the other hand, there was little they could do without risking an even more massive revolt. For years, then, they had to content themselves with limiting the democracy of 208 to that one Local, preventing, as well as they could, 208 activists from reaching out to Teamsters in other Locals.

In 1970, the year of the climax of the antiwar and student movements, and of the ebbing of the black movement, they saw at last a chance to smash 208. A brief national wildcat strike over the terms of the nationwide freight contract was ambushed in Los Angeles. The employers fired all who took part in the city—something like 15,000 people, members of Local 208 along with members of several other Locals in the Los Angeles area. In a dramatic and soul-searing strike, in which the strains were so great that marriages were torn asunder, houses repossessed, and reputations smashed and built, the rank-and-file workers forced the employers and the union officials to cancel almost all these firings. However, the effort exhausted them, and left them unable to respond militantly enough when the President of the International Brotherhood of Teamsters (and crony of President Nixon and of the Mob) Frank Fitzsimmons put 208 into trusteeship a few months later. That is, Fitzsimmons fired their elected officers and replaced them with an administrator with dictatorial powers—who let the companies attack the gains the 208 members had won over years of struggle.

The drivers resisted (and suffered far less than anyone would expect) and got rid of the trusteeship in under two years. They elected new officers, fully anticipating that the new leaders would bring back the glory days of the local—only to find that, instead, the new officers carried out a policy of honest but nonmilitant unionism that let the International and the companies slowly squeeze the life out of the Local and continue to attack the drivers at work.

At this time, then, the history of 208 merges with that of the Teamster rank and file in general, and in particular with the efforts of Teamsters for a Democratic Union to create a social movement among Teamsters all over the country—a struggle that in many ways resembles that of Local 208 in the 1950s.

Studying
a Rank-and-File
Local

The first stages in studying a group are to hear about it and then to set up contact with it. In my case, this came about in 1970 when wildcatting Los Angeles Teamsters, finding their enemies more powerful than expected, asked striking students from local colleges to help, and I was among a number of teachers who joined the effort. A lasting tie was forged between rank-and-file Teamster militants and university-based activists. Specifically, a few university activists set up a newspaper, *Picket Line,* to publicize the struggles of rank-and-file workers in Los Angeles and to help groups of workers come together. While I worked on *Picket Line,* I had at first little contact with 208, focusing instead on the Steelworkers Union and on the American Federation of State, County and Municipal Employees (AFSCME). However, after two years, *Picket Line* collapsed, and I decided that a full-scale study of 208 would benefit the rank-and-file movement in both the IBT and other unions. I approached the officers of Local 208, and asked if such a study would be acceptable. They themselves agreed, and I was presented first to a stewards' meeting and then to a full membership meeting, both of which approved the project. Their discussion was full and complete, so that the rank-and-file approval of my study was a conscious one, based on a reasonably accurate picture of who I am and why I wanted to do the study.

For well over a year, I actively studied 208, receiving cooperation from rank and filers and officers alike. I went to its monthly membership meetings, its monthly stewards' meetings, and its monthly executive board meetings to see what business each dealt with, what were considered important issues, how items were discussed, and what were the nature of disagreements and politics within the Local. I spent 14 days being driven around by business agents and Local officers, seeing how they conducted day-to-day dealings with management and how they related to rank-and-file members and to stewards. As we traveled, I discussed with them many facets of unions as well as their thoughts and beliefs. I attended grievance hearings and an arbitration of a deadlocked grievance. I went to meetings of a rank-and-file group that was running a 208 Business Agent for the presidency of Southern California Teamsters Joint Council 42, and took part in working sessions where mailings were sent and leaflets written in behalf of this candidacy.

I interviewed officers, business agents, stewards, and rank and filers of various degrees of activeness and varying views on union and sociopolitical affairs. I researched the history of the Local through documents and through interviews with past and present members. I talked with managers of trucking companies to get their views of the Local and to discover their problems. I interviewed members of other Locals, particularly rank-and-file activists. I also spent a day traveling around with a business agent from another Teamsters Local.

I observed what happened when 208 organized the workers at a trucking company. As the process of organizing went along, I had numerous conversations with these workers, and learned their hopes and their fears—and how they interpreted the actions of 208 officials involved in the campaign. Later, I observed—and helped—a strike which developed when this company's owner went back on a previous offer, and talked at length with the strikers and with other 208 members who came by to help.

In writing this book, I have discussed its contents with officers and rank-and-file members of 208, and have shown them drafts for their comments and suggestions. Such a book is nonetheless necessarily incomplete. At any given time, there are over 5,000 members of 208, and I have talked with only a few hundred of them. Inevitably, too, I talked more with the active members. At one point, I tried to systematize my findings by writing and passing out a questionnaire to all the drivers at selected barns; however, too few of the questionnaires were returned for this method to work. Also, I talked often with business agents and officers of the Local, both because they are crucial to understanding the Local's dynamics and because in 208 the officials are men who were central to the rank-and-file movement that took over the Local in the early 1960s. To some, this may make the book seem to give too much attention to the officers and too little to the rank and file, and indeed, there were times when I found myself slipping into the perspective of 208's officials. Yet, such a shift in perspective was in some ways beneficial, since it helped me to understand the officials' views and thus to see their fundamental inadequacy in regard to the most basic problems facing truck drivers.

After I moved to New Jersey, I kept in touch with events in 208 by letters, phone calls, and tapes, as well as by a trip back to Los Angeles. In addition, I received the *Southern California Teamster* (the official Joint Council newspaper) and the rank-and-file *Grapevine* when it began to come out.

In 1975, when two national rank-and-file Teamster groups, Teamsters for a Decent Contract (TDC—oriented to the Master Freight Agreement negotiations) and UPSurge (composed of United Parcel Service workers), formed, I worked with Teamster activists in New Jersey and New York in their efforts to build local TDC and UPSurge groups and their later efforts in Teamsters for a Democratic Union (which developed out of TDC). Of course, as an outsider, I could help only in limited ways, although the stories I told about 208 and its activists' strategies proved useful. Through this participation, I developed yet further understanding of the dynamics of Teamster unionism.

The chapter on TDU is based on my observations in New Jersey, discussions with national TDU and UPSurge leaders, and discussions with Los Angeles TDU activists, many of whom belong to Local 208. In addition, I had access to TDU and other rank-and-file newspapers and leaflets, and to various other documents. My own experiences as a rank-and-file activist in the American Federation of Teachers also helped me to understand 208.

Finally, if my study has succeeded, it is only because, in addition to the above, I had constant contact with socialists who are activist members of the IBT and who helped me with advice and suggestions. Their breadth of experience and knowledge has given a much wider viewpoint to my analysis of 208 than would otherwise have been possible. This is important. Many of the problems which 208 members face come from the isolation which the IBT bureaucracy tries to maintain between Teamsters of different locals and between Teamsters and other workers; for me, as for them, such isolation can be broken only by establishing broad ties among activists from many different locals, unions, and parts of the country—and this is one of the main tasks of socialists. Without their contributions, this book would be far weaker, as would the rank-and-file movement.

The Structure
of this Book

Chapter 1 deals with union bureaucracy, since the bureaucratic nature of the Teamsters provides the context in which Local 208 developed. In chapters 2 and 3, I give an overview of Local 208 and discuss what truck drivers do at work. These chapters also introduce the reader to terms such as "yard" and "barn" (which are simply two ways to refer to trucking terminals) and to the formal structure of Teamster locals. Chapters 4 and 5 tell how the rank and file took power in 208, and how they used this power. Chapter 6 discusses how changes in the freight industry provoked changes in the Teamsters Union that undercut the basis for 208's particular brand of rank-and-file unionism. This led to a long and bitter wildcat strike and then to seizure of the Local by the International—as is discussed in chapters 7 and 8. After this trusteeship, 208 settled into an honest, democratic, but nonactivist mode of unionism, which threatens to undercut the bases of the Local's democracy (chapter 9).

Since 1975, Teamster activists have organized a national rank-and-file group, Teamsters for a Democratic Union (TDU). Chapter 10 discusses how TDU formed, the problems it has faced, and its achievements, both nationally and in Los Angeles. It ends with a discussion of what TDU means for 208. In the last chapter, I discuss the implications of 208 and TDU for workers' activism; for social theory; and for American politics. Some readers, particularly those with a primary interest in social theory, may want to read this chapter *before* reading about Local 208.

Part 1

Background

Chapter 1

Bureaucratic
Unionism

MUCH OF what is interesting about Local 208 contrasts starkly with American unionism in general: 208 is democratic, alive, and effective; most American unions are relatively undemocratic, stultified, rigid, and ineffective.

In order to understand the obstacles 208 has faced in building and maintaining its brand of unionism, we must consider the forces that render most unionism bureaucratic and discover the history of how the labor revolt of the 1930s was tamed and bureaucratized. We shall look at the legal framework, and see how Federal labor laws smother union activities in legalism, insulate the bureaucracy from rank-and-file unrest, and push the unions toward contract-centered approaches. Contractual unionism is a cause and sustainer of bureaucratization: long-term legally binding contracts with no-strike clauses convert union officials into policemen who disorganize the rank and file and push them to resolve all issues through grievance procedures and contract negotiations. As a result, unions become grievance-processing machines in which workers themselves retain little power and in which officials become the sole source of initiative and defense; this, in turn, causes lower-ranking officials to become legalistic, depending upon higher-ranking officials for aid, which puts weapons in the hands of the higher officials while convincing them of their superior wisdom. The contract-bargaining process reinforces all these tendencies, and also leads officials to monopolize power in their own hands out of fear for the consequences for the union if negotiations are bungled.

The institutionalization of the bureaucracy is supported by the officials' own experience. Higher officers spend many years as officials, during which they are isolated from the dangers and frustrations of the workplace and during which their main social contacts outside the bureaucracy are with high-status employers, government officials, and professionals. Further, their very successes in winning gains for the workers lead them into self-satisfaction and paternalism toward the rank and file. Finally, the effects of their experience are reinforced by a system of ideas that has grown up—business unionism—which functions as an "official doctrine" that justifies their actions to themselves, the public, and the rank and file. (The term "official doctrine" is from Selznick 1969.)

This model is by no means universally accepted, and I present here no serious discussion of alternative views. Some analysts argue that union leaders do a good job, and are reasonably democratic.[1] Others argue that the problem with unions is not their bureaucratization, but that their very nature forces them to act against the interests of workers.[2] Further, the theory of labor bureaucracy is hardly my own invention. Many have written similar analyses.[3]

Finally, in describing the forces that tend to bureaucratize unions, I am *not* arguing that they must succeed in doing so, or that bureaucracy is unavoidable. These tendencies are strong, but they alone do not determine the outcome. Workers themselves can affect what happens, and can prevent or roll back bureaucratization. Indeed, Local 208 is of interest precisely because it shows that this can be done, and gives us insight into what happens in the process; and TDU (discussed in chapter 10) is a promising attempt to eliminate bureaucracy from the Teamsters altogether.

Union Bureaucracy— The Historical Setting

Most major unions in the United States were formed or reshaped during the Depression of the 1930s. The United Auto Workers was born in the sit-down strikes of the late 1930s; the Steelworkers also grew out of this period, although with less rank-and-file involvement. The Teamsters Union itself, while it existed for many years before the great crash, was reshaped into a powerful industrial union after the 1934 Minneapolis strikes, led by revolutionary socialists, showed that freight workers could fight for unions and win.

Those were days when union leaders fought employers—if for no other reason than because employers were constantly trying to destroy and weaken the unions. Furthermore, in most unions, the rank and file were militant and aggressive, since the struggles for unionization taught them they had strength and gave them experience of how to organize themselves to wield that strength.

However, those days did not last. As the employers came to see that they could not break the unions, they learned how to tame them. Many union officers were glad to help in this. These officers longed to solidify their own rule; continued power of the ranks appeared as a threat to their continuance in office. Even more, they saw the militance of the ranks as a threat to the profits of the employers, and thus, they believed, to the return of prosperity. The best example of this approach was Clinton S. Golden and Harold J. Ruttenberg, high officers in the Steelworkers' Union, whose book, *The Dynamics of Industrial Democracy* (1942), is a powerfully written argument for cooperation between union officials and employers in the interests of increased production.

The Second World War greatly strengthened the tendency among union officers to surrender members' interests—and also weakened the capacity and will of the ranks to resist.[4] After all, the argument that workers should give up their right to strike for the duration of the war was a compelling one to all who supported an American victory. The companies used this period, and the unwillingness of the ranks to retaliate, to break the power of the ranks. They set up new work rules "in behalf of the war effort" that took away many gains won in the 1930s. They insisted that union stewards and officers enforce the contract upon their own members—thus making the stewards take on the role of disciplinarian in support of company interests. Top union officers were given posts on government committees set up to increase production, and there hobnobbed with corporate owners and cabinet members.

The union officials were, by and large, happy to go along with company demands that they discipline the workers, since they supported Roosevelt's foreign policy and accepted the logic that victory required workers to restrain from strikes. They pledged not to strike "for the duration," so almost all strikes during the war were wildcats—and many wildcats occurred. In 1944, 2,120,000 workers staged 4,956 strikes,—more of both than in 1937 when the sitdowns had established the CIO.[5] But in 1944, unlike 1937, union officials actively intervened to order strikers back to work under threat of expulsion from the union and discharge from the job. The result was to open a wide gulf between the officials and the ranks, and to change the composition of local union officeholders and even of stewards. Those who supported the ranks quit their positions in disgust, or were removed by their superiors. The remaining officers, and many stewards, learned how to restrain the rebelliousness of the ranks. Higher union officials would insist that they continue to do so after the war.

Even the long strikes over postwar contracts did not disturb this new bureaucratization. The employers made sure of this. They generally did not try to run struck plants, thus avoiding forcing the unions into mass picketing or sitdowns which might have let the ranks taste power again and weakened the officials' hold over the unions. Shortly thereafter, under pressure from employers, Congress passed the Taft-Hartley Act. Its main thrust was to reduce the ability of the rank and file to wage struggles on their own (at least, if they chose to obey the law), and to motivate union officialdom to keep the ranks in line.

Critical to the growth and solidification of the union bureaucracies' power over their memberships, and of their complacency toward their own approach to unionism, was the long period of relative prosperity from the end of the war until the late 1960s. During this period, corporate profits were high. This meant that relatively weak struggles or even merely the threat of a strike would often suffice to convince a company to raise wages and perhaps even set up a new fringe benefit. Further, any workers not satisfied with gains of this magnitude could be redbaited, with some success, since this was also a period of cold war—and the Communist Party had discredited itself among militant workers by its support of speedups during the war and by its defense of Russia.

Thus, the union bureaucracy had time to consolidate its power over the ranks; and the ranks were not pushed to rebel, for even if the union leaders usually gave away working conditions and collapsed before the speedups and the job losses of automation, at least those who kept their jobs could count on inching ahead financially every year.[6] And, those who lost their jobs (at least if they were white) would usually find a new job opening up before unemployment benefits ran dry. During this period, then, the bureaucracy became entrenched. In addition, in the Teamsters, the bureaucracy reorganized itself internally. It entered this period as a loose collection of regional bureaucratic baronies, but changed into a centralized bureaucracy by 1970. This is discussed in chapter 6. There were some real struggles by the rank-and-file against the bureaucracy and against the employers, but by and large they remained localized. Indeed, one of the best examples of such a struggle is that of the activists of Local 208.

However, the prosperity of the postwar period came to an end. The economy began to run into difficulties in the mid-1960s, and employers reacted with demands for greater worker productivity and with price increases. As a result, working conditions and jobs were under attack, injury rates increased, and workers could no longer count on a slow but sure increase in real income. Thus, their militancy increased, leading to a wave of strikes, both sanctioned and wildcat, in 1970. Meanwhile, the union bureaucracy at first responded to the new conditions by a business-as-usual approach—then moved to the right. Thus, the IBT under Fitzsimmons tried to smash the 1970 wildcat. When Nixon set up economic-control machinery a year later, union officials accepted positions on a Pay Board designed to hold workers' wages below the cost of living. Fitzsimmons, it should be added, stayed on long after other unions officials had been forced off the Board by the disgust of their ranks and their lower officialdom.

Other unions' officials were no noble knights, however. When auto workers at the Mack Avenue Chrysler plant wildcatted in 1973, the supposedly "progressive" UAW bureaucrats indeed mobilized. Over a thousand union officials got up early in the morning, went to the picket lines, and beat up strikers! (Serrin 1974:324–26; Weinberg n.d.)

Amid pious statements that "you can't kill the goose that lays the golden egg," top union leaders throughout the country told members to go along with the massive layoffs of 1974–1975, and to cooperate with company plans to increase productivity (and thus to reduce the number of workers needed to do the work). "Times are rough," intoned IBT officials who helped Great Lakes Express cut the hourly wage by 20 percent, and I. W. Abel of the Steelworkers agreed as he put "productivity commissions" into the contract along with a no-strike-even-at-contract-time clause. The unions had been built upon the rejection of precisely this logic during the 1930s—something not mentioned by the bureaucracy.

And there it is—the capsule history of the establishment of labor officialdom's power over the members, and of the pro-company uses to which this power has been put. Let us now consider some of the forces that have spurred on the growth of the bureaucracy as a force over, and opposed to, the rank-and-file worker.

Legal Framework for Bureaucracy

American labor law has grown out of the conflict between labor and employers. Its guiding principle is that every concession to labor is accompanied by clauses that allow or pressure unions to bureaucratize.[7]

The Wagner Act is the basis for labor law. It was passed in 1935, after mass strikes by Minneapolis Teamsters, West Coast Longshoremen, and Toledo Auto-Lite workers had made it clear that unions would be built either legally, or as quasi-revolutionary organizations. The Wagner Act, therefore, let unions be set up in a peaceful and orderly manner—which means that, if the employer obeys the law and bargains in good faith, the rank and file will not have to strike to establish their union, and thus will not discover their potential power. Instead, by setting up procedures through which a government agency certifies the union as the workers' sole bargaining agent, the law makes the government appear the source of workers' rights—and hides the true source in the power of workers to disrupt production or take other forms of direct action. Further, the Wagner Act sets up procedures that make it almost impossible for the rank and file to decertify a union for negotiating a poor contract or for failing to process grievances, which means that union officials can often safely sell out their members. Finally, the Wagner Act set up the National Labor Relations Board to decide disputes, and the NLRB, appointed by the President, is not noted for its support of the rank and file versus the wishes of the labor bureaucracy or employers.

The Wagner Act was amended once the upsurge of the 1930s had been curbed. The Taft-Hartley Act of 1947 lets employers sue unions for breach of contract. Thus, it puts financial pressure on union bureaucracies to make sure that members observe the contract and, in particular, obey no-strike clauses. The Act also lets union officials off the hook; when they oppose the action of the ranks, they can always claim they fear that lawsuits may bankrupt the union. Taft-Hartley also prohibits secondary boycotts, which means that effective class-wide support for a strike, through refusal to work for a company that handles scab goods, becomes illegal. For example, before Taft-Hartley, if a steel company were struck and an auto manufacturer used scab steel, it would have been legal for the strikers to ask Auto Workers locals to strike until their employer quit using scab steel products; this meant that a militant local could often win even against the will of the international union.

Today, winning a strike requires much more dependency on strike benefits and on other help from the international union, so that the ranks become more reliant on the bureaucracy. Taft-Hartley also prohibits mass picketing during a strike, which means that strikers, atomized at their homes, are unable to maintain as effective solidarity as they otherwise might, and that they do not discover the potential power of masses of strikers. Finally, Taft-Hartley prohibits Communists from holding union office and thus helps employers and union bureaucracies redbait activists more effectively.

Another law, the Landrum-Griffin Act, was passed in 1959, ostensibly to break up union corruption and to maintain union democracy. It has failed in both of these goals, partly because the Federal Government has only a very weak support for union democracy. Yet in many ways, Landrum-Griffin was a mistake from the point of view of the employers who lobbied for it, since it was based on the view that a few leaders were responsible for stirring up the rank and file, and that unions could thus be tamed by giving the ranks more say.

This view was quickly found to be an error. The "mistake" mattered little, however, since the law puts enforcement of its key sections in the hands of the Secretary of Labor, who almost always uses it to protect the interests of employers and union officialdom.[8] Landrum-Griffin also contained provisions further attacking the secondary boycott, and particularly attacking certain secondary boycott tactics that the Teamsters had been using.

It is not any one specific provision of these laws that has had the most effect. What is important is their tendency to smother union activity in a cloud of legalism. This is true both at the international level and all the way down to the local level. Union officials must constantly ask their lawyers if they can do what they want without a lawsuit. And they can always try to delay actions demanded by the rank and file through claiming that they must check with the lawyers first. The effect is to hand power to the officials and labor lawyers and to remove it from the rank and file.

Contractual Unionism and Bureaucratization

The tendency of union officialdom to put itself above the members is strengthened because they negotiate legally binding contracts.*

Almost every labor contract in America contains language that prohibits strikes during the duration of the contract. Some allow a few narrow exceptions, as in the case of deadly dangerous working conditions or, for example, in the Master Freight Agreement's allowance for strikes should an employer fail to

---

* It is worth keeping in mind that the United States and Canada are the *only* countries in the world with legally binding labor contracts, and that, when the British government decided to weaken the power of shop stewards and the rank and file in the British labor movement, it did so through laws aimed at pushing British unions into an American style of contractualism. In Britain, however, the pressure of the rank-and-file forced the unions to fight the Industrial Relations Act actively; after a number of major strikes, the law was largely crushed.

pay health and welfare premiums. No-strike clauses are, of course, of extreme value to management, since they promise stability of operations between negotiations. The effectiveness of the 24-hour wildcats used by Local 208 during the 1960s will show how important such stability can be. Further, a no-strike clause in a contract can be used by management to pressure union officials to police their members; the officials find themselves constantly telling workers that the union cannot let them strike or take other direct action to protect themselves. Thus, the legal justification for the IBT attack on the 1970 wildcat was that it violated such a no-strike clause. The employers fought very hard to get such language into contracts in the first place, and hang very tough to keep it in the contracts whenever it is challenged. For example, the Los Angeles trucking companies tried for years to gut the 24-hour strike clause. Also, the long 1978 coal strike was in large part a result of employer's insistence on strengthening the no-strike clause in the mine contract.

Even more than the no-strike clause, the grievance procedure has pushed unions toward further bureaucratization. Of course, the two are related, since the inability to strike legally requires some other way to resolve disputes over the meaning and application of a contract. Thus, every labor contract sets up one or another form of grievance procedure, and indeed the day-to-day functioning of most unions revolves around the processing of grievances. The results are profound. The power of the officials mushrooms, that of the ranks dissolves; among the officials, bureaucratization prospers and democracy is stifled.[9]

Grievances are handled by stewards and paid officials of the union, which means that solving problems is taken out of the hands of the workers and put in the hands of the union bureaucracy and company management. Thus, the rank and file fails to become actively involved in any fight with the employer; it becomes dependent on the bureaucracy to do its fighting; and rank-and-file workers come to have a legalistic, rather than combative, view of how to defend themselves.

The officials of a union thus come to see the grievance procedure as central to their activities, and to ignore the basis of the union's power in the workers' ability to disrupt production. Business agents, whose time is taken up with preparing cases for grieving and with trying to convince employers to give in before the grievance goes to higher stages of the procedure, become grievers rather than leaders. Higher-ranking union officials, meanwhile, spend much of their time and energy on dealing with those grievances that lower-level officials could not resolve. The most important cases tend to be settled at high levels of the grievance process, by high union officials and high company officials. This means that the union bureaucracy has a potent weapon with which to punish dissidents. An individual militant can be fired and his or her grievance deliberately lost, or a militant local can find itself constantly losing grievances.

In addition, the quasi-legalism of the grievance procedure reinforces the legal thicket imposed by the demands of labor law and thus helps to convert the entire officialdom to legalistic thinking and a reliance upon lawyers' advice. No longer do they think like leaders of combative workers and rely upon the organization and mobilization of the rank-and-file.

Finally, grievance procedures subtly corrode the bonds of trust needed by the ranks if they are to mobilize themselves successfully. They make lying a common thing in union affairs. After all, if one relies upon a grievance to retain one's job, and if events as they happened fall under contract language that lets the company fire one, what could be more natural than to lie about what happened—perhaps even to the steward and other union officials, and certainly when going through the grievance hearings? Indeed, in many instances, lying becomes vital for both the workers involved and the union. As an example, if a company catches key union activists in a contract violation and fires them, this can severely threaten the union's strength—particularly if other members will be intimidated away from activism. Under such circumstances, the most effective course of action is probably to strike the company or take other direct action to get the fired members' jobs back; but if the anti-action orientation of the international or the local prevents this, then it is necessary to go through the grievance procedure. So, one lies—and indeed, in such a circumstance, one has to lie. It can be justified in many ways, not least of which is simply the fact that management lies, too. However, the problem is that workers, unlike employers, are totally dependent upon solidarity and mutual trust for their power. And unfortunately, once lying to the employer is accepted as legitimate, it is very hard to stop.

After all, if one may lie to an employer, why should one not be able to lie to Fitzsimmons or some equivalent pro-employer bureaucrat who would use the truth to throw the local into trusteeship? And if one may lie to Fitzsimmons, why not to all his allies in the officialdom who will act as he does? And, if one may lie to them, who is to say that the head of one's own Local can be trusted any more? Or the business agent? Or the steward (who may be in the agent's pocket)? Or even those rank and filers who support the steward?

It should be emphasized that this analysis of the effect of the grievance procedure on trust is not an abstract and moralistic one. The problem, rather, is that a tactical necessity—lying so as not to be destroyed by the legalistic grievance procedure— creates a major strategic problem—that of preserving trust and solidarity among the rank and file when the active unionists among them have all learned to be expert liars. For example, at one planning meeting of the Williams Joint Council campaign (see chapter 9), one activist proposed lying to Hiring Hall drivers so that they would get angry and join in a demonstration the group was planning. Such proposals, even when rejected (as this one was), weaken solidarity.

Let us turn now to another process which strengthens the power of the officials over the ranks, and of the higher officials over the lower ones. This is the process of contract negotiations, and it both pushes the officials toward contempt for the rank and file and solidifies the power position of the bureaucracy.[10]

The logic of contract bargaining is that the union and the employer negotiate on the basis that, if agreement is not reached amicably, a strike or a lockout can develop. A mistake can hurt the union members and officials through loss of jobs, income, or working conditions. Thus, the union tries to coordinate activities in the bargaining unit—which, in the case of most major industries, means nationwide coordination—to put maximum pressure on the company while not giving it a chance to weaken the union's position. This requires considerable centralization of decision-making during negotiations. Further, in many cases, the interests of certain Locals or groups of workers are traded for gains for others, and this seems to require discipline within the union to let the bargain stick—at least, this is how it seems to management and to higher union officials. Further, union negotiators have developed a perspective that their major bargaining chip vis-à-vis the company is the offer of labor peace during the term of the contract, and thus that their credibility as bargainers requires that they observe all contracts to the letter.

The upshot is that the power of officialdom over the rank and file is increased to ensure the observance of contracts by the members and to give the leaders tactical flexibility during negotiations. In fact, this centralization is taken to extremes among the negotiators themselves. The major guideline of union negotiating tactics, as practiced in almost all unions in this country (and as taught in labor education centers as well),[11] is to have the chief negotiator do all the talking. Those members of negotiating committees elected by the rank and file, or chosen by participating locals, are supposed to channel ideas through the high official who heads the team, and to say nothing in front of management. Further, the key portion of negotiations, almost always occurring in the last few hours before the contract expires, is conducted by top union leaders and top management negotiators quite out of view of the negotiating committee. This practice is justified by the claim that the committee's presence inhibits free discussion and limits the willingness of negotiators on both sides to float trial balloons and to retract those that do not work out. But the real effect is to remove the negotiations from rank-and-file influence or observation. Indeed, the negotiating committee sometimes votes its approval without even knowing key provisions in the new contract. Thus, in the negotiations that ended the 1970 autoworkers' strike against General Motors, the committee had very little time to decide whether to accept the contract worked out between the management and the top union officials, which was reported to them by Leonard Woodcock, President of the UAW. The following description and quotations from two committee members make this clear:

It was time to vote—even though most negotiators had no real idea of many of the details of the contract. Neal Madsen: "Nobody had time to analyze it. I mean, what was catch-up pennies and what was make-up money. . . . There was too much to digest in too short a time. You've got to understand that everybody was tired." Astorga: "At the time they gave us the proposal, after going around the clock, they just laid it down there in loose papers. And no member of the committee knew exactly what we had, to be truthful . . . not even the people who told what we got—they were not certain either.'' (Serrin 1974:272)

Let it be clear: this method of negotiating, with power in the hands of the officialdom, talk funneled through the head of the union, and secret negotiations, harms the membership. Weaker contracts result, and in the long run the bureaucratization of the union is increased. Even in the short run, and even where the union official in charge of negotiations sincerely tries to win a good contract, this manner of negotiating hurts the members. I say this on the basis of two different sets of evidence and analysis. First, in my observations of Local 208, I observed a number of negotiations, both of contracts and of specific matters falling within the context of the Master Freight Agreement. In those negotiations in which the rank and file was not present, the terms reached were no better than one would expect. In those cases where the stewards were involved actively in the discussions (rather than by channeling their ideas through the chief negotiator), the results were considerably more successful; indeed, the stewards were able to win on demands that the chief negotiator urged be dropped as futile.

Second, there is an argument based on the very logic of negotiations. If the company hears only the chief negotiator, it hears one set of demands and determines its compromise from there. But if it also hears demands coming from rank-and-file negotiating committee members, it must see that the chief negotiator's demands are mild compared to those which will be made if the negotiating committee takes over the bargaining. This line of analysis also challenges the approach of the labor bureaucracy to the activities of the rank and file during negotiations. The officials always urge caution—stay at work and obey company orders. Above all, they say, do not strike until and unless we tell you to. In doing this, they throw away their best bargaining tools. For the mobilization and anger of the ranks is the real threat to the company, and it is precisely through rallies and scattered walkouts that the power, combativity, and determination of the workers is organized and is made visible to management and to government.

In short, it is such actions by the rank and file that can attain maximum concessions. The labor bureaucracy, however, tosses this weapon away—and, indeed, books such as Beeler and Kurshenbaum (1969) give detailed instructions to the bureaucracy's novices on how to ensure that the power of the ranks does *not* affect negotiations.

Where a group of officials voluntarily gives up its most effective weapons—and does so consistently, year after year and in union after union, while teaching newcomers to its ranks the same practices—there is more involved than incompetence. It adds up to the bureaucracy, as an institution, siding with the employers against the workers.

Union Bureaucracy— The Bureaucrats' Experience[12]

Let us consider the negotiation process from the viewpoint of a union official. There he or she is (but almost always he, given prevailing practices), arguing as an equal with corporate vice presidents or even presidents, or with the owner of a small company. In doing this, he learns about the details of company finances, and about the personalities of the company's officials—matters of which the members of the union are ignorant (and which he will only tell them in piecemeal ways to buttress his own arguments). Further, the outcome of the negotiations will vitally affect the lives of thousands of workers, and he is their spokesman, strategist, and tactician. They seem indeed to depend entirely on his abilities as a negotiator, on his ingenious ploys to wring new concessions from management. The result is predictable. When a settlement is reached—and particularly if it is reached without a major strike in which rank-and-file initiative becomes a factor—he looks upon it as his own. His wisdom, wiliness, and understanding of the opposition's weaknesses seem the key. The power of the rank and file—and the company's fear of that power had the negotiator's control over the ranks been shattered—is forgotten, even though it was the unseen presence that led the company to make concessions. Further, if the official sees the gains as his own victory, then what could be more natural than that he begin to look upon the rank and file as a bunch of ignorant workers who would be nothing were it not for his or her leadership?

In addition, negotiations often involve publicity and news conferences, discussions with high government officials, and public praise for the labor leader's statesmanship and responsibility whenever he makes a concession that will improve the profitability of the company.* This can rapidly lead to a swelled head. And yet, when the "statesman" presents the new contract for ratification, the ranks are not grateful. Indeed, they criticize many of the same provisions which the press and public officials have been praising as an important contribution to economic growth and the health of America. Faced with a choice between accepting the views of high officials who are praising his great leadership, and those of a group of ungrateful workers who do not know the "true facts" about the finances of the company and the industry and who have no education in the dynamics of the national economy, the labor leader almost always chooses to go with the views of the wealthy and powerful—and his contempt for the rank-and-file increases.

Furthermore, the union official exercises considerable authority within the union. Local leaders look up to him, obeying orders and taking advice. So do staff members, including those with considerable education. This buttresses the negotiator's self-image as a natural leader and statesman, and increases his dislike of any rank and filers who question his judgment.

The *interests* of labor bureaucrats have also come to differ from those of the rank and file, and in several ways. First, the job security of officials is greater when the ranks have less say in what the union does and pay less attention to union affairs. Thus, in many Locals where the ranks have no real voice or interest in the union, the Local's officials have held their jobs since the 1940s, whereas in Locals with more active and

---

* Pressures toward a sellout based on the leader's desire for prestige as a "statesman" have operated somewhat differently among the Teamsters. Hoffa's poor press notices were too overwhelming for him to have been motivated by the desire for prestige; rather, he was influenced by the other factors discussed in this chapter, and by the fear that if he got tough with employers the government would attack him even more. Fitzsimmons, on the other hand, has been obsessed with the desire to appear statesmanlike in order to gain respectability for himself and the rest of the Teamsters officialdom. Thus, he toadied up to Richard Nixon and refused to leave the Wage Control Board. The price was paid by Teamsters and, indeed, by all workers. In fact, I encountered even many conservative and bureaucratic officials in highly bureaucratized Los Angeles Locals who were sickened by the spectacle.

empowered ranks, leadership changes at least once or twice per decade.

For higher officials of unions, too—who tend to hold their jobs for a long time if they go along with the top leaders and do not make trouble—too much democracy can be bad for job security: they can be voted out of office, and so can their sponsors. Of course, the threat of democracy to the officials' jobs is greater to the extent that they abandon the needs of the membership at contract time, in grievance procedures, or in other ways.

In addition, the very working conditions of the bureaucracy are opposed to the interests of the ranks. After all, defending the members' interests takes much effort, even in routine matters, and when the economy is having a hard time, it is indeed difficult to work out effective strategies for fighting the employers and the government. Thus, in Local 208, the business agents often work from 4 A.M. to 8 P.M. or later, and the stewards' meetings keep the officials up until 11 P.M. or midnight. Higher officials who try to do a thorough job have to work endlessly. Thus, numerous observers were impressed by Hoffa's grueling schedule.[13]

Third (and in any book about the Teamsters, it is necessary to mention this) corruption is involved in the bureaucracy's opposition to rank-and-file interests. If employers offer bribes to union leaders, in return for concessions, these are sometimes accepted. The members' interests are thus sold out. There have been many well-publicized cases of high union officials in the Teamsters, and in other unions, making such deals. Similarly, pension funds are sometimes looted in behalf of the business interests of union officials. I should point out that I saw no indication of bribery of current 208 officials.

Job security, working conditions, and corruption, then, are among the ways in which the officials and the ranks have opposing interests. However, another conflict is even more important: the interests of the ranks require the officials to take risks in behalf of gains that do not benefit the officials. Salaried union officials all share one characteristic—they do not work at the same kinds of jobs the members do. Thus, the bureaucrats are not the ones who suffer from speedup, injury, layoff, heat, noise, pollution, and harrassment. The workers' interest in ending these ills is immediate, direct, and often urgent; that of the officialdom is at best second-hand, and thus much more subject to compromise or postponement. This divergence takes particularly strong form during the social and economic difficulties of the present era. During crisis periods, the bureaucracy is forced, by the employers' attacks upon the living and working conditions of the membership, to choose sides. The officials must decide whether to take up the weapons of class conflict to combat abuses they barely feel themselves. To do so means to strike and remain on strike in the face of abuse from employers, press, intellectuals, government officials, and others who have praised their statesmanship in the past; to confront Taft-Hartley injunctions, contempt of court citations, fines, and jailings; and to deplete the union's treasury and reduce officials' salaries in order to finance the strikes. By not doing so, they can avoid a confrontation by abandoning their members' interests amidst the acclaim of all elements of "respectable society."

The history of the labor movement in recent years has given eloquent testimony that the labor bureaucracy understands the thrust of *its* interests. The crisis of layoffs makes officials choose—ignore the contract and protect your members, or avoid a fight—and they choose to take junkets to Washington, testifying in behalf of Band-Aid remedies for a hemorrhage, while thousands of workers are laid off and the companies successfully attack working conditions and (in some instances) even pay scales.

At contract time, the leaders of the unions have to decide whether to fight for no-layoff clauses, for wage increases to keep up with the cost of living, for living-wage pensions, and for livable working conditions. But they choose to avoid that fight, and the mobilization of the rank-and-file needed to win, by settling cheap.

One might ask how they can live with themselves. After all, many of the high officials of the labor movement were themselves militants in their earlier years, and seem to have consciences even yet. Thus, the question is how can decent human beings sell out those they are supposed to defend, and think that in doing so they are doing good? Relatedly, how can the officials defend themselves with arguments that gain some support among the rank and file?

To answer, we need to examine the ideology of the labor bureaucracy. *We must look at the systems of ideas developed to justify and rationalize the bureaucracies' actions.*

Business Unionism—
The Ideology
of Bureaucratism[14]

Business unionism is the name usually given to the set of beliefs currently held by labor officialdom. Like any ideology, it has various versions, and thus the different groupings within the trade union leadership see their situation through slightly different perspectives. However, certain ideas are common to all forms of business unionist thought, and these ideas form the structure upon which the variants are built.

It is important to understand, too, that the rank and file tends to accept many of these beliefs, although very often the ranks show by their actions that their acceptance of the implications of business unionism is tentative and contradictory. This is to be expected, since business unionism is an ideology opposed to rank and filers' interests and serves to keep them passive in the face of their enemies.

What, then, is the content of business unionism? What is this set of beliefs that encourages labor officials to act so often against the interests of their own members?

First, business unionism holds that there exists a basic harmony of interest between employers and workers. Employers need workers to do the work, and workers need employers to provide jobs. Further, this harmony of interests is rooted in a capitalism that may not be perfect, but provides most workers with a decent life and a chance for advancement (for their kids, at least). Even further, the health of capitalism depends upon the employers' making solid profits so that they can reinvest and thus provide more jobs (and more products).

Business unionism adds that unions are needed, in this situation, to haggle with management over the terms of sale of labor; left to themselves, employers will not give workers a fair shake, but will pay the lowest wages they can, and beyond that, will set up abysmal working conditions. Unions are also needed to establish tolerably fair procedures in regard to firings and layoffs; in their absence, supervisors tend to act like dictators.

Unions also have a *political* role, as business unionism sees it. They lobby for such social legislation as minimum-wage laws; they also fight for narrow sectoral interests—as when the head of the UAW urges Congress to reduce anti-pollution laws so that auto manufacturers can earn profits and thus presumably increase employment, or as when Teamster officials argue for more restrictions on the railroads so that more freight will move by truck, or as when the head of the Steelworkers Union argues in favor of import duties so that Japanese and German workers will be laid off instead of American workers.

There is also a role for the worker in business unionism. What it is depends on the specific variant of business unionism under consideration; for instance, in the unusual form of business unionism adhered to by 208's leaders in the 1960s, the rank-and-file was to be very active and to have a significant voice in union affairs. However, by and large, business unionism sees the ranks as passive and as having little voice.*

An example of this appears in the view of the union expressed by Teamster officials. Sam Romer phrases it as follows:

Beck was a great admirer of the arts and science of big business. "I run this place just like business," he told an interviewer in 1938, "—just like the Standard Oil Company or the Northern Pacific Railway. Our business is selling labor. We use businesslike methods." A decade later, he reiterated this theme with significant overtones for a labor leader committed to the democratic process: "Unions are big business. Why should truck drivers and bottle washers be allowed to make big decisions affecting union policy? Would any corporation allow it?" (1962:35)

Hoffa made his view on this question clear in 1961, when he fought for—and obtained—the previously mentioned change in the Constitution of the IBT that allowed only elected officers

---

* Indeed, the thrust of business unionism is always to reduce the activity and influence of the rank and file, because an active and powerful rank and file will try to defend its interests, which will always threaten the profits of the employers. Thus, in the 1960s, even Blackmarr, then Secretary-Treasurer of 208, ended up restricting the possibilities for strategic discussion in Local 208 in order to keep the ranks under control.

and the business agents of most Locals to be delegates to Teamsters Union conventions.

The views of higher Teamster officials are also visible in their relationship to the relative democracy and activism of Local 208. Hoffa tried to push the Local into relatively nonactivist channels, while keeping it as an ally and threat to the potentially anti-Hoffa union bureaucrats of Southern California. Subsequently, Fitzsimmons and the higher officialdom of Joint Council 42 and of the Western Conference have approached the task of containing or smashing 208 somewhat differently. They have threatened to do away with the practice of letting Locals elect business agents, claiming that elected BAs are unable to keep the rank and file sufficiently passive. They have cooperated with employers in attacking the 24-hour strike clause. And they have thrown 208 into trusteeship as well.

Thus, business unionism views the union as an organization of professional unionists who haggle with management while cooperating with it to ensure that workers stay at the job and work productively, and business unionism views the rank and file as incompetent to manage their own affairs—and dangerous when they try to do so. Indeed, as Beck said in the above quotation, a business union *is* much like a business.

We should hardly be surprised, therefore, when union officialdom sells out the membership, or when it tramples on democracy in its constant efforts to render the rank and file powerless. If the health of the union depends on the employers' profits—and the officials' ideology tells them that it does—then, in hard times, the employers' demands for higher profits through lower real wages and higher productivity fall on ready soil. The union bureaucrats accept arguments, and spout forth plans, to hold down workers' wages relative to prices, and turn contract negotiations into legalized fleecings of the members in which the bureaucrats try to hold the members inactive while they get sheared. After all, in the tenets of business unionism, the officials should make the decisions since they are the professionals and the workers do not know their own best interests; and all that we have discussed, such as the officials' experiences in negotiations, the legal structure of labor relations in the U.S., and the interests of the labor bureaucracy, serve to strengthen the officials in their beliefs.

The Rank
and File

We have seen in this overview how union bureaucracy is an institutionalized force that acts to minimize the workers' activism and thus serves as a "shock absorber for capitalism." However, since competition forces employers to attack working conditions and pay levels, the bureaucratization of unions does not eliminate class struggle. Instead, workers are impelled to fight back. Often, rank-and-file workers do this by fighting to democratize their unions and to transform them into worker-run organizations through which they can defend their interests. Teamsters Local 208 was one of them. We shall turn now to its story, and see how its battles point to the development of a radical workers movement in the United States.

Chapter 2

Teamsters
Local 208

LOCAL 208 has over 5,000 members at more than 200 different workplaces, primarily trucking companies. Most members are truck drivers involved in carrying freight in the Los Angeles area, a situation which differs somewhat from that in other cities, where long-distance drivers and dockhands are members of the same Local as the local-freight drivers. Teamster Locals in Los Angeles, however, are organized by craft. Thus, dockhands and clerks are usually in Local 357, local drivers in 208, mechanics are in 495, road drivers in 224, and so on.

A Local with workers at many different companies needs stewards—union representatives among the workers at each workplace. In 208, usually one steward and one alternate are elected for every 40 drivers. Smaller barns have a steward and possibly an alternate. Others have more than the formula would give them, others less. Then, too, some stewards are lazy, others energetic. A steward's task in any Local has many parts. When a driver thinks the company has violated the contract, the steward upholds the union's point of view, going with the driver to argue with management. If the problem remains unresolved, the steward writes up a formal grievance, gives it to the business agent, and takes part in the formal grievance process that follows. The steward also takes part in all negotiations with management over specific applications of the contract to the steward's particular barn. Further, the steward acts as a message carrier between the union officials and the members, and presents the members' views to the officials. Stewards also act as leaders of the workers in discussing, or taking action to deal with, some new company policy. In Local 208, a stewards' council meets once a month to discuss particular grievances or the meaning of a particular clause in the contract, or to hear a speaker.

Local 208 has seven elected business agents (BAs). At the present time, the President of 208 is on salary and also acts as a business agent. BAs are the paid officials in charge of handling grievances, going to barns to talk problems over with management, helping stewards deal with hard problems, keeping stewards in touch with the Local's policies and activities, and so on. In Local 208, where the rank-and-file is not powerless and the officials are not in league with the companies, BAs do not get hefty salaries and expenses while doing little work. Instead, they often work from 4 A.M. to 8 P.M., handling an enormous array of discussions with rank and filers and stewards, meeting with management officials up to half a dozen times, investigating and deciding how to handle grievances, and assisting with such projects of the Local as its organizing drives or Blood Bank. Further, they attend formal grievance hearings to present the cases from the barns they are assigned to. The hearings for 208's grievances (which are the lion's share of Southern California grievances, since 208 does not back down on members rights) take about one week per month. For this work—and the pace is grueling—they were paid in 1975 about $18,000 each (plus a car allowance of about $2,000 and another $1,000 for expenses), less pay than a full-time driver with reasonably high seniority.

The top-ranking officer of the Local is the Secretary-Treasurer, a paid elective position. The Secretary-Treasurer is in charge of the BAs, the office staff, and the Local's affairs in general. He is called in on difficult negotiations, helps in grievances, maintains relations with other Teamsters Locals and with higher union officials, and sets much of the tone of the Local.

There are also an elected President, Vice-President, Recording Secretary, and three Trustees. The President chairs all meetings and presides over the affairs of the Local when the Secretary-Treasurer is away. He carries much influence in the Local, and works with the Secretary-Treasurer in determining policy. The other five officers are working truck drivers with various duties and leadership tasks; with the President and Secretary-Treasurer, they make up the Executive Board, which meets monthly and officially sets the Local's policies and approves expenditures. It also hears all charges brought against members, whether for acting in ways contrary to the duties of a member (such as "snitching" to management on another driver or crossing a picket line) or, simply, for failing to pay dues on time.

Democracy in 208

There is considerable democracy in Local 208. Members feel free to disagree with officers, both in small discussions and in open meetings. Beyond that, they feel free to organize for changes in the Local and to run for office without fear of being victimized—in 208, running for office does not involve the risk of being attacked by "goons" or of losing one's job. Indeed, even the breach between the few active supporters of the trusteeship of 1970–1972 and the bulk of the members has not seriously impaired this openness. Thus, one person who was a business agent under the trusteeship was later able to function quite ably and successfully as a steward in spite of the hostility of past disagreement. Another person, who had helped set up a rank-and-file opposition caucus to the trusteeship but then abandoned it when offered a BA's job by the trusteeship administrator, was nevertheless even elected to a BA job in the 1974 elections. Outright leftists speak at meetings, often get widespread support, and certainly do not seem to fear reprisals for their views. The members and officers of the Local are very proud of their democracy and openness.

One way to judge democracy in a union is through the relations between officials and members. In this respect, 208 is unusual; the officers and the BAs do not act like a separate order of human beings whom others should respect, nor are they treated as such. Also, BAs in 208 do not negotiate with management behind the members' backs. Thus, BAs always enter a company through the loading dock and ask drivers about their problems and grievances, about the general affairs of the Local, and about their families before going in to talk with management. They always take stewards with them too, so the working members will know what went on. After the conference, the BAs usually tell the drivers what happened with management. This is in contrast to most other Locals, where BAs enter and leave by the front door and confer with management alone, unless they want a steward present for a specific purpose. In many locals, a BA or steward who does not think a member has a winning grievance will refuse to process it; in 208, BAs and stewards will always process a grievance if a member insists upon it, sometimes winning what seemed hopeless cases.

One cause—and result—of 208's democracy is that a large number of members are actively involved in its affairs. Hundreds regularly come to meetings; hundreds serve as stewards and alternate stewards; hundreds actively discuss Local affairs. And even more members take active part in the affairs of the union at their own workplace. Even so, the activists are in a minority. But activism in 208 remains far greater than in most locals of any union—a state of affairs which keeps the Local healthy and effective.

Democracy in 208 also shows in its reliance on elections. Stewards are elected at their barns by co-workers, rather than appointed by Local officers as is true in many union Locals. Business Agents are elected by the membership as a whole—which is very rare in the Teamsters Union, where BAs are usually appointed. Thus, it is hard for the Secretary-Treasurer to build up a machine of supporters, since the BAs depend upon rank and filers' votes for their jobs, and thus must orient more to the membership than to the head officer. Elected officials also tend to be more diverse in outlook and approach than are appointed ones; thus, many minority viewpoints are represented among officialdom. In 208 there is genuine openness; members' views influence the actions of officials, who assume that every member has a right to hold and build support for his or her views. They consider officials to be their employees rather than their masters.

Local 208's experience contradicts the common belief that democracy in unionism is ineffective, and that placing power instead in the hands of full-time professional union leaders will improve the lot of workers. The Local has, by far, the best work situation in Southern California. Drivers in 208 are more secure in their jobs, are less often subjected to pettiness, and are able to take longer breaks than are those in other Locals. Further, many yard practices that are the envy of drivers elsewhere have been won by the Local; such patterns as the five-day, Monday–Friday week are absent in other Locals in the Los Angeles area. Indeed, many drivers who transfer to other, less democratic, area Locals want to return to 208 and its better working conditions.

Grievances and How They are Handled

The method of handling grievances is central to the way 208 officers and members regard their Local. Indeed, it is hard to overemphasize the importance to the drivers of grievance-handling. As an example, if one asks members what the Local was like in the 1950s before the rank-and-file movement took over, the most common response is that it failed to deal with grievances; if one asks what the rank-and-file victory meant, one is told that drivers won grievances and that the Local would back them up.

What, then, is a grievance? Any answer to that question tells much about the outlook of the answerer. The answer of a bureaucratic-minded official is that a member's grievance is a contract violation by management that the business agents agree to grieve through the formal system of hearing boards. Another answer—common in 208—is that a grievance is anything that can be interpreted as a contract violation and then put over on management as being such, whether by argument or by formal procedure or by threat. A third outlook sees grievances as "beefs"—that is, if management does something a member feels is wrong, that is a grievance regardless of its contractual status, and the test of a union is whether or not it can win such "beefs"; many in 208 hold to this view of grievance, and, indeed, the success of the Local in winning "beefs" made it stand out during the years before the trusteeship.

In fact, many people underestimate the importance of grievances. Actions by the company can deprive workers of their jobs, threaten their safety, keep from them overtime money rightfully theirs, or assign them to unpleasant work when seniority should entitle them to much better assignments. In such cases, the workers' only defense is to grieve the matter—whether through the formal procedure or through more active means. Indeed, often the main basis for workers' feelings toward their union is its success or failure in curbing the company on such issues.

The procedure by which grievances are handled is also important. Since it provides a legalistic way to try to solve such problems, it tends to take them out of the hands of the members and put them into the hands of stewards and business agents. The formal grievance procedure is enormously time-consuming, and puts most of the burden of defending members on the stewards and BAs. They prepare cases for presentation to a board composed equally of managers and Teamsters officials, who tend to view cases as legalistic interpretations of contract language. As a result, members' livelihoods and safety depend on the lawyer-like qualities of stewards and BAs rather than on their own actions or even on the leadership of their elected stewards and officials. The result is loss of active involvement in the affairs of the union, and a barracks-room lawyer approach to grievances.

The contractual grievance procedure begins when a worker makes a demand the company refuses to accept. The worker then takes the matter to the steward, who discusses it with management. If no agreement is reached then, or in later discussion in which the BA takes part, a formal grievance is filed. Such grievances, for Southern California, are heard monthly in quasi-judicial proceedings in a motel meeting room in Long Beach (thus, they are called Long Beach grievance hearings). Half of the grievance board consists of union officials from Locals not involved in the grievance in question, the other half of management representatives from companies not directly involved in the grievance. After the business agent, and other Local members involved, and the managers of the company have made their presentations, the grievance board goes into "Executive Session": it sends the parties to the dispute out of the room while it discusses the case and votes on it. If the case is deadlocked, it goes to San Francisco for the quarterly Joint Western grievance hearings. Cases not resolved in San Francisco (most are) are sent to national hearings, left open for either side to take direct action, or sent to arbitration. Needless to say, rank-and-file workers feel left out in the cold while this process goes through its paces.

Strategic
Discussion
or Muddling
Through

Unfortunately, the freight contract gets weakened every time it is renegotiated, and gets weakened even further as IBT officials and company managers on the hearing panels reinterpret its language. The International becomes more and more employer-oriented, the rank and file is sold out and, in addition, denied any voice in the affairs of the International.

The question is how to change this—but the question is discussed far less often than one would expect. In part, this happens because the grievance procedure keeps almost every active unionist too busy with the absolutely vital day-to-day problems to have the energy to tackle the longer-range problems; nine full-time officials of Local 208 spend scores of hours per week, and hundreds of stewards and rank-and-file activists use their spare time on grievance handling. Work, work, work—and problems get solved only to come up again the next day. Muddling through thus becomes so difficult that it prevents strategic discussion.

This lack of strategic discussion also comes from one basic approach of 208 members—and, indeed, of most unionists—to unionism. They see their problems in very *specific* terms rather than as needing a general solution. Thus, time after time, they discuss their problems in terms of a specific manager who is a slave-driver, or a given Joint Council officer who is rotten, or a particular new rule by management that is irrational and a "pain." From this perspective, of course, strategic discussion is of little value. After all, if the union's task is to solve each specific problem as it comes up, then the only issue is how to organize and what tactics to use in each case. Questions of strategy seem irrelevant. Meanwhile, a grievance procedure based on the view that problems are specific and not part of a general attack by the employer reinforces this narrow perspective. This perspective, however, greatly weakens Teamster members' attempts to come to grips with the very real unity of employers' plans to weaken drivers' strength and the equally real problem of the International's continued degeneration.

Finally, the lack of strategic discussion is, in part, intentional, and represents a blunting of the thrust of the rank-and-file movement that transformed 208 in the early 1960s. When the rank-and-file organized to take over the Local and obtain effective representation, they saw that they had to develop means to discuss the problems facing them. There were always unplanned discussions—often in coffee shops during workbreaks—but these involved only a few people at any given time and place. The members set up two major forms of more widely attended discussions—membership meetings and the steward's council. However, these did not work out as anticipated.

Membership meetings are usually amorphous affairs; all sorts of issues are raised from the floor, and most never really get discussed or decided. When a recognizedly important issue does get raised, the discussion is sometimes very thorough, and always uninhibited, but such an issue is normally of an immediate character. Longer-range issues are widely viewed as "too political"—and do indeed involve crucial political questions such as who wields what power for what ends, and how to organize the power of the Local's members to take on the International bureaucracy.

Such topics are shunned, for several reasons: they tend to divide the membership; they seem possible to postpone; they are risky; and they would require mass mobilization of the membership, even to the point where the Local's officers might not be able to control the results. Thus, there is a feeling among the rank and file, as well as among the officers, that such topics are dangerous or utopian—and, besides, there is always so much pressing business—so strategic issues do not get discussed.

The stewards' councils are subject to these same forces. In 208, the stewards tend to be among the more involved members, and often express their frustration at the undoing of their efforts by the International bureaucracy. Further, the Local's bylaws clearly state that the steward's council shall "set up and carry on programs designed to advance the Local in all matters of progress" (Article XIX, Section 11), indicating a desire that stewards deal with strategic issues. And yet, the officers of the Local have successfully restricted the agendas of the steward's council to the education of stewards in use of the grievance procedure and to other day-to-day topics and, until recently, have succeeded in keeping agenda-setting in their own hands. Thus, strategy is not discussed at steward's councils.

While strategic discussion could also develop around a Local 208 newspaper, a method proposed by a few leftish members of the Local during my study, the officers of the Local defeated this proposal for a number of reasons—including, again, the possibility that strategic discussion might "get out of hand" (see chapter 9).

Haunting Echoes

While democracy and activism in 208 were still strong when I observed the Local, I realized, in listening to drivers closely, that most of them viewed the days before the trusteeship as even better. Currently, they get good grievance representation through the formal procedure; then, they not only had formal representation but also were able to take direct action on problems with the backing of the Local. Now, they win if the contract says they are right and if the grievance committee agrees; then, they were able to win rights not in the contract. Now, the union serves as a grievance agency *for* them; then, it was often a matter of "doing it themselves" and winning, too. In short, everyone agreed that 208 was a good local but felt haunting echoes of an even better past.

Even in the period before the trusteeship, the freight contract was inadequate. Then, however, it was less of a problem than it is now, since 208 drivers were less restricted by it. Now, their rights are limited by what grievance panels say the contract means; then, they got what they were strong enough to win. Specifically, in the 1960s, the drivers at any given barn used strikes, or took such direct action as turning in trucks for every possible necessary repair, to win their demands. In such actions, they would be backed by the Local; usually, the BA would go in and negotiate for them while they continued their action, but sometimes the BA would "vanish" and so be unable to order them back to work. Such direct action worked. It solved the problems in a hurry, and in favor of the drivers. Beyond that, it led to high morale, to the view of the union as one's own, and so to a high level of interest and active involvement by the membership. It is precisely this rank-and-file activism which is missing from the legalistic, contractual approach of the post-trusteeship period.

The Good
and the Bad

Local 208, then, is a local with much to teach about unionism. But to learn from it requires that we exaggerate neither its bad points nor its good points. Local 208 does not offer the total answer to the problems facing Teamsters. Its enemies have been very powerful and very smart—too powerful to be overcome by any one local, and too smart to allow the apolitical activism of 208 to break the isolation of being only one Local. The drivers of 208 have won many victories, but many have since been eroded. Indeed, even one of the Local's crowning triumphs, the defeat of the trusteeship and the return to office of rank-and-file oriented activists, has suffered such erosion, and has even become a new sort of chain, through the transformation of the post-trusteeship leaders into contractual legalists.

Nevertheless, 208 shows many successes. A rank-and-file movement was able to come to power in the Local and to maintain an activist membership over a long period of time while preventing rebureaucratization. Further, 208 has improved the lives of thousands of drivers. And it has reintroduced the themes of solidarity and activism into the Los Angeles labor scene, and opposed the attempts by the IBT to violate these themes by siding with the growers against the Farmworkers. Whatever its failures, 208 still provides a core of activist unionists trying to work out new solutions to the drivers' problems; members have, for instance, been centrally involved in attempts to build Teamsters for a Democratic Union.

Thus, there are failures, and there are successes. In the context of American unionism of the last generation, even the failures of 208 are among the more successful actions of the labor movement; the successes point out a path for all. The basis of 208's successes has been the existence of a large number of rank-and-file members and stewards who are deeply involved in the day-to-day struggles in each barn and in the internal political life of the Local, within a context of democracy, rank-

and-file initiative, and activism. Historically, the sources of this activist core, and of the Local's democracy and openness, lie in the fight during the late 1950s to create a local that would truly protect and represent the membership, a fight that involved the creation of a powerful rank-and-file movement. Socially, the source of this activist core lies in the nature of local freight driving and the creation, by chance and by choice, of social clubs and other community-building networks. The shaping and actions of this activist core, and the democratic traditions and institutions built by these militants, provide the key to Local 208.

Chapter 3

Drivers
and Driving

TRUCK DRIVING has a lot in common with other work—it is a source of income, an activity that is sometimes dull, sometimes intolerable, and sometimes rewarding, and a source of new friendships. Further, like any work, it is a focus of struggle when workers fight employers' attacks and try to create a little elbow room amidst the obstacles which management provides. The pains and dangers of driving are specific to driving, as are the rewards. Drivers have different forms of social relations than have most other workers. Because of these differences—in problems and in relations with other workers—drivers have their own ways of fighting management and their own specific resources with which to wage their struggles. Yet, the special problems of driving remain just specific forms, in one industry, of more general problems of relations between workers and their work and between workers and their employers. Thus it is representative of the general problem of the context in which labor–employer struggles take place.

What Do
Drivers Do?

It is important to understand what short haul drivers do. The description given here is of driving in Los Angeles in 1974; this differs somewhat from driving in other cities, partly because of the strength of Local 208 (which has made the work easier) and partly because the spatial and highway organization of the Los Angeles area, and the laws of California, differ from those elsewhere.

When you come to work at your barn, the first thing you do is park your car. (Most companies have parking facilities, but a few do not, and in these latter, your first problem is to find a parking space.) When, finally, you walk up to the loading dock, you see a concrete-roofed loading dock with trailers at loading bays. On the dock itself, piles of freight wait to be loaded, and there is an enormous uproar and clanging of bells as freight is moved by forklifts, by hand, and (in larger barns) by the loading dock's equivalent of the assembly line—a never-ending loop of carts, nearly always in motion, which carry freight from where it was unloaded from an incoming truck to where it will be loaded on an outgoing truck. (Smaller barns may be much quieter.)

When you get into the terminal, the first thing you do is go to the timeclock and punch in. Then you are given your assignment for the day. What follows is given in this description of work at a large, if temporarily relaxed, terminal, as related by a driver in a good mood. It describes driving at its best. For obvious reasons, this quotation must remain anonymous.

(What do you do during a day's work? Today, for example?)

Today was very easy, I took an interline to Sam's Transportation . . .[1] [After getting my assignment] I went out and found a tractor and hooked it up to the trailer. This takes between 10 and 45 minutes, depending on the day and how much time it takes to check the equipment. First, I went to the bank in Los Angeles; this took 45 minutes including driving time. Then I went to the coffee shop for 30–45 minutes, for breakfast, to talk with other drivers about what's going on. I have different stops, since I don't want the employer to have an easy time finding me. It's an unauthorized stop.

At Sam's, it takes 15 to 30 minutes to block your bills in regard to where to put your freight. You handstack the small stuff on carts. The heavy stuff *they* do with a forklift. I was at Sam's from 10:30 to 12:15, with 15 shipments and six to seven thousand pounds. Then they signed my bills and I went to lunch.

(Did you have a break at Sam's?)

They had one 11:30 to 11:45, so I sat down with them and didn't count it as my break. You're allowed a 15-minute morning break, 30 minutes for lunch, and 15 minutes afternoon break. All else is unauthorized. I counted my breakfast as my morning break. I have no set lunch; today I went to the Golden Key, which is where I often go if I'm in the neighborhood. Though not too often. I don't want to set a pattern; that can lead to trouble. Lunch was 45 minutes, I talked with a couple of farmers from Minnesota. My father-in-law used to farm a section and a half in Minnesota. Then I went to [a commercial warehouse], where manufacturers store goods, and we distribute them. I picked up 100 cartons of furniture pads at 45 to 50 pounds per carton. You put the truck in spot, they run the stuff to you in a forklift and you hand-stack it. The forklift operator has a bill of lading and you check it with your tally sheet and then sign it. This took half a trailer, and it took 45 minutes to do it. When they put the work in front of me, I load it as soon as possible, so I can have more time for my own business.

I got pretty hot, and stripped to the waist, that's why I'm drinking so much this evening.

I got back in the truck, called the dispatcher on the radio, and was sent to Bellflower to pick up 10 shipments of dishwashers and garbage disposals. It was a 15- to 20-minute drive. I used a manual-hydraulic pallet jack to load it. It took half an hour to load it, including an interruption to talk to a line driver a few minutes. Pallet jacks are not dangerous.

Then I went to Frank's Cafe in the Plaza without calling in, had coffee and read the sports page; it took 20 minutes.

Then I called the dispatcher and said I was coming in; it was 4 P.M. Usually they ask how much room you have left, and may send you to get more.

I went to the yard, turned in various paperwork, finished by 4:30, and left the yard. I got paid for the full eight hours.

We haven't had a policy of unloading the truck in our yard for a number of years. We don't even punch out. It's never been grieved; we take it for granted.

(What problems do you run into?)

It varies with the area. If you have a bobtail* run downtown, people want you to run freight up 20 floors, or down. They try to con you into doing it without hitting them for an inside-delivery charge.

On CODs, I just call in and let the office manager say, "Collect it or bring the freight back."

Or having a pain-in-the-ass at a place I'm stopping at. I don't let this bother me; some do.

Just don't get emotional over it and you'll have no problems. If one comes up, have the dispatcher handle it.

That is what an easy day was like in 1974. This driver, a few hours after he got off work, was cheerful but, not surprisingly, tired.

As a comment on the power of 208's democratic unionism, working conditions for drivers remain like this in 1981. This

---

* A bobtail is a one-piece truck, as opposed to a tractor-trailer combination.

contrasts sharply with the experience in other areas, such as New Jersey, where company control has greatly reduced drivers' freedom on the job.

The Meaning
of Breaks

A number of sociologists who have read the above discussion have reacted by viewing the breaks drivers take as "goofing off," and as a sign of the laziness of workers and thus of the need for tight supervision if work is to get done. Some drivers have worried that outsiders will react negatively to the idea that workers take long unauthorized breaks. Thus, it is worth considering how these breaks fit into the pattern of production and the efficiency of work.

These breaks do not seem to me to be laziness or inefficient at all. They seem instead to be part of a highly efficient rhythm of work. Driving a truck produces a lot of tension in the driver, as does loading and unloading a truck while being careful to minimize breakage and to protect one's safety. Drivers tell me that this leads them to a pattern of working very hard and intensely for a time, "getting way ahead of schedule," and then breaking off for a considerable period and relaxing. This relaxation may take the form of talking at a restaurant, but can also involve getting a haircut or going Christmas shopping at a time when stores are not crowded. Nor is it really robbing the company. Thus, a driver who works in an Eastern state told me that in his Local, management, aided by union officers and stewards, successfully cracked down on such "theft of time." This has made work less pleasant but did not increase production. My informant, at least, moves less freight than before, because the lack of long rest periods makes it impossible to produce the bursts of high-effort work. He tells me that this is true of his co-workers as well. This is not due to a deliberate slowdown, either. Slowdowns have been used by drivers in his barn, both as collective actions and as individual responses to management actions, but this is not such an instance. Over the long term, they try to do the job effectively.[2]

Driving

Drivers' own words best present the many contradictory aspects of driving. Thus, this is what John Butler said when I asked how he liked driving:

I detest it. How it is, you've got to do other things to keep your mind active. Partly it's the low caliber of management. It wasn't bad when it was a means to an end, to an education.

Ray Smith answered as follows:

The pressure of the job can lead to trouble. If you have home problems, the pressures of the job can lead to more trouble. In the last two days there have been two accidents, one where the brakes gave out.

You have more freedom in driving. The company doesn't follow me, since if I don't want to work I call in and tell them I won't come. And you are meeting lots of people. When shagging [not driving the same route each day] always meet new people. You have interesting conversations every day.

You have to learn how to pace yourself and to take care of yourself.

John Franklin described his work as follows:

Driving is a freedom type of job. In a sense, you have no boss, so you can take coffee breaks and lunches. . . . Wages are decent. Guys are drivers because they enjoy driving, and freedom, and the wages are good.

(What are your discontents?)

I wish I was discontented; then I'd answer it.

(Does it get boring?)

No. I enjoy driving, and try to go to a different area of town each day for variety. On a regular run, it gets boring after a year or two. Being shag, with our choice of runs, each day is different.

(What's interesting?)

The people. Your co-workers, management, union officials, people on the street. . . .

(Where do people get hurt?)

Lifting. Mostly from carelessness, when they step between the back of the truck and the dock. Or the overhead doors come down and you fall and break your ribs, or you slip on oil or water. Or you drop stuff on your feet, or a forklift occasionally hits you or runs over your toe. Mostly straining back, or hernia, from lifting. Also, hypertension goes along with driving, due to traffic alertness. On an average day, you come close to having an accident twice a day, since you daydream or the other person goofs.

The good side of driving, then, includes the relative freedom from supervision, being "out and around" rather than cooped up in one place. Drivers meet friends in coffee shops or while waiting for their trucks to be loaded or unloaded. On rounds, they go into factories and offices and are able to see the ways in which modern production is carried out and meet people from widely different backgrounds. The pay is relatively good. This all adds up to relatively interesting work and a well-based sense of independence.

The bad side of driving includes numerous injuries, odors from some freight, and the noise level of traffic (particularly on Los Angeles freeways). Handling freight is also hard work, and can create vulnerability to numerous diseases. For instance, the changes in temperature involved can contribute to arthritis. Further, the tension of driving can affect one, both psychologically and physically. All of this is worsened by management violations of seniority, "miscalculation" of pay checks, and verbal harassment.

In addition, some drivers feel a lack of status and a bad public image. Others see themselves as at the end of the line, believing that things will never get better and that they will never advance to a better job.

Still another complaint common among drivers is that management does not know how to run the business. They want to please the customers and to see that freight is not lost, but they feel management makes this impossible. They sometimes comment on how the company, in a drive for profits, in effect sabotages its own handling of nonprofitable freight—picking it up late, or "losing" it amid the jumble of the loading dock. Felix Santoro described one such instance as follows (the quotation here is from my field notes summarizing a much longer description of what happened):

Even after the strike I was working real hard because I got along real well with the salesman. I was way overworking, sometimes I would overload my truck, and transfer it to an empty trailer they had sitting nearby for a 12 noon starter to pick up. It was fun, I was really able to do a good job, without too many hassles. The salesman and I really built up that route.

Then, they changed the run from a 10 A.M. start to 8 A.M. and wouldn't tell me why, even though I asked all the managers. The run has gone down hill. There is no sense in it. They lost a lot of money this way; they used to make my week's wages in one day.

Drivers

Let us now consider how the milieu of driving affects drivers' style of unionism. Local 208's is a tough kind of unionism, ready to use fists instead of words in a quarrel. The history of the Local gives many examples of this, ranging from large-scale violence against strikebreakers to fights between individual drivers over union policy. Some of the roots of this toughness lie in the nature of the work. The combination of relative freedom from supervision and hard physical labor is the key, creating an individualistic and aggressive attitude, building physical strength, and tending to recruit people who already have macho styles. Further, while in a factory a worker is always surrounded by co-workers who are potential supporters in a fight, a driver is often out of touch with other drivers from the same company. Thus, drivers who are hassled by a company spotter or by supporters of a different union faction have to deal with the problem alone.

Thus, a tendency toward militancy grows out of drivers' working lives. But the same isolated working conditions make this militancy very slow to take political-strategic form, since strategic thought must grow out of many discussions among the same people over a long period of time. A driver, however, may run into another driver once a month or less. While this is often enough to keep up on events at each others' barns, and to allow complaints and discussion of immediate problems, it is not enough to allow full-scale analysis of such problems. Nor does it allow serious discussion of strategies for dealing with such problems. Further, it usually requires a long and deep acquaintance, and a sense of totally shared fate (such as might exist in a mining community), to develop enough trust to dare discuss the full political and personal meaning of common problems.

The lack of regular sustained contact with co-workers also produces a way of viewing union affairs in terms of individual morality and courage. Thus, I often encountered an emphasis on "the kind of guy I am" among drivers; usually the speaker would describe himself as someone who speaks straight and comes out with what he thinks, not someone who hides his thoughts. This comes in part from machismo, but even more develops out of the kinds of brief, occasional conversations drivers have with one another on the job. In any case, such personalizing, and with it the view that union officers' sellouts come from their personal failings (expressed in the common expression about the International's officialdom, "the whores run deep") leads to a failure to analyze union problems more deeply. If the problem is that the officialdom is made up of "gutless wonders" and "corrupt bloodsuckers," one need not look deeply into the dynamics of the bureaucracy. One may remain puzzled about why almost every reform candidate turns into a sellout within a year or two of election to office, and about why all the higher officers of the International seem to be in bed with the companies. One may spend time wishing for the return of Jimmy Hoffa—widely viewed as corrupt, but nonetheless straightforward and tough with the companies—rather than in trying to figure out forms of struggle that might create effective unionism and restrain the tendency of officials to sell out. Thus, the personalism bred by driving is another major source of the relative lack of strategic thinking even among very tough and, in some cases, even radical drivers.

To some extent, these factors—episodic contacts and personalism—are reversible by conscious effort or by chance. In particular, when drivers begin to meet on a regular basis and to discuss union problems, some of these forces even reverse their effect. Then, drivers are not prevented from getting close to each other because they are out and around. Instead these contacts become a source of wide knowledge about events all over the city; once the personalism becomes a known problem, the question turns to how to establish power over little-known officers who speak of reform but perhaps will sell out; and so on.

Driving
as a Milieu
for Organizing
Militant
Unionism

Militant unionism depends primarily upon the organization of the rank and file. Organization is needed to create solidarity and plans with which to fight the employer, and to determine plans for removing nonmilitant or sellout union officials as well as for pressuring activist officers. In many ways, driving is an occupation that makes such organization possible.

First, drivers are out and around, and thus not under the eye of management. Thus, within the limitations mentioned, they can get together at coffeeshops and discuss their problems. When the problem concerns poor union administration, drivers from different barns in the same Local can get together and talk—often they already know each other from coffee stops, which makes such meetings easier. Further, there is a grapevine to spread the news of the union's sellouts and the drivers' successes far and wide. Successes of drivers in a given barn, whether in defeating their company on an issue or in facing down a union business agent arguing on behalf of management, spur similar efforts at other barns. And activist drivers hear about other activists, easing efforts to organize an activist caucus within the union.

Second, the trucking industry is still made up of a large number of different companies. In particular, there are far more barns than paid union officials. In Local 208, for instance, there are several hundred barns. Since business agents have so many barns to cover, they can learn little about any but the very biggest barns. This makes it obvious that drivers need a steward system to deal with management, and that day-to-day dealings between company and union must fall into stewards' hands. The implications of this are many and profound. Many potential leaders are being trained at any given time by being stewards and barn leaders. Salaried union officials are limited in their ability to affect what goes on in the barns. The existence of many independent power centers in a Local makes it hard for a bureaucratic machine to maintain control. Finally, the large number of barns gives drivers a certain freedom to be more militant and risk their jobs—especially since there is a grapevine to aid a fired driver in finding a new job and barns whose rank-and-file drivers are well enough organized to pressure their employers to hire a good unionist. (In fact, such networks helped many of the hundreds of drivers fired after the 1970 wildcat find new jobs.) Further, the large number of barns in a given Local means that if union officers help a company fire an opposition member, they may well find this same oppositionist hired by another barn in the same Local. This weakens one of the strongest weapons of union officers against the rank and file and strengthens militancy.

Also of great importance to drivers' struggles in 208 has been the existence of a hiring hall. The hall means that a fired or laid-off worker can work on a day-to-day basis while looking for a steady job; even if he becomes unemployable on a steady basis, he can find work to keep himself alive. Thus, again, drivers can take greater risks with their jobs. The hall is also a constant source of discontent, since casual drivers have very little protection on the job, less steady work, and thus more financial problems then have company drivers. Further, since corruption in a Local usually leads to the necessity to pay kickbacks to the dispatcher to get work out of the hall, discontent grows up early and strong there. Further, the hall is a natural center of communications and organization, since hall drivers go into almost every barn in the area and meet many more drivers. Finally, hall drivers who have not gotten work on a given day or who are waiting to be dispatched spend much time talking together. Thus, it is a natural source of strategy formation, since it combines lots of problems and lots of time to talk about them among people who have come to know each other well.

These characteristics of driving as a milieu can be clarified by showing their similarities to those of subsurface coal mining, which has been the soil for rank-and-file activism since the mid-1960s (Yarrow 1980). Communication is facilitated in both milieus by the small number of workers per workplace per shift, so many workers know everyone on their shift or at their workplace. In both industries, workers have a considerable opportunity to talk without fear of supervisors' listening in; in both industries, workers are at the job a considerable time before "production" begins, and there are many opportunities during the working day to talk together. In both industries, the production process itself forces workers to exercise considerable judgement, which fosters independence and gives the workers a resource in struggle: the power to control the speed of one's machine lets one cut productivity. (Managements have tried to find ways to reduce workers' control over their work, but so far they have not succeeded sufficiently to affect the workers' power resource.) Both industries are dangerous—and cost-cutting and productivity pressures increase the hazards. Both industries have lots of small workplaces in which leaders and strategies are discussed.

The two industries also have differences. Drivers are out on the streets and in other companies' loading docks during much of the day, which encourages communications among workplaces. Miners are under the ground at work; but kin and friendship networks carry news and ideas among mines. Miners have more of a monopoly of skills than drivers—although the ability to handle double trailers, and knowledge of customer locations and good routing, is also a skill that gives local drivers a power resource. The collective nature of miners' work, however, is a major difference between the two occupations: for miners, threats to safety affect all the miners as a unit, and the actual process of mining coal also involves miners' acting in unison. Collective work processes also make it easy for miners to exert group pressure on each other. For drivers, the processes are more individualized, and collective pressure on a driver who is on a freeway is relatively small.

The miners have been able to defend themselves against management through workplace cohesion and a loose network among mines. Drivers, lacking this cohesion at the workplace, have built a national rank-and-file organization to strengthen their defense against management.

In summary, driving is a milieu with characteristics like episodic encounters, hiring hall conversations, and multiple workplaces. This milieu makes Local-wide organizing relatively easy and encourages militancy, but retards serious strategic discussion except and until organizations like TDU or movements like that in 208 in the late 1950s provide a context in which it can occur.

Part II

History
of Struggle

Chapter 4

Rank-and-File Rebellion in the Late Fifties

FOR THE first half-century of its existence, Local 208 was fairly typical. Formed in 1900, it was chartered as Local 208 in 1903 by the newly formed IBT. The Local grew stronger over the next several years and won contracts with some of the largest drayage firms in Los Angeles. However, in 1907 its power was broken when employers refused to deal with it any more and succeeded in winning the ensuing strike. The employers were pressured into confronting the drivers by the Merchants' and Manufacturers' Association (M & M), and were spurred on by financial assistance to those holding fast—as well as by the threat of a boycott by the M & M against any company signing with the union.[1] Then as now, the immediate employer in the freight industry may be only part of the drivers' problem: the employer, even the trucking association, are only the first circles of the opposition. When the chips are down, the entire class of employers opposes strong and effective unionism.

Local 208 remained in existence, a skeleton of its former self, until the Depression. During the 1930s, it experienced several strong, but brief, surges of membership. Working conditions and pay at this time were abysmal; for example, drivers were expected to make most repairs themselves, on pain of being fired; they received pay only while actually making deliveries, not for the often considerable waiting time between dispatches; their pay was 32.5¢ per hour; and, of course, union membership had to be kept secret.[2]

In 1937, the Teamsters struck Pacific Freight Lines, the largest trucking company in California, to force it to recognize the union in the Los Angeles area. The strike was won after a

long struggle, characterized by violence and by secondary boycott pressure from the more organized Teamsters of Northern
California and newly organized West Coast Longshoremen.
Notably, control remained in the hands of Seattle Teamster
leader Dave Beck and his lieutenants rather than with the strikers. In the years following victory over PFL, much of the Los
Angeles freight industry was unionized. Most of the new membership was put into 208. However, even with the frequent use
of trusteeships, central to Beck's rule, a Local of 15,000 members was potentially too powerful to control. Thus, during the
early 1940s, a number of specialized locals were carved out from
208. By 1948, 208 had become a relatively homogeneous organization of drivers of local freight.

Local 208
Under Filipoff

In February 1948, the International named John Filipoff the new
Secretary-Treasurer of Local 208. He was to remain at the head
of the local for 11 years, first by appointment and later by election. The inadequacies of the Local in representing the drivers'
interests during the Filipoff regime were the initial target of the
rank-and-file movement which transformed 208.

   Defending workers in their disagreements with employers
is a basic responsibility of a union; the main flaw of Local 208
under Filipoff was its failure to represent the drivers, who, as
a result, were harassed, overworked, cheated out of benefits
and protections contractually due them, and fired arbitrarily. A
few examples will point up the conditions of that time, and
indicate how individuals' reactions paved the way for change.

   First, there is this brief description (taken from my interview
notes) by Mauricio Terrazas of 208 during the period 1946–49.*

There was no democracy at all. They ruled it from the top. One guy
I worked with was paid $10 each meeting to work over anyone who
raised stuff from the floor.

---

* Terrazas joined the local in 1946 and was a member until 1949, at which point he got
a job in another Teamster jurisdiction. He became a 208 member and activist again in
the 1970s.

(What was the Local like in terms of protecting the members?)
Very bad. In the hall, they were selling jobs at five to ten dollars a day.
(Grievances?)
They didn't follow through. There was no protection.

Nor did things improve. One day in the mid-1950s, a driver for Pacific Motor Transport (PMT), who had been sick, was told by his doctor to keep out of the rain. In the middle of his delivery run, it started to rain. He called the dispatcher's office and was told to finish his deliveries and come back to the yard. When he returned to PMT, he was sent out again. After this, he was sick at home for two weeks from his exposure to the rain. When he came back to work, he was fired. He called the union office, and was told that a business agent would be down in two weeks to see what he could do.

At this point, a driver who was to become one of the activists in the rank-and-file movement stepped into active unionism. Eddie Dietrich took the phone. He talked to the business agent about the driver's case. The BA again said he would come to PMT in two weeks. Dietrich told him no one was going to work until he arrived. The BA called Filipoff to the phone; Filipoff repeated the BA's words. Dietrich hung up. In 18 minutes, two carloads of union officials showed up. As Dietrich remembers, "I told the guys not to go in, and I'd break anyone's leg who tried, with a two by four. Or, if I couldn't, I would pay somebody who could. I had the majority of guys with me, and I threatened the minority with a two by four. The union officers went in alone to talk to management. They came out and said they'd get him another job; this one stinks anyway." After work, Dietrich and five other men went to the 208 office, talked to a BA, and asked for a copy of the contract. The BA said the office had none. The PMT drivers threatened to tear the office apart if they did not get one. Filipoff backed up the BA; the threat was renewed; the officers gave the drivers a copy of the contract.[3]

At about the same time, John T. Williams, who would later become a leader of the Black Caucus, and still later an officer of 208, was driving for Southern California Freight Lines, while also trying to get through law school. Always tired, always busy, Williams fell asleep one night during a long wait for another truck to pull out and make room for his rig. The dispatcher found out about this, and when Williams went to work the next night at his normal midnight starting time, he was told to stay at the terminal. They fired Williams in the morning; nor was he paid for the many hours he was at the terminal waiting to be fired. The Local did not try to defend him or even to get him his pay for that last night; it just told him to work out of the hiring hall.[4]

Jim Henderson, who would become one of the hiring hall activists, had similar experiences. He held one job for about a year and a half, but the company had destroyed his letter of hire. Since the union did not stand up for him, he had to compete with drivers with less seniority to continue working and finally lost his job and had to go back to working out of the hiring hall.[5]

Thus, the problem the drivers faced is clear. Their livelihoods and their health were constantly threatened or attacked by their employers, and their union would do nothing about it. This is a common experience, shared by millions of other workers. However, the drivers of Local 208 fought back, with considerable success.

Round One:
The Fight
for Stewards

The first fight came over the issue of stewards—full-time workers who serve as union leaders on the job. A union is strengthened when shop-floor activists are provided with the protection of the title of "steward"; further, stewardship can provide a way for rank and filers to organize in their dealings with the union local's officers; and activist, committed stewards can fight the harassment of workers, day by day, on the job.

In the early 1950s, Local 208 did not have shop stewards, and the contract between the employers and the Southern California Teamsters included no provision for them. A number of drivers felt stewards were needed, because the paid business agents were not representing them well, and set out to get them. Opposition came from both the employers and the Local's officers. The officers, fearing any form of rank-and-file organization, saw stewards as a threat. Stewards could provide a leadership able to pressure the business agents actually to leave their offices and do their proper jobs—defending the members. Further, stewardship could give members experience with grievance-handling and with dealing directly with employers, thus breaking the officials' monopoly on such knowledge and establishing credible opponents in elections. Thus, when members from various barns raised the issue of stewards at Local meetings, Filipoff opposed them, claiming that since the BAs acted as stewards, there was no need for stewards at the barns, and that stewards, having no contractual protection, would be fired. Although Filipoff eventually gave in on this issue, the idea that a rank-and-file contract committee was needed to formulate such demands as contractually protected stewards had been firmly established.

Employer resistance was often overcome by direct action. Thus, early in 1955, at Pacific Intermountain Express (PIE), the drivers simply got together and elected stewards. When the company refused to recognize them, the drivers fought back. PIE management had a rule that drivers should check their trucks every day before going out on the road, and take faulty equipment to the repair shop. For two weeks, therefore, all 37 drivers would, in the afternoon, bust lights, pull wires, or take even stronger actions; in the morning, they would "find" the breakages and take the trucks to the repair shop. Then management gave in and recognized the stewards. Similar actions were taken at other companies at about the same time.

The new Southern California freight contract negotiated later that year, with the aid of the first major strike since 1937, contained provisions for a stewardship system. At first, while the Local accepted stewards, it ruled they were to be appointed. In some yards, this had no real effect; the drivers were well enough organized to elect stewards and make their decisions stick. But in many yards this was impossible. In any case, many drivers felt that the principle of elected stewards should be made the formal policy of the Local. This issue lasted for several years, and became one of the main demands of the rank-and-file movement developing in 208 during this period. It was finally won at the union meeting of October 1958, when, amidst an election campaign, Filipoff made a number of concessions to the membership in a vain attempt to save his office.

Opposition
at the Job Site

One of the keys to organizing the 208 rank and file was through the various workplaces, with activist drivers from different barns slowly getting to know and work with each other through the meetings of the Local. A close look at how the drivers organized at the two most important centers of rank-and-file opposition, Pacific Motor Transport (PMT) and the hiring hall, shows how they fought and organized.

During most of the period covered in this book, PMT, a trucking subsidiary of the giant Southern Pacific Railroad, has been the largest single trucking company in Los Angeles. At one point it had about 400 drivers on its seniority list. It is also extremely complex: it has a regular local freight pickup-and-delivery operation, a separate operation to move freight between the railroad and the harbor, a separate "pig yard" to put containers on and off railroad cars, and an operation to deliver freight from the railroad to local receivers and pick up local freight for the railroad. (A container is a trailer that can be put onto a flatcar and then shipped by train to another city; or it can be loaded into the hold of a specially designed ship and transported to the other side of the earth; or it can be hitched to the back of a tractor and thus be a normal trucking operation. Since the process of loading trailers onto trains is called "piggyback," the area this is done in is called the "pig-yard.") This complexity creates considerable potential for labor-management conflict. For example, the difficulty of running a yard-wide seniority system with separate managements and dispatch facilities for each of four separate operations creates room for grievances and disputes; if overtime, for instance, is to be assigned, is it offered first to the driver with highest seniority in the given operation or to the driver with highest seniority in the entire PMT barn? Then there are the complexities of the annual bids, in which drivers choose their starting times and the area of the city in which they will work for the year, and such issues as assigning vacation times. From the drivers' tactical point of view, if they are not well organized, they can be whipsawed if management takes them on one operation at a time; or they can be fooled if management violates yard-wide seniority provisions unless they have enough communications across operations to detect such violations.

The sheer complexities of PMT's normal workings, then, motivate the drivers to organize strongly in self-defense. However, in the early 1950s such organization did not exist, and management walked all over the drivers. In the words of Eddie Dietrich: "We didn't pick on them just to pick on them. The problems were real. People would be fired for nothing. And had to pay damages if you got in a small accident, or lost a handtruck, or got a traffic ticket. And the union was doing nothing about it."

In 1953, PMT drivers made their first attempt to organize. They set up the PMT Club, a combination of social club and drivers' representative. The Club had a baseball team, bowling, and special events for drivers and their families. It was organized to form a uniform front toward both company and union. Members would meet with management over problems directly, and tried, with some success, to resolve them. Sometimes the union would try to get on the bandwagon.

After a year or two, the PMT Club fell apart over personal jealousies and hostilities. However, it left a number of lasting results: drivers knew each other better than did drivers in other barns; they had been through a collective experience of dealing with management and union officials, and some had learned important lessons about leadership.

Shortly afterward, PMT's management took two actions that would make a complex situation more complex and spark reactions leading the drivers to organize on a new and more effective basis. The company merged with Pacific Freight Lines (PFL), and it pioneered "piggyback" operations in Southern California.

In September 1955, PMT acquired PFL and merged the operations of both into one yard. The 70 PMT drivers and 200 PFL drivers, some of them veterans of the 1937 strike, were confronted with thorny problems. PFL drivers had to adjust to a new management, dispatch system, and working rules. The drivers were confronted with a major shakeup in their relative seniority, at a point when procedures for dealing with mergers had not yet been formalized. Drivers with PMT prior to the merger felt it unfair—especially as they had had no prior warning that seniority lists would be dovetailed—for newcomers to be granted their PFL-hire dates as their PMT seniority. They tried to organize to challenge this, and their anger was intensified by their inability to reach the officials of the Local. They tried to challenge the dovetailing in court, which of course spurred PFL drivers to organize in self-defense.

The PFL merger led to increased drivers' organization. It could have bred long-lasting and paralyzing enmity between the two sets of drivers, but this did not happen, for several reasons. First, the newly enlarged PMT prospered. Thus, seniority disputes were less important than if there had been layoffs. Second, both groups of drivers were able to see the possible pitfalls of enmity. Third, the normal level of problems with management was increased by the uncertainties and complexities of the newly merged company, which constantly reminded drivers of their need to be united and provided frequent problems over which to deal with management in a unified way.

At about the time of the merger, PMT pioneered piggyback operations, which grew rapidly over the next few years. For this, a whole new section of the yard was set up, and new rules established. In particular, new safety practices had to be worked out, leading the drivers' interest in their safety and the company's interest in productivity into a number of head-on collisions. Thus, drivers in the "pig-yard" were faced with the need to organize themselves. Their response was to elect a steward, Eddie Dietrich, and to back him when it came to trouble. Local officials objected (this was in the period when stewards were to be appointed), and at first the other three stewards in the PMT yards were afraid to introduce elections. However, when they saw that elections worked at the pig-yard, they introduced them throughout PMT.

Then, the newly elected stewards and their supporters set out to organize the yard. In large part, this meant talking to the drivers—hours and hours of discussions about what could be accomplished by sticking together, about the rights of the drivers under the contract and how to win and defend these, and about the affairs of the Local and how to deal with its problems. These discussions created a very tight barn, one where drivers and stewards would back each other in their fights with management and with the Local's officers. So tightly was it organized that on one occasion, when the Local's officials put up a picket line at this highly union-conscious barn, the drivers would not walk off the job until Dietrich, their steward, had given his okay.

PMT drivers began to go to union meetings, where they would oppose Filipoff's policies and put forward their own proposals. They came to know other drivers who supported them or made their own proposals. In particular, they found that drivers who worked out of the hiring hall were an important opposition group.

It was no accident that the hiring hall was a major center of rank-and-file organization and militancy. The economic and social nature of the hall made certain of it. There, drivers on layoff or lacking a steady job were dispatched to trucking companies temporarily needing extra drivers to handle a particularly heavy load of orders. Thus, a hall driver was in a very bad position: he could potentially be forced to pay off the hall dispatcher for work or be discriminated against by the dispatcher for union militancy; and his economic situation was insecure and, in a recession, potentially disastrous. But he was also in a relatively good position: He was not tied to a regular work schedule, had time to talk things over with other hall drivers while waiting for a dispatch, and came to know drivers in those barns to which he was often dispatched.

In addition, according to John T. Williams, hall drivers "are the most militant people—that's why they were fired in the first place. Furthermore, the people at the hall have nothing to lose. They don't have jobs to lose, and they know how to go a week without a paycheck. And this adds up to militant strength. . . . A guy with a regular job may be a better leader because it may reflect skill at self-protection, sometimes. But as to militancy, a hall guy's family may well have already left him, so he can take risks." Also, a disproportionate number of hall drivers were black (there has always been much racial discrimination in the trucking industry). Even by the mid-1950s, blacks had gotten much experience in defending themselves through strong actions, and in supporting each other in a pinch. Already, they had a high degree of militancy and motivation to reshape the union. Finally, contracts between the employers and the Teamsters union were not designed to deal with the problems of hall drivers—something that business agents and stewards at trucking companies usually did not understand. Or else they were unwilling to go beyond the contract to attack hall drivers' problems. This meant hall drivers were forced to become experts at using the contract and grievance procedure where they could, and at fighting back outside the contractual channels when they had to. Thus, when they mobilize, hall drivers are very powerful. In the mid-1950s, they mobilized to force the union to defend them, to clean up the dispatching process, and eventually to defend the hall's existence.

Organizing among hall drivers at this time centered around Eddie Barrett's car in the hall's parking lot. His car became a social center and the place hall drivers came to discuss everything from specific grievances to reshaping the union. In particular, when a driver was fired by a trucking company and came to the hall to get work, the activists around Barrett's car would do what the union should have: They would talk with him at length about why he had been fired and, if they could find a way to defend him, they would write up a grievance and then press the Local to process it. From such experience, John T. Williams and Eddie Barrett, elected hall stewards in 1955, became key men in the developing rank-and-file movement.

Thus, when the rank-and-file of 208 began to organize, the hall became a main center of the action. Drivers would stop there to find out what was happening and what was planned. Both regularly employed and hall drivers would bring news of events in various companies—which created a very effective communications network. Drivers at a given company would arrange for hall activists to get temporary jobs at their company, either to "work underground" in the fight with management, or simply in order to give the activist (often under virtual blacklist by the dispatcher) some work.

Filipoff's forces counterattacked in a number of ways. An early method was to call drivers seen hanging around the activists' group into Filipoff's office downtown and to tell them to stay away from the group or they would not work. However, Filipoff's strongest counterattack, an eloquent testimony to the potential power of a hiring hall to a rank-and-file movement, was his closing of the hall in November 1958—something that is not easy to do, particularly during a recession.

However, in the year 1958, Los Angeles Dock and

Office Workers Local 357 had been ordered by the National Labor Relations Board (NLRB) to repay six months' dues and initiation fees to members who had used its Hiring Hall over the previous couple of years. The grounds were that the Local had violated Taft-Hartley provisions on closed shops. Filipoff claimed this ruling equally endangered Local 208, and threatened to wipe out its treasury; thus, he convinced the November membership meeting to approve the closing of the hall. He planned to bring in a privately owned commercial employment agency under contract to the union—which would insulate the Local's administration from rank-and-file charges of discrimination and misconduct in the Hall's operations.[6]

In practice, what happened was that the hall was closed for a year, during which time hall drivers had to scramble for jobs. By the end of that year, they had organized the Local's members to vote to reopen it.

Local-Wide
Struggle
Develops

Strong organization at the hall or at the barn level can do much to protect drivers; however, this alone is not enough. The Local, with its influence over what happens to grievances, may back or attack the drivers of a given barn to influence the balance of power between them and the company. Thus, soon after drivers began to organize in their barns, they began to try to obtain the Local's backing. When they did not, and even met opposition instead, they turned to changing the Local. At first, they pushed for specific changes, like elected stewards, but they came to see there were many such specific issues and that to make the needed changes would require organization of the rank and file throughout the local, ousting of the Local's officers, and hard work by a lot of drivers.

In this process, the development of tight barns was a crucial asset for the insurgents. A tightly organized barn, ready and able to take such direct action as slowdowns, sabotage campaigns, or walkouts, provides protection against collusion between management and Local officers to fire the more committed drivers and intimidate the less committed. Further, a tightly organized barn provides a base from which to reach out to other drivers in other barns. A barn where the drivers have learned how to protect themselves has prestige; building such a barn helps develop self-confidence and new skills. And a tightly organized barn can intervene effectively in Local meetings and elections.

What happened is fairly straightforward. Drivers from the hall and from the tightly organized PMT began to attend Local meetings, to make proposals, and to speak up for what they thought right. Fairly quickly, they came to meet each other, and also met other groupings of active unionists from companies like Denver-Chicago and TCD. Informally at first, the insurgents came to know each other, discussing plans for upcoming Local meetings, methods they had used in dealing with management, etc.

As time went on, the insurgent opposition grew more organized. Activists began to meet at the Olympian Coffee Shop after Local meetings to discuss what had happened. Then they started meeting *before* Local meetings, to discuss what they should propose, how to plan tactically for maximum effectiveness, and so forth. By the middle of 1958, they had a strong base in the Local, and were often able to get proposals through. Thus, in 1958, California had a referendum on a "Right-to-Work" proposal. Drivers working out of the hall proposed that the Local set up a committee to oppose it, and Filipoff supported this, mainly to pacify them. The insurgent drivers set up the committee, and then used it not only to organize against the "Right-to-Work" initiative but also to activate new rank and filers and to establish the insurgents' reputations as good unionists.

Indeed, with the Local election approaching, they won approval for elected stewards as well as for a Stewards' Council to provide a "complete training course in such subjects as the responsibilities and duties of a steward, grievance procedure, details of your contract, bargaining and negotiations, basic leadership, parliamentary procedure and many others."[7]

At this point, the officialdom split in two. The strength of the rank-and-file movement and its potential threat to incumbent loyalists was enough to tempt 208 President and paid business agent, Sid Cohen, to run for Secretary-Treasurer. He declared his candidacy with attacks on Filipoff and a promise to keep his door open to the rank and file—yet with no real acceptance of the demands of the activists. However, deciding that here was at least a chance to shake up the bureaucracy, the activists gave Cohen their support. Their support increased when, in response to a 12-point program issued by John T. Williams, who was campaigning only to spread propaganda, Cohen issued a 10-point program of his own, embracing such central rank-and-file demands as bylaws, use of Robert's Rules of Order at meetings, rank-and-file committees to administer charitable and social activities, contractually supported stewards and stewards' councils, and "Business Agents . . . chosen from the rank-and-file." Cohen's program, it must be noted, evaded the question of who would choose the Business Agents; and Williams' platform had also contained, as Cohen's did not, planks against employer and union racism and for political action by the Teamsters.

Office, Office, Who's Got The Office

In spite of Filipoff's last-minute concessions to the rank and file on stewards and minor issues, and in spite of Hoffa's appearance in Filipoff's behalf (Filipoff was one of only two Hoffa men among the Southern California Teamster leadership), Filipoff lost the election with 1,149 votes to Cohen's 1,269. However, losing an election did not necessarily mean one simply left office. Filipoff's attempts to retain it disrupted the operations of the Local for months, brought its affairs to the front pages of Los Angeles newspapers, and led to attention, if briefly, by the U.S. Senate probe of the Teamsters' Union. However, while these events made news, their significance rests primarily in their outcome: Filipoff was finally ousted. While attention was focused on the feuds and maneuvers at the top, it was at the bottom, in the self-organization of the rank-and-file drivers of Local 208, that the real action was taking place.

Briefly, this is what happened: Filipoff claimed that the election had been rigged and that over 1,600 members had signed a petition stating they had voted for him. Therefore, he refused to vacate his office. Cohen went into court, had 208 put into receivership, and then fired most of Filipoff's business agents. Both contenders were subpoenaed to Washington to testify before the Senate Committee chaired by John McClellan of Arkansas. Such notables as Robert Kennedy, then committee counsel, and Pierre Salinger, who would become Press Secretary in John Kennedy's administration, claimed that Hoffa must be a Red since 208 had supported a strike by the "Communist-linked" Furniture Workers. Cohen's ally, business agent Red Savage, testified that he had not wanted to support that strike, but that Filipoff had ordered him to. While in Washington, meanwhile, Filipoff, Cohen, and Paul Collins (a PMT driver and Cohen supporter, later appointed a BA) got together in the IBT offices with Mike Singer, a Los Angeles-based troubleshooter for Hoffa, and reached an agreement: Cohen would return to being the President and BA of 208, as he had been before the election, but would have the same salary as Filipoff; Filipoff would again become Secretary-Treasurer; there would be no animosity toward Cohen or Red Savage for their actions.

However, on his return to Los Angeles, Cohen repudiated the deal and asked for police protection. He then took over the direction of the Local under the court-ordered receivership. Two weeks later, Filipoff formally withdrew his claim to the Secretary-Treasurership. The receivership was withdrawn, but all was not to quiet down so easily. A number of rank and filers, some previously active in the fight for stewards, had supported Filipoff, feeling that Cohen was too weak to run a local. They had started a newsletter, *208 News*, to rally support for Filipoff and cut away at Cohen. For example, they published reports on how the stewards' program was going nowhere, on how the companies were taking advantage of Cohen's weakness to violate seniority provisions, and on how grievance after grievance was being lost. Their pressure was sufficient, in the context of Cohen's failure to move ahead with the rank-and-filers' program that he had embraced during the election campaign, for the Filipoff majority on the 208 Executive Board to try Cohen and Savage on charges of not enforcing the contract and of misappropriating funds. As a result, the anti-Filipoff section of the rank-and-file activists picketed the Teamsters' building during Cohen's and Savage's trial. John T. Williams acted as Cohen's "attorney." Cohen was found guilty, nevertheless, and was kicked out of office. He appealed this action to Southern California Joint Council 42, which—as it was composed of Teamster officials of the anti-Hoffa faction—reinstated Cohen.

Cohen's Regime and the Rank and File

Cohen's regime was a period of great progress for the drivers of 208 in their attempt to reshape the Local. This progress was not due to Cohen—basically a bureaucrat with no desire to organize a fighting Local—but rather to Cohen's inability to oppose the active unionists effectively.

Cohen's weakness was due less to his personality than to his having gained office as an "out bureaucrat" attempting to take advantage of a rank-and-file upsurge. He got little support from the rank-and-file activists, who had no respect for him nor illusions about his motives. He had been supported only because his campaign offered drivers a chance to unseat an incumbent who had entrenched himself, over the years, through favors to supporters, while failing to defend the Local's membership. Thus, once in office, Cohen was confronted with a choice: he could abandon complacent business unionism, join up with the rank-and-file activists, and attempt to take the lead in changing the Local; or he could attempt to use the power and patronage of his office to build up his own machine, making peace with the Filipoff supporters insofar as possible.

As almost always happens in such cases, Cohen tried to set up his own machine, but failed. He was not cut out for the job of reestablishing bureaucratic control over a rebellious membership. Besides, the conflict over the disputed office had left Cohen in a poor position to make peace with 208's longtime officials, especially as the minority rank-and-file faction which had supported Filipoff would only support those officers who refused to make peace with Cohen. Also, Cohen was caught in the web of IBT top-level maneuvering; replacing a pro-Hoffa official in a region run by anti-Hoffa officials, his natural path lay in allying himself with the regional bureaucracy, especially since he owed his office to the anti-Hoffa Joint Council. Yet, in opting for the regional bureaucracy (for which he was rewarded in August 1959, by Einar Mohn of the Western Conference of Teamsters, with a job as trustee of the new Western Master Freight Division), he ensured himself of the enmity of Jimmy Hoffa and his supporters. The chief reason for Cohen's failure to establish his power however, was that the rank and file of Local 208 were strongly enough organized to put through such important planks of their program as bylaws and elected BAs, to keep Cohen's supporters from election to Executive Board positions, and finally to oust Cohen from office.

The Fight
for Bylaws
and Its Results

The drivers made Local bylaws a major goal. This did not come from any abstract desire for constitutional structure, but rather reflected their ultimate goal—a union that would help them to defend themselves. For years they had found that it took a major fight to make the union act helpfully, and felt that a prime obstacle was the lack of spelled-out rules, which had allowed the Secretary-Treasurer to make his own. Furthermore, they hoped that in the process of writing a set of bylaws, they could put through a number of specific reforms in the Local, such as to have business agents elected rather than appointed. They also hoped to use the bylaws to structure the Local so as to encourage an active union in which members would participate and become involved in defending themselves, develop solidarity, and learn to work well together. The hope was to structure activism into the bylaws through the new steward system. Stewards were to continue to be elected and to be quite numerous (one steward and one alternate for every 50 members, elected for two-year terms). A Stewards' Council would be set up, with broad powers to initiate action, vote on issues, assist in the formation of contracts, and so on. Stewards would be required to attend monthly meetings of the Local as well as monthly Steward's Council meetings. (Just as requiring stewards to attend meetings was an attempt to legislate active union involvement, so, in their attempt to create solidarity, the rank and filers also spelled out working rules and union obligations, enforced by fines and suspensions from the union, such as that no member was to tell management about other members' activities nor to work under subcontractual conditions.)

It will be recalled that Cohen had embraced rank-and-file demands for bylaws as part of his election campaign. Thus, shortly after his election, members raised the question of bylaws at the monthly membership meeting; they assumed Cohen would work out a proposal on setting up a bylaws committee, and present it for approval. After some months, however, it grew clear that Cohen did not intend to set up such a committee, and that the drivers had another fight on their hands. They thus introduced a motion for an elected bylaws committee. It was ruled that it would take a reading at each of three successive membership meetings to pass the motion. As a result, the rank-and-file group had to mobilize to keep the proposal from being scuttled, an effort made more difficult by the fact that their proposal was opposed by the candidate whom they had supported for election just a few months before. However, at a meeting in early summer 1959, attended by over 400 members, the bylaws committee's proposal was passed and the committee elected. While varying in their attitudes toward Cohen, all committee members were rank-and-file drivers who favored bylaws of some sort.

In addition to the difficulty of holding frequent meetings of a committee of full-time working truck drivers, which was worsened by stalling on the part of a few Cohen supporters, the bylaws committee faced the problem of moving from a general political mood, a thrust for greater rank-and-file control, to its representation in rules of procedure that would, in practice, enable the active unionists to shape a participative, democratic, and effective Local. How this mood and this difficulty affected the bylaws committee—and its results—can be seen in the comments of two leaders of the movement for bylaws.

One, Pat Patton (interview of March 25, 1975), sat in on many Committee meetings:

The bylaws came out of disenchantment when we made proposals at meetings and we'd be ruled out of order. And they'd say, "We don't need bylaws, we've got the International Constitution." We wanted working rules, like you couldn't seek a job without going and registering through the hall, and rules about how to pass motions. In the early stages of our interest in this, we saw bylaws could give control to the

Executive Office, *or* to the Executive Board, which was new to us. And people were against having BAs on the Executive Board.
(What kind of Local were you trying to create?)
One that gave a voice to everyone, and better educating of those who were interested enough to come about how to deal with business and make proposals. So individuals with good ideas could get them over.
(Was the kind of effective unionism you developed in mind then?)
We assumed that if we could take care of our own business we'd be more effective in defending the members' interests. The central interest *then* was how to develop and explore ideas among ourselves.

The second, John T. Williams (interview of March 29, 1975), chaired the bylaws committee:

The bylaws reflected the divisions at that time. That was the first time I know of where you had rank-and-file members on a bylaws committee. This was unique, and difficult. The people had no experience at it, so it was difficult. So we looked at other bylaws as guidelines, and therefore *we were still controlled in that way.* Thus there was a risk of the rank and file being a cover for the bureaucracy's bylaws. To deal with that, we tried to get bylaws from locals that were somewhat advanced. We'd hear of a local with the rank-and-file active, and send for *their* bylaws. Or someone's Dad would be in a Local, and we'd get their bylaws. And the Joint Council had a "draft bylaws" model which suited them. And had we gone too far, the bylaws would have been dumped.
(What was in people's minds during the struggle?)
A surge for rank-and-file participation and control. The bylaws were a way to get it—and bylaws the rank and file had a say in. During this same time, a demand was going on for a rank-and-file contract committee, and BAs elected by the rank and file.

The bylaws committee met weekly for over a year. After working up a proposal for a section of the rules, it would report to the members; the members would discuss the proposal, and the committee would work on it some more. Finally, with all sections prepared, the committee organized an all-day bylaws convention with catered lunch and dinner, at which the bylaws were discussed by hundreds of drivers, amended, and finally approved by vote of the membership.

The Rank and File
During the
Cohen Period:
Further Actions

During the period between creation of the bylaws committee
and the bylaws convention, drivers were active in numerous
ways. Early in this period, for instance, black rank-and-file
Teamsters, including many members of 208, set up a black caucus and went public with charges of racism against the companies
and the union. Within 208, black hiring hall drivers were a particularly active group.

According to John T. Williams, a leader in the Black Caucus
(interview of July 26, 1973):

I saw no black BAs in the Joint Council—now there are about a dozen.
Many companies didn't hire blacks, and the hiring hall didn't send
blacks to certain companies. No Teamster office employees were
black. We brought charges against Beer Local 203 at the Joint Council,
and it became a national issue. They ruled that attorneys could represent each side, and Local 203 got an attorney, but we didn't. The
NAACP, ACLU, and some law professor all wanted to come in as
advisers to me and two other hiring hall rank and filers who fought the
case. There was a three-day trial with the news media there, then it
was postponed for two weeks. But the pressure was so heavy that a
number of blacks got jobs in 203 at this time, and the trial never
reconvened. They had planned to ''sell'' me to 203 during this, so that
I would go to the Beer Local and 208 would give them extra for taking
me out of their hair, but this didn't happen.

This led to formation of a Joint Council civil rights board, which
included Williams and a number of high Teamster officials; the
board was a ''safe'' one—the officials made sure that it did very
little—but the fact of its existence, combined with pressures
from the black caucus and its numerous white supporters, led
to such victories as getting Greyhound to hire black drivers. The
combination of a black caucus and an active multiracial rank-
and-file movement in which blacks played an active role therefore succeeded both in mobilizing the entire movement behind
the demands of the blacks and in intensifying black involvement
in building an active and effective union.

Another action centered on elections. In December 1959, an election was held for six of the seven Executive Board positions in Local 208—the Presidency, Vice-Presidency, Recording Secretary, and three Trustees. The rank-and-file caucus ran a slate of candidates, and found itself facing a problem very common in union elections—eligibility rules are written so as to exclude a great many members from candidacy. In this case, a member must have been "in good standing" for two years, which meant that he could not once in those two years have been late in paying dues—a provision that made ineligible many of the caucus's most involved members, particularly those who worked out of the hiring hall and so could not have been on dues checkoff. The caucus decided that anyone they could elect, no matter how little active, would keep an opponent out and make it more difficult for Cohen to entrench a machine; success this time in electing even a not very desirable rank and filer would spark others to run in the next election, when the activist candidates might win.

The caucus also had to make sure that the election was conducted fairly. Traditionally, the election committee had been appointed by the Local's President. The caucus did not trust this procedure. Here, their strong support among the membership and their strong base in several barns and in the hiring hall paid off. They mobilized a large number of drivers to attend the nominations meeting, and thus were strong enough to pass, after a heated debate, a motion that the election committee be drawn by lot from those in attendance at the meeting.

Another problem concerned unity. An election is more than an occasion to win office. For a caucus of working drivers, it could provide an opportunity to publicize ideas on improving the union, and to win other drivers' agreement and future support. This required a somewhat unusual sort of campaign, one focusing on the issues rather than on the personalities or past exploits of the candidates. The desire of candidates to seek votes for themselves alone on the basis of their personal qualities, or of their disagreement with some of the more controversial parts of the platform, had to be transcended. This was made easier because the slate had developed naturally from a caucus that had fought together over a considerable period of time. The election was just one more in a continuing series of battles. Even so, the lure of office was a threat to the unity of the caucus. Since the slate included less active caucus members with little experience in a common struggle, and even drivers who had no real connection to the caucus and who had been run largely because they happened to be eligible, the problem was serious.

The major vehicle the caucus used to overcome this built-in disunity and to publicize its ideas was a newsletter, *Rank & File News*. In it, they presented their picture of the election campaign and their ideas on changing the union. Not incidentally, by linking in print the names of their candidates to the views of the caucus, they effectively pressured slate members to support and present the program.

This program, presented while the bylaws committee was working on its proposals, emphasized an active membership and leadership by working drivers rather than by officials. The activists outlined this program in the December 12, 1959, issue of *Rank & File News*:

Editorial

As one of the largest Teamster Locals in the Southern California Council, our local 208 have every right to give strong leadership to the most advanced programs for the welfare of our members.

UNITY

We cannot achieve these natural and substantial gains without the support of an active rank-and-file membership; a membership standing together. . . .

RANK-AND-FILE LEADERSHIP

Believing firmly that no Executive Board member can serve two masters; a salaried business agent and also represent working truck drivers—it is imperative to separate all business agents from our Executive Board if you, as working truck drivers, expect to get a fair shake of the [document illegible].

CONTRACT NEGOTIATION

Only when we have a contract negotiated "with the rank-and-file" can we expect a contract "for the rank-and-file." A rank-and-file Contract Negotiation Team of Working Truck Drivers. . . .

COMMITTEES

The fullest participation of the membership is best expressed through active, rank-and-file Committees . . . Committees on finance as well as other Committees to assist the membership. . . .

GRIEVANCES

One of the most serious complaints of our members is grievances as well as out-right contract violations by the employer; All grievances must be met with STRONG ACTION!—not WEAK ANSWERS!

STEWARD'S PROGRAM

Our Steward's Program must be revived and reactivated. A potent Steward program, with the backing of the Executive Board and the membership, shall be an effective link in advancing all segments of our local. . . .

HEALTH & WELFARE PROGRAM

Our present Health and Welfare program is in urgent need of complete overhauling; we have out-grown this present out-dated program. Complete hospitalization for ALL SICKNESS is a protection your family needs. . . .

May we also take this time to sincerely thank you for your encouraging support for our team.

Your support and your VOTE is a badge of confidence. . . . May we uphold your trust with dignity, with courage, with determination, and with the ability to warrant your continued support.

In the election, the rank-and-file slate won the Vice Presidency, Recording Secretary, and two of the Trustee posts, which, in theory, gave them a majority on the Executive Board. However, in practice, the weakness of the slate's connection to the caucus enabled Cohen to woo half of the slate's victors and to maintain control over the Executive Board. However, his control over the Local itself, shaky to begin with, was considerably weakened by the caucus's electoral successes and by the remaining effective caucus members on the Board.

The next year, 1960, was one of maneuvering and infighting on the Executive Board; charges and countercharges were filed on financial irregularities and other matters. During this same year, the bylaws were finally passed; but many of their provisions, such as the steward's council, were not put into effect.

From the viewpoint of the drivers, then, things stayed bad, with the union still not adequately representing them, and so support for change in the Local continued to build. Some of the former Filipoff forces were led by Edwin Blackmarr. Blackmarr had been a BA and then hiring hall dispatcher before Cohen was elected Secretary-Treasurer. He quit as Dispatcher and went back to driving when Cohen took over. Blackmarr and his supporters drifted into alliance with the rank-and-file caucus; both opposed Cohen, and the Filipoff supporters were coming to see the need for bylaws, elected BAs, and greater rank-and-file involvement. But then, early in 1961, the constant battling and wrangling in 208 led to the involvement of Jimmy Hoffa.

Intervention
by the
International

Hoffa had never spent an unthreatened day in office. He was constantly under attack by the United States government, whether by Congressional committees or by the Justice Department. Further, he always had enemies within the Teamsters Union, including the top-level officials of the Western Conference of Teamsters. In Southern California Joint Council 42, Filipoff of 208, and Frank Matula, Jr., of Local 396, were, around 1958, his only major supporters. Filipoff's defeat by Cohen left Hoffa even weaker.

Thus, the conflict in 208 gave Hoffa an opportunity to build support in Southern California by allying with the insurgents. Both he and they would be walking a fine line between basically incompatible interests. Hoffa would not and could not take actions that would threaten the basis of his bureaucracy's power in the union. Yet the natural course of development of the insurgent rank-and-file movement centered in Local 208 was to attack the bureaucracy's power and, in particular, probably to take eventual actions to spread the power of the rank-and-file throughout the Joint Council. At such time, Hoffa would have to intervene against 208 lest the membership in other areas of the country, where the officials supported him, become infected by 208's example.

However, in 1960 and 1961, these worries were in the future, and Hoffa had ways to head off insurgencies before they developed too far. The constant charges and countercharges among the 208 leadership both brought the Local to Hoffa's attention and gave him the opportunity to intervene in its affairs. He sent a top assistant, Bill Fontaine, to investigate. Fontaine spoke to drivers in coffeeshops and trucking terminals, and reported back that the drivers were up in arms about not being defended by the Local. Thus, the insurgents might get out of hand; in any case, there were enough of them to make an alliance valuable. So Hoffa appointed Mike Singer of Teamsters Local 626 to act as informal "overseer" for 208. This meant that Singer would make "suggestions" to Cohen (who would remain Secretary-Treasurer)—and that Cohen had better take Singer's advice.

In a few months, Singer made important changes in the Local. For one thing, he made the business agents work. He made them give full reports on their activities, and chewed them out if they were not solving the members' problems. In the classic tactic of those in power who decide to make a conciliatory response to an insurgency, he offered jobs to several leaders of the rank-and-file movement. Some came onto the payroll as organizers, and conducted several organizing drives, including one aimed at G.I. Trucking. G.I., one of the major trucking companies in the Los Angeles area, was originally set up after World War II, at the instigation of the Motor Trucking Association of Southern California, as a strike-breaking company. Although G.I. remained nonunion, Singer got considerable credit among the drivers for trying to organize it.

Another of Singer's cooptation tactics was to appoint John T. Williams as "Health and Welfare Coordinator" for the Local. Thus, by one move, he removed Williams from the hall, gave him a taste of union office, gave a union position to a black, and helped build the alliance between Hoffa and the insurgents. By assigning Williams to help members with their problems—with the promise that the first time Williams failed to do this, he would be fired—Singer ensured that his overseership would get credit for those individual problems that Williams solved, and for Williams' innovations such as a Local bloodbank.

Another of Singer's moves was more complex. He arranged that the head stewards from the major barns each spend two weeks as an assistant business agent, going with the BAs on their daily rounds. They were paid as BAs. This action had several goals. First, it trained stewards to be more effective in defending members, which also aimed to take the edge off discontent. Second, it showed the stewards, and through them the rank and file, the difficulties, even for a conscientious BA, of winning grievances. Finally, it whetted the appetites of many stewards for union office, and in particular for the post of business agent, while giving them experience so that they could make well-grounded criticisms of any ineffective incumbent. Subsequently, no administration could take it easy—but opportunism and ambition for office became an open part of 208's political life.

Singer also initiated the use of 24-hour strikes by Local 208 members. The 24-hour strike stemmed from a contract clause allowing one unauthorized absence from work every nine months without drastic penalty. Of course, should all the workers at a trucking terminal just happen to take their 24 hours at the same time, the company could lose an enormous amount of money from unmet timetables, and from dissatisfied customers whose freight hadn't been delivered as promised. The 24-hour wildcat became a major tactic and threat for 208. In fact, as a way of maintaining an active rank-and-file, it had central implications for 208's later development, although it is probable that Singer did not see this when he introduced it to the Local.

From the viewpoint of the rank-and-file movement, Singer's overseership was a victory that laid the basis for major defeats a decade later (See Chapter 7). Singer made changes in the Local that benefited every driver. On the other hand, the "model for victory"—if you make enough noise, the people in charge will grant your demands—was misleading. The thrust of the rank-and-file movement had been toward developing a far stronger "model for victory"—if you organize your own rank-and-file power, and take your own actions, you can defend yourselves, take power in your union, and go on to bigger and better things. Further, Singer set up the first stage of an alliance with Hoffa—an alliance which over the years led to a fatal reliance on so-called friends at the top rather than on the drivers' own strength.

These dangers were not evident at the time, and many activists in 208 saw Singer's leadership as crucial to their successes.

Singer, however, was powerful only because Hoffa said he was, and in May 1961, Hoffa and Singer quarreled. Reportedly, the quarrel was over Singer's ambitions to become an International Vice-President, in which independent actions by some of the activists in 208 may have been a complicating factor. However, it may well be that he had done his job too well—that is, that he had been too effective in helping the rank and file. Singer was then removed from his role in 208.

The rank and filers who had been trying to transform 208 were outraged. They were also angry at the prospect that Cohen would be back in control of the Local, and that failure to stand up to the employers would again be the pattern. Their response was to seize the 208 office, and lock Cohen out of it. In the words of Pat Patton, at that time Recording Secretary of the Local and a leader of the rank-and-file movement (interview of July 31, 1974):

No one would explain why Singer had been removed, so we decided to lock it up until he was back. I arranged to get the key to the office, and called people to come and bring buckets for toilets, and sleeping bags. We barricaded it, and told everyone that it was closed.

Hoffa called, and told me to knock it off, that I could be tried on charges if it continued. So we screamed at each other, with me saying we'd stay in the office until Singer came back.

So they broke in, the cops removed the panels to the hall and broke in. We asked the cops to search us and to examine the office to establish that nothing was being taken out and that nothing had been destroyed.

[A high Teamster official] called a special executive board meeting the next night. . . . At the meeting, [the high official] said nothing, and used a lot of words saying nothing, except that it had been bad publicity. I pointed out that Cohen had called the cops, and that this is where the publicity and the headlines came from.

After the meeting, [name deleted] and another guy attacked me and John Butler. [Name deleted] beat me, and Butler did a beautiful job on the other guy.

Patton had asked six men to take part in the lock-in; all but one had come. Presumably, then, the insurgents could easily have organized a much larger demonstration, but did not. In any case, the headlines they had stirred, at a time when civil disobedience was just coming into use in the civil rights movement, counteracted any negative effects on rank-and-file morale of the loss of Singer, and the movement continued its series of victories.

The Rank-and-File
Movement
Comes to Power

Shortly before Singer was removed, the Local held an election for delegates to a special convention called to reelect Hoffa as President of the IBT and to revise the constitution of the International. This election provides evidence of the support for the rank-and-file movement, which ran a slate of seven delegates and three alternates—one candidate for each spot on the ballot. Although hurt by the decision of some rank-and-file activists who had been rejected for the slate to seek election as individuals, the rank-and-file slate won four of the seven delegate positions and all three of the alternate slots. Two other rank-and-file activists were elected as delegates, as was the pro-Cohen Local President. Cohen himself came in eleventh.

The rank and filers were in a position of strength. They decided the time was ripe to attack the appointed BA system, which they saw as the cause of the Local's poor representation and as giving the Secretary-Treasurer the ability to create a patronage machine. The activists had not originally proposed elected BAs because they feared it would goad Cohen's forces into throwing all their strength into defeating the entire bylaws project.

Their campaign to pass a bylaws amendent for elected BAs was a model of tactical skill. Their problem was to get a resolution to amend the bylaws onto the floor of the Local meeting, and to make sure the meeting was not adjourned before the vote. The insurgents had majority support—won and organized in the course of the previous several years of struggles—but still could not be sure of mobilizing the two-thirds majority needed to pass an amendment. Thus, precise tactics at the time of the vote were necessary. John T. Williams described them (July 26, 1973):

We organized what was going to happen very carefully. We had "light artillery" people to surround the opposition leaders on the floor, hassle them, and take their attention away from what we were doing. We had a General Headquarters on the floor for communication, coordination, and making decisions about what to do next. And there were "heavy artillery" people to make speeches, motions, and so forth. We ran test motions to see where things stood, to see how strong we were. On the BA election motion, their spies had told them it would come, and they didn't want to call on us. So we put all our heavy artillery on one mike, and they wouldn't call on anyone at that mike, but we had Manny Magan on the other mike and their chair called on him and he made the motion.

This degree of planning and organization, and the understanding among the rank-and-file activists that such tactical precision was needed, had of course developed out of many previous battles.* An inexperienced activist would have seen no necessity to maneuver to get a motion brought onto the floor for a final reading and a vote; he would have thought it obvious that the chair must follow the rules and bring it up. However, had the activists not maneuvered and obtained a vote, the incumbents could have forced them to reintroduce the motion and go through three readings of it again. Similarly, the test motions, along with organized "headquarters" on the floor to interpret them, were critical because the balance of support was very close. As things worked out, the vote was one or two votes shy of the needed two-thirds, but the insurgents made such a long, sustained uproar that the Local President finally ruled that the motion had been passed.

The actual election of business agents, scheduled for six months later (January 1962), was the focus of much attention and energy. However, a danger remained that the International might refuse to allow the relevant changes in the bylaws when it reviewed them.† That it did allow them was the result of

---

* It should also be understood that Cohen's following the rules was also a product of this struggle. As many locals discovered during the TDC and UPSurge campaigns in 1976 (see ch. 10), the officers may just rule motions out of order, or adjourn the meeting early. Cohen's overall position was too weak, the insurgents too strong, and the national attack on Teamster corruption too sharp to let him get away with this.

† In October 1972, Teamster Local 853 in the San Francisco Bay Area passed a set of bylaws written by the rank-and-file to give themselves more say in the Local. It took two-and-a-half years, a petition, and a mass lawsuit by members to get the International to act on them. When, in February 1975, a letter finally came from the International stating that most of the changes had been approved, the rank and file still had to pressure the Secretary-Treasurer of the Local to put them into practice.

Hoffa's extreme difficulties at this time. Locals (or, in some cases, groups within Locals) were trying to secede from the IBT. For a short period, it seemed as if the pressure of the Federal attack on the Teamsters, combined with the AFL-CIO's willingness to raid the IBT, might spark a widespread revolt from the rank and file and dismember the union. Specifically, after the 1961 Special Convention reelected Hoffa and increased his power in the union, a number of Locals in Cincinnati bolted from the union, and groups in St. Louis, Louisiana, Cleveland, Chicago, and Tucson met to consider doing the same. Members of San Francisco Local 85 were said to have booed down a proposal that Hoffa be invited to speak on the progress of Western Freight Agreement negotiations. Local 85 and East Bay Local 70, it was rumored, might leave the union over discontent at being forced to take part in Western area-wide negotiations that would produce weaker contracts than they thought they could win on their own.

In this context of nationwide discontent, for the International to veto 208's election of BAs could have sparked a revolt that might have spread far beyond one Local. In addition, it would have alienated some of the few allies Hoffa had in the West. The danger was underscored when Hoffa personally presented the Western Freight Agreement results to 208 before the ratification vote on the new contract. In part because the agreement failed to give wage-parity with San Francisco, members hissed and booed Hoffa, and almost mobbed him. Some yelled "AFL-CIO" in a reference to secession. They then voted, 800 to 150, against the proposed contract.* Thus, the election of BAs, although unwanted by the officials of Joint Council 42 and

---

* According to articles in the *Los Angeles Times* and Kennedy aide Walter Sheridan (1972:190), the next month saw some members of 208 circulating petitions to leave the Teamsters Union, and other members circulating petitions to have 208 put into trusteeship by the International. However, no one I talked to remembers any such petitions being carried around by anyone. They all are sure that the organized rank and filers took no such action. It is impossible to be sure of the truth, to know whether anti-Hoffa forces told lies to the newspapers, or whether the newspapers lied for their own ends, or whether my informants are suppressing memories of a moment of disloyalty to their union (whether disloyalty on their part or disloyalty by other Local members), or whether a few people passed such petitions but the activists never took the matter seriously enough to remember it. But whatever the truth, Hoffa had to take these reports, and the clear evidence of discontent, into account, particularly when early in November the AFL-CIO made an offer to assist any Southern California secession.

by most other officials of the Teamsters Union, was approved for Local 208.

This battle won, the rank-and-file activists turned to the election itself. They ran a full slate of seven candidates for Business Agent. Thirty-two other candidates also ran, including a slate of Cohen's appointed incumbents. Of the insurgents' slate, five won. Four of these had been working out of the hiring hall since Singer's departure and thus had extra time to campaign, as well as to make frequent contact with hall activists and other hall drivers, whereas activists Pat Patton and Eddie Dietrich, who had continued to work at TCD and PMT, were not elected BAs. Only two incumbent Cohen-supporters were elected. By the beginning of 1962, then, the rank-and-file movement had elected five of its leaders to positions as full-time officials, with the responsibility for dealing with employers over members' grievances; it had a number of powerful barn organizations, which already were beginning to make effective use of the 24-hour wildcat; and it was strongly backed by most members of the Local.

Time was indeed running out for the Cohen regime. Cohen's President, Cam Ferrell, who had been earning his living as an appointed BA, quit as President after losing in the BA election. William Croysdill, recently elected BA on the rank-and-file slate, was appointed Acting President.

Meanwhile, activist BAs were going into the yards and co-operating with the drivers in ways that neither Cohen nor the employers were used to. Cohen attempted to restrain them. The rank and filers replied with formal charges that Cohen was not representing them but defending the companies. Unable to take the heat, Cohen "got sick." In June 1962, he resigned.

Croysdill was appointed Acting Secretary-Treasurer. He resigned as BA and appointed Dietrich in his place. A section of the Executive Board refused to support the rank-and-file caucus on this appointment of Dietrich, and brought charges to oust the rest of the Executive Board on the grounds that the bylaws stated that BAs were to be elected. They also charged that Croysdill had packed the Executive Board with his faction when vacancies were to be filled. They organized a 30-person picket line demanding that the Croysdill faction leave office, warning that otherwise they would seize the office forcibly. After the police prevented their planned seizure, they then filed suit in court. However, the whole affair was settled out of court, in September, when Hoffa appointed one of his top aides, Jim Harding, to take over the affairs of the Local until the Executive Board election at the end of the year.

When Harding came in, he asked the BAs to sign resignations in case it should be decided that any be removed; the BAs refused, noting that they had been elected by the membership and thus were not accountable to Harding. Harding and Hoffa, anxious to forge an alliance with 208's rank-and-file movement, did not push the issue.

The next month, the rank and filers called a meeting of some 20 activists and key stewards to put together a slate for the forthcoming election. They decided to run Ed Blackmarr for the Secretary-Treasurer spot, on the basis that Croysdill would very likely be defeated. They also chose, by election, their other six Executive Board candidates.

In the election, Cohen loyalists were decisively defeated. Blackmarr came in as Secretary-Treasurer (a position he was to hold for eight years); with him were elected Patton as Recording Secretary, Dietrich as Trustee, and Al Quintero as Trustee. Croysdill, the insurgents' Presidential candidate, lost, as did Vice-Presidential candidate Alex Maheras (a PMT steward whose name will recur many times in this book). A second rank-and-file slate, composed of those who had resisted Croysdill's appointment of Dietrich as BA, elected John Butler as President and also won the Vice Presidency and a Trustee spot. In general, supporters of this second slate had been less involved in the rank-and-file movement, and were thus less sophisticated about the politics of unionism and the steps needed to maintain rank-and-file control, but more concerned with being scrupulous to the letter in finances and in following procedures. By the end of 1962, then, the rank and file had come to power in Local 208, in a divided and factionalized but nonetheless real way.

Overview of the Process

The most important process in the fight to take over Local 208 was the development of a large number of activist unionists, and the formation of organizational ties among them. In particular, a number of barns became strongholds of unionism, able and often anxious to take on their employer or reshape their union. The most active drivers in these and other barns formed a formidable local-wide rank-and-file movement. Further, in the course of their struggle, many of the participants learned ways to function in union politics and ways to fight the forces that encourage bureaucratization. Thus, Local 208 members developed a politically skilled group of activists, many of whom have both remained active and have also trained a new generation of active unionists.

Another important process was mobilization—why and how the drivers fought back. Before the drivers began to struggle, their employers had enormous power over them, and often used it in ways that hurt them. The union did not defend them, and often would even hinder their attempts to defend themselves—for instance their attempt to set up a stewards system. As a result, in those workplaces, such as PMT and the hall, where employers' power was most galling, the drivers formed social clubs of a sort, then used these clubs to mobilize to defend themselves. As the word of their successes spread, other drivers organized their barns; from there, the process snowballed into a large rank-and-file movement.

The process of taking over the Local was also aided by splits among union officials within the Local and within the International, as well as by Hoffa's troubles in controlling the IBT. The split let the activists use Cohen to oust Filipoff. The activists prevented Cohen from solidifying his control, maintained their forward momentum, and crushed his weak attempts to oppose their programs. The split within the International prevented Cohen from obtaining upper-level help, and indeed gave the insurgents some outside help. The activists of 208 remained, however, in a very different relationship to Hoffa than to Cohen. While Hoffa's troubles let them take over 208 more easily than would otherwise have been the case, they were an isolated group in one Local and thus unable to stop Hoffa from consolidating his position within the IBT. They became boxed-in, an offbeat wing of the Hoffa forces, shielded by their powerful ally from employers and from hostile forces in the Teamster bureaucracy; when Hoffa went, their umbrella collapsed, and they found they had not maintained the momentum to confront their enemies successfully.

The rank and filers came into control of Local 208 only after years of struggle. They had already created a powerful force—a barn-based, organized, sophisticated group of rank-and-file activists—to keep their elected officers in line and to oppose the subtle pressures toward bureaucracy that so often turn fresh breezes into stale odors. With control of the Local in their hands, the activists were ready, willing, and able to turn their attention to their employers and clean up those workplace conditions that isolated barn organizations had been unable to correct, as well as build fighting organizations in those barns where the drivers had not yet organized.

Chapter 5

Rank and Filers
in Office

THE DRIVERS in Local 208 had built a rank-and-file movement to take on their employers and to force their Local to back them. Having taken over the Local, they proceeded, from 1963 to 1970, to push management around. In part this was done through the contractually established grievance procedure. The trucking companies were accustomed to sell-out, incompetent Business Agents. In those barns where the rank-and-file movement was not established, they were accustomed to lazy, timid, or inept stewards. Thus, management did not know the contract, nor how to present a case successfully at a grievance hearing. Suddenly confronted by the newly elected militant business agents, who had backgrounds as stewards in militant barns, the companies were caught totally unprepared. Nor were they ready to deal with the new style of stewards, who became more aggressive, as they saw that the Local officers and BAs would support them, and more and more competent, as the Stewards' Council meetings and their own experience trained them to present cases and to gather evidence in ways that win grievances.

Thus, in a situation where management had been running over the workers, aggressive policing of the contract meant that use of the grievance procedure could make up lost ground. To the extent that management remained incompetent, drivers could even establish rules that went far beyond the contract, then encode them as "past practices" that, being outside the contract language, were hard for the companies to remove through the grievance procedure.

Rank-and-File
Unionism
in Action

Gains due to management's incompetence were, however, possible only as long as management remained incompetent. In the words of Alex Maheras (interview of March 15, 1974):

208 and its membership had a ball. Management didn't have experience with militant members or agents, so we got things that stretched the contract out of recognition. But, slowly, employers got educated; we hurt ourselves in reality. Managers stay in longer, or go to other companies, but we're always having to train stewards.

But use of the grievance procedure was by no means the only way the activists fought management. Far more important was the use of such direct action as strikes and sabotage campaigns. As an example, consider the following account (excerpted from my field notes) by Archie Murrietta, one of the leaders of the 1970 wildcat and now the President of Local 208 (interview March 25, 1975):

People at PMT loved to fight. The motivation was to keep the yard a good one.

When Dietrich and Alex [Maheras] left the yard, and Tobin died in '68, I at 28 years became the leader of the yard. It was scary. I saw Andy and asked him to come in. And I got more friendly with George Alexander and Butch. In the Pig Yard, we were less active.

We were proud of PMT's record, and we'd get prestige through it and people would tell us . . . people would fight to become steward. *Pride.*

People would fight to become stewards.

It's still true.

(What about short strikes?)

It was a matter of prestige, emotions, togetherness. We had four 24-hour strikes. And about one safety stoppage per month at the Pig Yard. This would lead to laughter at managements' faces when we were eating lunch, and was great for our morale. It got so they would come and ask us in advance for our OK before asking anyone to do any dangerous work. Blackmarr would encourage us on fighting like this.

And we could use safety for other things. Like to save _____ 's job. He had backed up to pick up a trailer, which rolled back a little and caught on the train. The train started at that moment, and dragged the trailer, and this knocked over 15 trailers. _____was fired. [A 208 official] made up a safety issue, and we struck, and he ended up with only a warning letter. He got his job back.

Ninety-five percent was the atmosphere of fun while learning something.

Blackmarr conveyed this atmosphere—fun, power, strength—to all stewards in the city. PMT had it from '55 or '56, of course. And stories about Blackmarr would make people want to have a piece of the action.

And meetings with management were long, and involved in setting policy, and so you got a sense of taking part.

The drivers of Local 208, backed by their union officials, pulled such short strikes time after time. They achieved results. Backlogged problems were resolved in a few hours, jobs were saved, particularly bothersome terminal managers lost their jobs. Working conditions improved, and companies found it harder to cheat drivers out of pay or benefits.

In particular, a number of companies had worked out devices to avoid making the required payments for employees' health, welfare, and pensions. Thus, when a driver retired, he might have trouble collecting his pension, or, if injured, he might have problems collecting health insurance payments. Specific instances of this were presented by BA Charles Brenner to the Trusteeship Hearings in 1970:

By falsifying the record I mean this: Sometimes an . . . employee of a trucking company works until the eighth or ninth of the month. The security fund does not know that. The only thing they know is when they receive a payment. Then the company, instead of saying that they terminated on the eighth of the month, which would mean that the company has to pay another premium, a month's premium for that particular month, they say he was terminated on the thirtieth of the previous month, which means the company does not have to pay the premium for the month that they actually worked.

As a result of that, when a man asks a business agent or myself, he says, "Look, I worked . . . December 8th. Now when is my health and welfare coverage stopped for me and my family?"

I tell him, "Well, under the Prudential plan you have 30 days from December 8th to January 8th. Under Kaiser you have all of December and all of January."

So he takes his kids, his wife or himself goes in the hospital, because he's not working, he's laid off, and when he gets in there the hospital calls up the security fund to find out if they can give him treatment and the security fund says he's not paid for the current month and they say no.

In the meantime, the dependent, whether it is a wife, child or the employee himself, cannot get any hospital attention and his illness becomes aggravated as a result of that.

So that was the reason we have to go in there and act fast.

We had one of our members who worked for [a company] from approximately—the last time he worked there was approximately '59 to '64. When he was 65 years old he came up and asked to be processed for a pension.

So he brought up the W-2 form, and sure enough on there it showed where he earned different sums of money for each year he's working.

The employer—when I accosted the employer, I said, "Look, you failed to make payments for this man. As a result of this, he can't get his pension."

They still haven't paid it. And I was advised by the legal department that inasmuch as four years has passed, that you can't do anything. Meanwhile, [the worker] died of malnutrition, because he couldn't get the money.[1]

Early in the Blackmarr regime, Pat Patton, the Recording Secretary, took a few months leave from his job as a truck driver to go on the Local 208 payroll to make examples of some of the delinquent companies. From then on, delinquencies in payments were often met by strikes sanctioned by the Local; once started, such a strike would involve far broader issues. In fact, the issue of delinquency provided a good "cover" against lawsuits by giving a legal pretext for a strike over issues on which the contract prohibited striking. Terminal managers sometimes found themselves conceding many of the drivers' demands in private conversation with the business agent (private to avoid witnesses to the fact that discussions strayed beyond the strikable issue of delinquent payments.) Thus, the companies had strong reason to keep their health, welfare, and pensions payments up-to-date and honest.

The atmosphere created by the many battles with employers had great effect on the Local. It built a desire to take part in Local affairs, and a willingness to take risks. The risks were real. One active and aggressive steward whom I talked to had been fired 10 times in 13 years by his employer—but management had been forced by the other drivers or by Local officials to take him back each time. In general, stewards in strong yards might get fired fairly often, but would get their jobs back (often with back pay), while an aggressive steward in a poorly organized yard might well find himself fired and working out of the hall.

When the rank-and-file movement took over the Local, they used their new power and the militancy of already strong barns to win victories over employers. As a result, drivers in many previously passive barns began to become militant. However, this process of establishing militancy throughout the Local, and broadening the membership's political support for the Blackmarr regime, was not spontaneous; it was conscious action. When they came into office, the leaders of the rank-and-file movement had much support, but also confronted much cynicism. Many drivers assumed the new officers would become as self-seeking, bureaucratic, or ineffective as their predecessors. Others were simply apathetic, feeling that neither the union nor anything else would improve conditions. To meet the challenge of convincing unmobilized members that activist unionism could work, the rank-and-file leaders took two main courses of action. First, as Murrietta's remarks point out, those barns which were already organized furnished living proof that it could be done. Thus, when a driver from an unorganized barn spoke with drivers from militant barns or with hall drivers working at his own terminal, he would hear stories of the militants' accomplishments, learn of how they had organized for success, and even hear that, when the drivers (or even management) called in a business agent, the BA would support the militants. Second, the new BAs were sent to *all* the barns to discover what the gripes were and then help members to deal with them. When it thus became clear that the Local would fight the company, and fight successfully, previously apathetic drivers organized more actively and started to initiate their own battles. This in turn led them into active participation in the Local.

Particularly interesting is that this process did not create a clique of militants who were "in" with the administration, to the exclusion of the rank-and-file, as happens in some locals when insurgents take over. Since the incoming officers were split between the Blackmarr faction and the Butler faction, the need for broad political support prevented such cliquism. More important, the dynamics of confronting management through strikes created activists in each barn who would not put up with any such clique. Further, the leaders of every sizable barn, as well as the most successful leaders of small ones, saw that, in an open situation, they might be elected BA; thus, they opposed cronyism for opportunist reasons as well as idealistic ones. In addition, as time went on, the pride of the activists in 208, and in its reputation as a fair, democratic, open, and militant local, itself became a powerful motivation to keep it that way.

The Stewards' Council played a key role in these processes. When a barn became active, its stewards would go to Council meetings. This drew them into the internal life of the Local, its politics and debates. The Stewards' Council also provided activists from various barns with a way to get together. Since two hundred or so stewards might come to any given meeting, and about a hundred came to most meetings, there was a powerful counterweight to any tendencies toward cliquism, as well as a convenient means of communication about any mistakes made by the officers or BAs. Thus, the monthly meetings of the Stewards' Council and the serious monthly discussions at membership meetings mobilized newly active members to take part in the Local's affairs and kept the officials on their toes. Of course, the existence of meetings only had such effect because the drivers had seen the importance of participatory unionism to their workplace struggles.

Also, new leadership of 208 actively organized drivers into their Local, which not only brought previously nonunion drivers the benefits of unionism, but enlivened 208 as well. The organizing drives and frequent strikes to compel an employer to sign a first contract involved active rank and filers from throughout the Local and also provided a valuable training ground for militant stewards, a number of whom took three to six months off from work to go on the union payroll as organizers. Later, stewards who had been effective organizers provided much of the leadership of the 1970 wildcat.

How the barns organized themselves during the Blackmarr years is crucial. The success of 208 came from having strong barns to serve as examples and to act as alternative power centers to, and watchdogs over, the Local's officials, at the same time that the energy and commitment of the activists came largely from the successes and excitement of the struggles in each terminal. How PMT and WesCar, two of the most active barns, organized themselves, may serve as examples.

PMT organized in the mid-1950s (see chapter 4). During the 1960s, the problem was how to maintain that organization, particularly since a number of its leaders had become full-time Local officials or had died during this period. To some extent, the problem solved itself; as the earlier remarks of Murrietta indicate, the excitement and success of strong action drew many PMT drivers into active unionism. Careful training also was involved. If a driver started to raise issues, or to complain frequently about management, stewards would ask him to help out. For example, when one of the stewards was away on vacation, they would give the driver a chance to come as an alternate to meetings with management. The more experienced stewards would also train the newer ones to function effectively, teaching them the niceties of the contract and the special arrangements forced from management. In particular, the head steward would have received extensive training from his predecessor. Such a training program was possible only because the stewards trusted each other; they had a ground rule that their disagreements would not be told to outsiders, and that they would back each other up.

Because the stewards were successful, active members tended to follow their leadership. The stewards in turn made it a point to talk with members and ask what they thought should be done. Wider solidarity among the drivers also developed from social contacts outside of work. In particular, a picnic ground at a winery near the PMT barn became a gathering spot for the drivers after work. Talk ranged widely, but problems with management and what to do about them were favorites.

WesCar was not a well-organized barn in the early 1960s. At the beginning of the Blackmarr regime, WesCar's drivers were dominated by a number of high-seniority men who did not want to rock the boat. However, comparing what was being accomplished at other barns to conditions at their own company—reputedly a "fortress of brutality"—led some of the younger drivers, along with some dockworkers of Local 357, to fight back at WesCar. Their ensuing struggle brought them into conflict with the older drivers as well as with management. Thus, in one strike still widely remembered, they threw a picket line up at the terminal over certain demands; when management agreed to these demands, they added a few more, and then kept the barn shut down until management gave in on these as well. In fact, before the strike ended, they had not only ended many annoying yard practices but had also won the removal of the terminal manager whom they held responsible for the bad conditions. This victory established the young militants as the leaders of the barn, but the split between the younger and the older drivers remained. In particular, 17 of the older drivers crossed the picket line.

The Local leadership decided to make an example of these 17, and at the same time solidify the militants' backing for the Blackmarr leadership, by bringing them up on charges of crossing an authorized picket line. However, the Butlerites opposed Blackmarr, holding that the strike had not been authorized. Nevertheless, at their trial before the Executive Board, the 17 were found guilty and fined. Drivers all over the Local thus understood that if they crossed a picket line they would be punished, an awareness which strengthened the position of militant stewards throughout 208. The officers' decision also became an issue in the election of Local officers that Fall, with the Butler forces calling it an example of Blackmarr's contempt for proper procedures, and the militants terming it an example of their policies' effectiveness. Blackmarr's slate won the election.

The episode turned the rift between the older and younger drivers at WesCar into a lasting one; it was not until eight or nine years later that, under the pressures of company attacks, some of the older drivers began to side with the militants. In spite of the problems with the high seniority drivers, however, the militants had been able to organize one of the most solid and militant barns in Los Angeles, and turned it into a major force within the Local.

Interestingly, the WesCar drivers had a gathering spot, just as did the PMT drivers. At WesCar, they met in the parking lot. They set up a tent with thick rugs and other amenities and created a very popular hangout. (Ultimately, "The Oasis" was burned down in 1972 during the election campaign between the Trusteeship and the rank-and-file slate, and the railroad that owned the parking lot would not let it be rebuilt.)

The process of creating and maintaining militancy in the barns, and in the Local as a whole, resulted in a very effective kind of unionism. Drivers in Local 208 became the envy of all other drivers in the Los Angeles area. They won good working conditions, power enough to conduct themselves with full dignity in their relations with management, and strong pride and solidarity. Drivers who left 208's jurisdiction looked back upon their days in 208 with longing. In short, active rank-and-file unionism greatly benefited the workers who created it.

Problems
the Militants
Faced

The members of Local 208 faced a number of problems in preserving the open, democratic, activist unionism that they had built. Forces were tending to rebureaucratize the Local from within; the rest of the International had to be coped with (since the basic thrust of the International's officialdom is to crush rank-and-file militancy and democracy); racism in both the union and management, and how to relate to the struggles of black people throughout the country, had to be dealt with. Finally, there was the problem of coping with changes: changes in the economy as a whole which, during the Blackmarr regime, went from relative prosperity to the early stages of a major crisis; changes in the trucking industry, both in its reactions to changes in the broader economy and in the growth of larger trucking companies; and changes in the policy and structure of the IBT stemming from changes in the trucking industry and the adoption of national contracts.

THE PROBLEM OF BUREAUCRATIZATION

Unions tend to be bureaucratic and to ignore the needs of their members for a number of reasons. For one, the officers can benefit. Sitting in an office is easier than dealing with members' grievances. Employers respect a "labor statesman"—i.e., an official who sells out members' interests—and if that official can set up a strong machine, he has security, the possibility of advancement within the international officialdom, and the benefits of gifts and other bribes from employers. Besides, militancy involves risks. If one pushes too hard, the employers may try to destroy the Local. Even before that, they will certainly use the structure of national labor law to tie up the Local in damage suits for breach of contract. The International may intervene and impose a trusteeship on a Local which gets too militant, or which, by its successes, poses a threat by inspiring members of other Locals to rebel. Thus, it is logical to minimize these risks by restraining the most militant sections of the membership, but the procedures set up to curb the militants—such as review of proposed actions by officials—strengthen the power of those who stand to lose their jobs and salaries if an action is too militant but who lose nothing from the continuation of the conditions that such a militant action would fight. It is, after all, the rank and file and not the paid officials who are injured or laid off by the transgressions of management.

Bureaucratization also stems from the structure of labor contracts. These contracts set up a grievance procedure to deal with workers' problems. As we saw in chapter 1, the grievance procedure means that power over grievances rests in the labor bureaucracy and in management. Working drivers have no say in the outcome; thus, by the grievance procedure, the power of direct action is given up in return for a legalistic decision-making process in which working Teamsters are not involved. And as we have noted, this produces its own effects. Where a local relies on grievance hearings to defend the membership, stewards tend to become contractual-legalists, and union officers become simply expert grievance-processors; leadership is in no real sense needed. In contrast, where organized strikes, slowdowns, and sabotage are used to defend members' working conditions and livelihood, the rank and file develops its own leadership. Further, such an action as a wildcat strike requires the support of all the workers and the active involvement of many participants; this enlarges the base of active unionists upon which militant and democratic unionism depends, and weakens the sense of hopelessness and powerlessness which upholds bureaucratic power. Power over matters that affect the drivers' lives remains in their own hands, rather than in the hands of grievance-processors. And the union officers are affected, too; they become involved in organizing job actions rather than grievance papers, and are kept on their toes through contending with the leaders of mobilized barns.

There was present in Local 208 a strain between these two methods of achieving results—that of direct action, which would tend to resist bureaucratization but would also eventually produce a head-on collision with the International's conservatism, and that of the aggressive use of grievance procedures, which would minimize risks but would also erode rank-and-file power.

As we have already seen, the militants in Local 208 were proud of their activism, found it effective, and would fight against its replacement by contractual legalism. Nevertheless, how they maintained their activism during the Blackmarr regime is not clear-cut, since the history of American unionism is one of bureaucratization of militant locals against the wishes of their activists. For 208, the bylaws and working rules—although less effective than they might have been—were important in keeping power in the hands of the militants.

The bylaws set up a system of stewards. Unlike stewards in some other Locals, those in 208 did not receive extra seniority and were not paid by the Local; indeed, the stewards often lost pay by taking time off from work for union business. Thus, stewards continued on the job as working drivers, and shared the dangers and hassles of the work with other drivers. This meant that stewards were attracted to the stewardship strictly by the wish to deal with the drivers' problems. Further, unlike some Locals, 208 had a relatively large number of stewards; thus, stewardships were less likely to become fiefdoms, the stewards had other stewards with whom to cooperate, and the number of grievances was not overwhelming. In addition, election of stewards meant that they were not dependent upon officials for their positions; rather, the natural leaders of an activist barn tended to become stewards, and the rank and file maintained control over them. Thus, it would be harder for a Secretary-Treasurer to build up a machine, and "hacks" would find it difficult to restrain the rank-and-file if he did. Then too, in many active barns, the excitement of being a steward—a leader in confrontations and struggles against management—was so appealing that there was constant competition for the stewardships, and constant pressure for stewards to prove themselves tough and effective.

The bylaws also set up a Stewards' Council. Potentially, the Steward's Council could have become a center of action, strategic discussion, and planning that would have reduced even further the power of the officers and business agents and possibly have led to continued consideration of the strategic dilemmas confronting the Local. Unfortunately, the Council became more or less a forum, where the Secretary-Treasurer or a BA would lecture on the contract or pension plan, and the stewards would discuss this and perhaps touch briefly on other matters. In this instance, the initiative and power of the drivers was limited by that of the officials, who used their lectures to the Council to maintain themselves as the most organized and best-trained group in the Local. The dynamics involved are indicated by the following quotations. The first is from field notes of a conversation in which John Franklin, the leading steward at one of the TIME-DC terminals in Los Angeles, described an event in the 1960s (July 24, 1974):

I proposed to Blackmarr that we educate stewards better, and [another 208 official] said, "No way I'm going to educate people to take over my job."

John T. Williams (March 29, 1975) saw the dynamics as follows:

(So the Stewards' Council never reached its potential?)
Right.
(Why not?)
The Stewards' Council had no basic format. It was very un-pinned-down. Depends on how aggressive the stewards are in seizing it. And the stewards had no guidelines, so they've become more or less a forum.

Any attempt to change the Stewards' Council leads to people seeing you as building a political machine. You need a caucus. And you need time. Lots of time. Or you need somehow to eliminate the fear of the administration.

The rank and filers' failure to develop coordinated action and discussion independent of the officials, and thus to organize its own organs for strategic thought, decision, and action, was to have severe consequences during the 1970 wildcat. However, this flaw had not become apparent earlier, since, even in its official-dominated form, the Stewards' Council let the active stewards establish close ties and communication and thus provided considerable counterweight to any bureaucratizing tendencies.

A number of rules regarding business agents also affected the strain between democracy and bureaucracy. Most important, perhaps, was the bylaws provision for elected BAs. Any BA wanting to be reelected had to act in ways the membership liked, and the Secretary-Treasurer was unable to set up a machine by offering supporters BA appointments. If the members in a barn wanted to take militant action, an elected BA was under heavy pressure not to oppose them; if a member had a grievance, the BA would have to present the case effectively; and if a Secretary-Treasurer tried to set himself up above the members, some of the BAs would probably fight him.

Further, while Business Agents received adequate pay, it was not enough to breed excessive opportunism. During the Blackmarr regime, BAs received a higher income than most low-seniority drivers, but considerably less than most high-seniority drivers. Unlike the case in some areas, in most instances a BA who lost his position would also have lost, during his term of office, his seniority at his previous job, and would thus have to become either a hall driver or the bottom man on the seniority list at a new job. This would mean a drop of income and security, but during the relatively prosperous times of the Blackmarr administration, enough work was available that the drop would not be disastrous. Thus, the officials of Local 208 had relatively little reason to forget democracy and to take drastic action to protect their jobs. (In more recent years, the economic difficulties and unemployment have increased the incentive to retain a BA job.)

This point was reinforced by the lack of corruption during these years; BAs did not amass large sums under the table. Underlying this lack of corruption was, of course, the power of the rank and file. In particular, a rule was made that BAs would never meet with management during strikes without a steward present. (This rule was ignored only in the case of "private discussions" over delinquent health, welfare, and pension payments.) Thus, sweetheart deals would be hard to organize, stewards would have a direct voice in discussions with managements, errors by BAs would become public, any BAs who began to be affected by the subtle flatteries of management would be exposed, and stewards would learn the techniques that BAs develop from their wider experience. Another rule was to rotate BAs' assignments. Thus, BAs were prevented from developing fiefdoms; furthermore, it would hardly be worthwhile to set up a corrupt sweetheart deal with management when the next BA would surely discover it, even if the stewards didn't.

The threat of corruption, it should be noted, was very real. It is worth a lot of money to a company to win even a few new work rules that let it increase productivity or reduce overtime costs. I was told by one of Sid Cohen's business agents that employers gave them saddles, top coats, tires, and other gifts. Gifts were offered to officials during the Blackmarr regime as well—but were refused.

Rules and bylaws alone do not prevent bureaucratization; the people concerned, particularly the rank and file, must be actively involved in their union. Otherwise, it is the officers who rule on any challenges to their actions, who arrange for the counting of ballots, etc. Thus, again, the nature of truck driving, and the experiences and personalities of the members of Local 208, become crucial. As previously noted, truck driving provides opportunities for drivers to talk about their concerns away from the view of management or union officials. Drivers used this advantage, and learned to use it well, during the rank-and-file struggles that led to the bylaws and the Blackmarr regime. Beyond this, they learned that the rank-and-file *can* organize itself, *can* take over its local, and *can* then win important concessions from management.

Further, the members of 208—both drivers and those who became officials—developed deep personal convictions that democratic, activist unionism is worth fighting for. The pride of most members of 208 in their Local serves even yet as a powerful barrier to bureaucratic tendencies. Victories breed vigilance.

Further, the officials were themselves products of 208's rank-and-file struggles. Blackmarr had a personality little suited to bureaucracy, and most of the Blackmarr regime officials whom I met were, in my opinion, far more suited to agitating and hell-raising than to quiet contract administration.

It should nevertheless be noted that the forces of bureaucratization did have some impact. The Local was less activist and more contractual by the end of the 1960s than during the early period of the Blackmarr regime. Yet it remained activist and democratic; and even the bureaucratization which had developed was creating rank-and-file forces to oppose it.

THE PROBLEM OF THE INTERNATIONAL

Militant, democratic unionism is very rare in the Teamsters, as in every union in America today. Militancy and democracy do not "just happen" to be rare; it is in the perceived interests of the labor bureaucracy to destroy them. Thus, the hostility of union officials created a major problem for Local 208. For example, the leadership of Southern California Teamster Joint Council 42, as well as the leadership of most locals in the Los Angeles area, opposed 208's militant unionism. They objected to letting the rank and file have much voice in union affairs, and were appalled when drivers took direct action against employers rather than ask officials to solve their problems for them. They wanted above all to stay in their offices, draw high salaries, make friendly deals with management, and avoid working too hard in defense of the membership. The example of Local 208 was a threat to them. Thus, by and large, these officials tried to destroy 208, or at least to render it ineffective.

In seeking to defend itself, 208 could have moderated its militancy and relied more on contractual legalism and less on direct action; it would thus have become similar to its enemies. That is, however, the current situation in 208 under the Maheras regime (see chapters 2 and especially chapter 9).

Alternatively, the Local could have allied itself with friendly elements within the bureaucracy, and let them act as an umbrella, especially against Joint Council 42. This was in fact the primary strategy of the Blackmarr regime, which allied with Hoffa.

Another possible course of action would have been to attempt to spread the rank and file movement. This would have involved mobilizing the membership of 208 to assist rank and filers elsewhere to take over their own locals. Over the course of some years, they might thus have developed real strength within the Teamsters as a whole. Such a path would have been

filled with conflict, and would eventually have led to a confrontation with the International, and thus to the threat of trusteeship
(which for 208 came in 1970 anyway). Such ploys as supporting
Hoffa against attempts to jail him, or threatening to leave the
IBT might have delayed this risk. Yet such a path would have
offered the chance of long-term success rather than strangula-
tion. Local 208 took a few steps along this path, but never really
pursued it.

The "Hoffa Connection" was in fact the Blackmarr leadership's strategy. The connection protected the local against
some of the cruder pressures from officials of neighboring bureaucratic locals, from the higher bureaucracies of the Joint
Council and Western Conference of Teamsters, and from employers. Thus, before signing the first and second Master Freight
Agreements, Hoffa insisted that employers drop pending lawsuits against use of the 24-hour walkout clause. Or, as noted
(July 3, 1974, interview) by John T. Williams:

*(Did the hostile officials use the grievance panels to undercut 208 by
giving unfavorable rulings?)*
Yes. Then a special panel came into being for 208. We had a special
208 blue ribbon panel. Hoffa appointed it at the Joint State Committee.

We supported Hoffa, so we could take our problems straight to
him and bypass the committees. And he would say to refile the grievance, and then he'd call the Joint Area Committee people and tell them
to pass it.

So Hoffa gave us a special panel. . . . When Fitz [Frank Fitzsim-
mons] came in, that panel, which was pro us, was ended. Though
sometimes the special panel *would* rule against us, and then the union
members would tell us why.

One reason this was done was that the Joint Council hated 208,
partly because we elected BAs and partly because we stayed together
. . . so they took it out on us in grievance procedure so we'd be kicked
out of office by the members. This went on from '61 or '62 to about
a year or year and a half before Hoffa went to jail, at which point he
set up the blue-ribbon panel.

Similarly, PMT stewards told me that Hoffa set up additional special panels to hear cases from PMT and WesCar, since
the militancy of the drivers at these barns had won so much that
the regular grievance panels would not deal fairly with them.

What did Hoffa get from the connection with 208? There

was, for one thing, the support of 208's delegates at conventions. For another, he obtained a base of support within the Western Conference of Teamsters, and within Southern California Joint Council 42, both of which tended to oppose him and his policies. Presumably, he could use 208 as an implicit threat; should the top Western officials become too great a nuisance to him, they might find Blackmarr appointed to high positions, or the militants of 208 turned loose to organize rank and filers in other locals, with Hoffa's blessing, support, and protection. In particular, Hoffa was putting together the first Master Freight Agreement during the early days of the Blackmarr regime, and in this effort, the Local's support was very helpful as a counterweight to opposition in San Francisco.

The connection also meant that Hoffa had support in his efforts to stay out of jail.[2] In 1964, a Hoffa Defense Breakfast was organized in Los Angeles to mobilize opposition to Federal attacks on Hoffa and the Teamsters. While the Breakfast, an enormous success in protesting what was being done to Hoffa, was organized by Teamsters from several Locals, 208 members (and John T. Williams in particular) were major driving forces behind it.

Similarly, when Hoffa went to prison in 1967, the most widespread of the many wildcat protest strikes in cities across the U.S. were the wildcats in Los Angeles, where thousands of 208 members picketed, carrying signs that read, "No Hoffa No Work." The Joint Council, attempting to use the protests against 208, sent people with tape recorders to gather evidence that Blackmarr or other 208 officials had instigated the walkout. However, the Local's leaders were much too proficient at hiding their tracks for the bureaucracy to prove anything of the sort.

A few weeks later, when trouble erupted over Fitzsimmons' handling of the Master Freight negotiations, Blackmarr wired the U.S. Secretary of Labor to release Hoffa from prison for a few days to settle the dispute. And Local 208 was a strong supporter of the "Free Jimmy" movement, and would almost certainly have supported Hoffa had he ever been able to challenge Fitzsimmons for the Presidency of the IBT.

Unfortunately for its long-run militancy, Hoffa's protection meant that 208 did not find itself forced to cooperate with rank-and-file movements in other locals. Yet, such groups did exist, and, as they organized, often came to 208 for help. Such was the case with groups from Locals 357, 389, 420, 598, and 986, and perhaps with others I have not heard of. However they received little help besides encouragement and some advice. As 208 had chosen not to fight the International bureaucracy but instead to ally with Hoffa, the active members did not really mobilize to help other rank-and-file groups; thus, when militant Teamsters came to 208 for aid, they were helped by friendly BAs or officers, but not by the Local as an official body or by its entire membership. Moreover, 208 officials had found that they could be burned if their involvement in such affairs became visible to local officials who felt threatened by the particular insurgency they aided. In particular, when a group of Local 598 rank and filers approached Pat Patton, he and Williams advised them and helped them to write leaflets and other materials. Patton was especially involved in defending one leader of the 598 group against being fired, and later in fighting his expulsion from the Teamsters. To this end, Patton tried to invoke Hoffa's aid. The limits of the Hoffa alliance and of Hoffa's supposed commitment to activist democratic unionism then became clear: Hoffa acted against the 598 rank-and-file group, holding that they had properly been ruled ineligible to run for local office, even though he did act to prevent their leader's expulsion.

At this point, the Secretary-Treasurer of Local 598 filed charges against Patton. When these charges were heard by the 208 Executive Board, the Butler faction opposed Patton, claiming that he was guilty of procedural violations. Patton was put on probation for a year. While this was no real punishment, it gave the officials of 208 a clear message—particularly since the charges could have been transferred to the Joint Council, composed of the officers of all the Teamster locals in Southern California, where Patton would have received severe punishment.

In the early 1960s a Los Angeles-wide caucus existed, which met monthly at a local hotel. This caucus had members from a number of locals, including 208. Its purpose was both to discuss issues, so that its members could grow beyond the confines of their locals' struggles, and to explore the possibility of loosely coordinated actions at Joint Council meetings and Teamster Conventions. However, this caucus was rather narrow. It did not attempt to weld together the rank-and-file of various local caucuses but, instead, aimed to reach the few top leaders of each. It therefore led to relatively little. In particular, it never led to any real alliance between the already mobilized rank and file of Local 208 and the still weak insurgents of other locals.

There *were* successes, of a sort, by some of these local caucuses—in several cases they elected their slates and thus took over their locals—but in most cases this just led to the "outs" becoming a new group of bureaucratic "ins." And, even where they did not become Joint Council loyalists, the movements remained at the level of "clean up the Union," never forging the rank-and-file activism that combines direct action against the employer with insurgency within the Local.

Thus, 208 remained isolated. No other insurgencies developed to spread democratic and activist unionism to other locals in the Los Angeles area. This isolation may well have come about because the activists in 208 chose to stand aloof from other locals' struggles. And, with Hoffa gone, the isolation would become serious.

The Hoffa Connection acted as an umbrella. While Hoffa was in power, it offered 208 a limited protection from its bureaucratic enemies. However, with Jimmy in prison, the umbrella was closed. And when the removal of the umbrella exposed the activists to the full force of their opponents' storms—when the special panels for 208 grievances were ended, and the International cooperated with employers' lawsuits, and there came threats of trusteeship—208 found it had failed to organize a rank-and-file movement in other Locals that would have let it successfully resist.*

Further, 208 found that, all the time it had been supporting Hoffa, he had been busy building up the strength of its enemy, the International's bureaucracy. In particular, he had (with 208's support) organized the Master Freight Agreement (MFA) which covered almost half a million workers in America's freight industry. The bureaucracy therefore became much more powerful as a national force, and the days of local autonomy were over. Under a national contract, much of the fight against employers

---

* In regards to the umbrella analogy, John T. Williams points out that the theme song (or mood music) of the 1971 IBT Convention, which elected Fitzsimmons IBT President and confirmed the Trusteeship of 208, was none other than "Rain Drops Falling on My Head."

becomes national in scope. Thus, to win a larger pay raise in a period of inflation, or to prevent union officials from removing the 24-hour strike clause from the contract, or even to prevent officials from letting employers reorganize their trucking operations in ways that lead to lost jobs, it becomes necessary to organize a national fight, and a nation-wide rank-and-file movement to wage such a fight.

Thus, in retrospect, reliance upon friendly bureaucrats to provide an umbrella was a losing strategy for the rank-and-file activists. As ever, the interests of the rank and file in militant self-defense were opposed to the interests and ideologies of the bureaucracy. Ultimately, this basic opposition surfaced in the 1970 wildcat, and, having relied upon friends at the top, 208 found it had not taken the steps necessary for defense from the bottom.

RACISM AND ACTIVIST UNIONISM

The Blackmarr regime coincided with a period of black struggles against racism. Rank-and-file activist unionism in Local 208 met some of the challenges of this struggle, but failed to meet many others. There was considerable racism in the local trucking industry in Los Angeles. Consider the following evidence, given me by black members of 208, of racist policies by the local trucking companies. As of the late 1950s, only four trucking companies hired black drivers. One result of this was that the hiring hall was disproportionately black. Even in 1974, according to John T. Williams, while blacks made up only about 10 percent or 15 percent of the drivers in the area, the hall was about 50 percent black. Further, until shortly before the Blackmarr forces came to power, the hall had practiced a racist system of dispatching drivers; if a company wanted to specify that no black drivers be sent, the hall would acquiesce. Even when the hall, under pressure from the rank and filers and the black caucus, stopped this practice, the problems of black drivers working out of the hall continued. For example, one black driver told me in 1975 that, at the company where he had worked since 1964, the policy had been that if a black driver were sent by the hall, the company would not let him drive, but would instead give him the contractually specified show-up pay and send him back to the hall. This same driver related an experience he had with one company. Dispatched there from the hall, he had worked on a Friday, Sunday, and Monday. As he did a good job, the supervisor asked him to fill out an application for employment and return to work the next day. However, when he arrived on Tuesday, he discovered that the supervisor had been fired for offering him the job, and there was no work for him.

Racism by the companies is still strong and takes many forms. Sometimes it surfaces when drivers are caught stealing. White drivers caught stealing are often (although by no means always) allowed to resign rather than be fired, and the employer may conceal the theft by giving a good letter of recommendation. Blacks do not get these breaks; they become unbondable (which limits available work greatly), and management makes sure that everyone hears why they were fired.

Further, a black worker who does have a job must put up with constant racist insults from white managers and with the strong probability that he is the person most likely to be blamed when something goes wrong.

However, racism in trucking is by no means limited to management. White drivers speak and act in racist ways, as do union officials. For instance, the hiring hall hardly opposed its client companies' racism. To quote one of my informants: "Management and workers and union officers are racist—and the union officers shy away from it." And John T. Williams notes (interview of March, 1974):

To me, the Teamsters is a racist union. If you look at the International Executive Board and International Organizers and Representatives, there are no blacks. Though all other big unions have some there. . . . In the last 10 years, it's just beginning to break a little. Though there are still no black secretaries in the offices.

Last Monday [at the grievance hearings], 3-Finger Jack from Local 235 said the company told him the next person they hire will be a black, and that when it does he will grieve it. This shows that (a) the company uses this to create problems; (b) the company wants to get off the hook, and to get the black community against the union; (c) if the union had been acting right, we wouldn't have waited for the Federal government to come in.

Among white drivers, too, there is still much racism. Drivers at barns or meetings often made racist remarks in my presence.

The following sequence of events at Western Gillette was told to me by a black steward there, Ray Smith (March 28, 1975):

When Western Gillette hired its first black driver, the whites cut his tires, stole his battery, and wrote "nigger" all over his truck. This went on until one day he got threatening. By the time they hired me, there were four of us. One of whom had swept the yard for 17 years before they let him become a driver. By 1965, when the revolt came, there were eight of us, and we had the reputation of being bad-ass niggers. When a white steward nominated me as alternate steward, some of his friends got on him. [A white driver] was walking on the dock with a gun, and someone warned me. I pointed out that if *I* came to work with a gun I would be jailed. That night me and my brothers met him in the lot and warned him off.

It should perhaps be added that, about a year later, Smith saved the gun-carrying driver's job by being the only steward who would defend him when he was fired.

Against this background, the question exists of how well the rank-and-file unionism of 208 worked on the need to end racism—a need which was as crucial for white drivers as for blacks. It is clear that, while there remains much racism in the Los Angeles trucking industry, probably no course of action by the drivers of 208 could have entirely eliminated it. The rank-and-file movement fought a number of instances of discrimination—with the lead in these fights being taken by the black caucus. During the Blackmarr administration, the Local opposed instances of racial discrimination by management, and tried to defend black drivers as well as white. The policy in this regard, and its limitations, are caught in the following statement of Williams:

In 208, Alex Maheras, and Blackmarr when he was in office, are without political awareness on this. They will claim they deal with grievances as they come up without regard to color, and they are right on this. That is what they do.

Take the case of three black drivers up at the Joint Western Conference. They were grieving to get jobs at System 99. I told them how to do it some. _____said there that the company never hired blacks and we're here for justice, and if we don't get justice here we know what to do about it. They got jobs and they got $750 back pay.

Alex later said they didn't need to go into all that.

I told two of the drivers about how, if you've got nothing to lose, you can only gain. Alex or Blackmarr would have gone strictly by the contract, and they would have lost the case and would still be on the street.

(Do BAs discriminate against blacks in 208?)

Not consciously. It's just that they have no social awareness to recognize what to do.

Thus, the rank-and-file movement of the 1950s brought into office a "colorblind" group of Local officials; however, with the employers consciously and systematically racist, a "colorblind" approach could not deal fully with the problem. But they also developed a rank-and-file militancy that served the interests of black drivers much more effectively than did the officers. As unfair acts by a company were met by direct action, management came to hesitate to discriminate. Further, a number of the movement's most competent stewards were blacks, who led fights against discrimination in their own barns. And the activist and aggressive representation that 208 developed successfully dealt with at least some of the black drivers' problems.

Meanwhile, during the late 1950s, black drivers in several Locals had organized a black caucus. During the Blackmarr regime, the caucus continued to function, although not too successfully. It succeeded in having blacks appointed as business agents in a number of Locals, and in forcing some companies to hire blacks, and proposed a civil rights resolution to the 1966 IBT Convention, which was passed (although it led to little). These drivers found that blacks who got involved with them would often be threatened, and in some cases fired. Others would be appointed to union positions, and told to avoid the caucus if they wished to keep their posts. Unfortunately, the black caucus never gained the involvement of large numbers of black activist rank and filers, and was thus rather limited in what it could accomplish.*

---

* Ideally, I would have liked to analyze in detail why this caucus was not more successful. However, this is hard information for a white to come by, and I was not able to spend the massive amount of time it would have required.

The Blackmarr
Regime:
A Summary

What, then, can be said of the activist, militant unionism that Local 208 drivers built from their struggles? It is clear that, for years, it succeeded in solving many of the problems drivers faced, and was, in addition, a form of activism that gave the activists much personal growth and dignity. Further, the drivers of 208 found ways to slow, and perhaps defeat, the tendencies toward bureaucratization that threaten all attempts by workers to set up their own institutions. Thus, in many ways it succeeded.

However, this success was built within a context, a situation that has now changed. Then, the U.S. was in a period of relative prosperity, and so relatively small struggles could win concessions. Then, the International union had only begun to set up the Master Freight Agreement, and had not yet consolidated the increased power which the MFA gave it; in particular, it had not yet eliminated those sections of the contract which allowed brief strikes at little risk. Then, too, the International's officials were divided and embattled, so that it was expedient for its President to ally with the 208 activists.

Now the companies, facing leaner times, harass the drivers for every iota of increased productivity and fight very hard not to make concessions. Now, the IBT officialdom has consolidated its position and sold out the drivers in contract negotiations. Now, most visibly since 1970, the companies, the government, the International's bureaucracy, and indeed such smaller bureaucracies as that of the Los Angeles area Teamsters' officials, have tightened the alliance against the needs and aspirations of the drivers. Against this combination of enemies, the activist and militant, but apolitical and isolated, unionism of 208 is an inadequate weapon. Struggle in only one Local cannot mobilize the massive forces needed against such strong enemies.

Chapter 6

Changes in the Trucking Industry and the Teamsters Union

THE TRUCKING industry has changed since the 208 insurgency began in the mid-1950s. This has greatly affected the International Brotherhood of Teamsters and Local 208. Trucking companies have grown much larger, and their managements more sophisticated. At the start of this period, the Teamsters were the most powerful single force in the industry, but the growth of nationwide freight companies challenged the union's position and threatened the working conditions and jobs of its members. This posed a choice for the Teamsters—either reorganize or suffer major defeats. In freight, the IBT was able to reorganize through Jimmy Hoffa's succession to power. Yet, however necessary, the reorganization of the IBT under Hoffa involved the bureaucratization of the Teamsters on a nationwide level.[1]

Large Companies

Trucking companies have grown larger since 1950: they handle a larger volume of business, serve a wider geographical area, and handle a larger percent of total freight. Growth has occurred both through internal expansion and through merger.

In 1951, there were 47,435 trucking companies in the United States. Only 34 of these had 500 or more employees. By 1971, there were 64,737 companies, of which 88 employed 500 or more.[2] A clearer picture emerges when we look at what has

Table 6.1 Freight Employees of Major Trucking Companies

| | Company | | | | | | |
Year	Consolidated Freightways	T.I.M.E.	Denver-Chicago	McLean	Transcon	Roadway	Yellow
1953	3,812	NA	1,680	2,138	502	NA	NA
1959	8,112	1,338	2,518	3,026	1,615	5,221	2,100
1966	12,432	3,079	3,047	5,240	4,444	7,977	2,746
1973	13,628	6,457*		9,660	4,520	16,107	11,500

* T.I.M.E.-D.C. merger.

happened to a few of the largest trucking companies, using data taken from *Moody's Transportation Manual.*[3] Tables 6.1 and 6.2 show that the large companies have grown greatly in number of employees and in the number of terminals operated by each. Along with the number of terminals, the geographical scope of the companies' operations has also grown. In the early 1950s there was only one company with transcontinental operations; now there are many.

Furthermore, trucking has become much more important in the economy (see table 6.3), and the politics of the trucking industry have become increasingly important to capital as a whole, so that the Teamsters are increasingly able to give essential aid to other workers by honoring their picket lines. Furthermore, the power of the union to improve wages and conditions for its members is increasingly a threat to the profits of American business, which has become increasingly dependent on trucking transportation.*

The growth of large companies posed a threat to the Teamsters. The impact of such growth on bargaining arrangements is considerable. In the early 1950s, most local pickup and delivery contracts, and a number of over-the-road contracts, were negotiated by individual Locals or by bargaining units composed of a relatively few locals in a relatively small geographical area.

* The growth of the trucking industry stems from major changes in economic organization since World War II. In particular: the reorganization of factories in single-level buildings, and the associated suburbanization of production (and people) and warehouses along highways built with Federal money; the development of interstates and freeways within cities; and the development of containers so that freight can travel long distances by rail and then go cheaply by truck.

Table 6.2 Terminals Operated by Major Trucking Companies

			Company				
Year	Consolidated Freightways	T.I.M.E.	Denver-Chicago	McLean	Transcon	Roadway	Yellow
1953	62	NA	14	37	6	NA	NA
1959	145	21	34	63	19	75	NA
1966	130	29	22	65	47	104	107
1973	190	55 or more*		107	63	246	149

* T.I.M.E.-D.C. merger.

As long as the companies' operations were not too much larger, this was reasonable, and gave greater potential control over the bargaining process to the rank and file. However, when companies grew larger, the position of the Teamsters was endangered. A strike by one Local, or even by all the Locals in an area, would shut down only a small part of the operations of the largest companies operating there, such as Yellow Freight or Consolidated Freightways. Thus, these companies could hold out for a long time unless the union were willing and able to extend the strike to other areas. But this was precisely what the localized organization of the union made difficult. The implication was obvious. Freight workers stood to be defeated piecemeal by the enlarged companies.

The experience of United Parcel Service is a useful contrast. The Teamsters did not move until recently to set up a national UPS contract. Thus, UPS was able to take on isolated locals or regional groupings and win concession after concession. As one example, UPS has forced the workers to let it extend the use of part-time workers. Part-timers now do almost all the "inside

Table 6.3 Employment in Railroads and Trucking[a]

Year	Railroad	Trucking
1947	1,352,000	551,000
1958	841,000	793,000
1974[b]	527,000[b]	1,186,000

[a] Robson (1959).
[b] U.S. Bureau of Labor Statistics (1977).

work''—such as sorting and loading the packages—and they get less pay and inferior benefits than full-timers. Over the long run, this has undercut the bargaining position of the full-timers. The company uses the weaker attachment of part-timers to their jobs, and the resentment of part-timers towards a union which allowed them to be given such a raw deal, as weapons to divide the workers. In addition, the threat of extending the use of part-timers to "outside work" forces the full-timers to moderate their demands on the company.

In the early 1950s, then, freight workers faced the strong possibility that they would face the same problems UPS workers still face (although the lesser size of even the largest freight companies compared to UPS* makes it probable that the threat was somewhat less severe).

Even under a national contract, the increased size of companies has affected bargaining power. Large companies have been able to set up several terminals in each major metropolitan area. A company then uses the threat of moving operations from one terminal to another as a whip to keep workers in line. Every demand by drivers or inside workers in New York is met by the threat to move most of the company's operations to New Jersey; northern New Jersey Locals are threatened with a move to New York or southern Jersey. In Los Angeles, trucking companies have set up satellites in Orange County and the desert regions north of the Los Angeles basin, and have transferred work there to curb Local 208. Of course, these actions are effective under a national contract only because the men who run the IBT let the companies get away with them. But it is clear that without bargaining units as large as the companies' operations the whipsawing would be even more effective.

The growth of the trucking companies has to a large extent been accomplished by a long series of mergers and acquisitions. Two or more trucking companies with separate terminals and different ways of doing things are turned into one company. The

---

* UPS employs more than 100,000 workers. It is important to note that conditions and wages at UPS have been maintained by the existence of better wages and conditions in freight. This has made it hard for the company to go too far in its demands without running into a massive revolt of workers demanding freight-level contracts. Thus, had freight workers been unable to meet the threat posed by company growth, conditions at UPS would have been worsened even more.

new company closes down duplicate terminals and standardizes work rules and management. During this process, there are many ways the employer can attack workers' jobs and conditions relatively easily, because the previously separate groups of workers do not know each other. Further, the improved efficiency of combined operations usually lets the company reduce its workforce by up to a third without losing business. The threat of layoffs, and the uncertainty about how the seniority list of the bought-out company will be merged with that of the purchasing company, make it easy for the company to pit "old" and "new" workers against each other. This greatly weakens the power of the workers to resist the company's new work rules. Furthermore, mergers usually involve consolidating operations among a number of different cities, and this lets companies whipsaw the different cities' Teamsters against each other—a situation further aggravated by the possibility that two or more of the newly merged company's terminals in a given metropolitan area might be in different Locals. The threat in the early 1950s was that the Teamsters Union would be unable to develop bargaining mechanisms that would enable it to coordinate its actions to meet the unity of such newly merged companies.

Changes in Employer Organization

The trucking industry has also developed more sophisticated managers, advanced its technology, and set up effective bargaining agencies for the companies. Changes in management are harder to document than changes in company size. In large part, I am forced to rely on the analyses of experts in trucking management, as well as on the descriptions of the older drivers who have experienced the change. The logic of events is clear, however. Larger trucking companies offer many opportunities for more sophisticated management techniques, and the rigors of a competitive industry, together with the pressures of banks and sources of other forms of loans or capital via stock and bond sales, force the companies to make use of such techniques. Higher wages due to union gains mean that the companies look into more efficient ways of using the time of their workers. Various contract provisions, for example, have forced management to use standardized and controllable dispatch procedures that minimize the chances of costly mistakes. As one example, if the wrong person gets overtime, the company may be forced to pay overtime both to the junior employee who does the work and to a passed-over senior employee.

In 1965, *Business Week* magazine described changes in the trucking industry that would interest potential investors and other businessmen. After describing the growth in company size and the mergers, the article went on to discuss changes in management. It pointed out that managers were increasingly recruited from colleges, and that the companies sent managers without college training to take courses on modern management techniques. This had led—together with the lessons of sad experience—to a greater emphasis on management's part on cutting costs and increasing productivity, replacing the previous single-minded attention to expansion. As part of this, companies began to use computers to plan the loading of goods, dispatching, and routing and billing, and they redesigned their terminals to cut the costs of transferring incoming freight to outgoing trucks. In addition, they have continued older methods of cost-cutting (such as increasing the size of trucks) and in particular using "semis" (with trailers that can be loaded and unloaded while the tractor is being used to haul other freight) rather than "bobtails" (single-unit trucks). Similarly, the companies have increased the use of "doubles" (two trailers pulled by one tractor), and they are lobbying for laws that let them haul three trailers in tandem.

It is clear that many of these changes have eliminated jobs. More efficient routing, billing, and dispatching mean fewer workers in those operations. More efficient terminals, and the increased use of pallets, chain-pulled "trains" of carts within terminals to transfer freight between loading bays, and forklifts, mean fewer freight-handling jobs. More efficient dispatching, the use of radios to keep in touch with drivers, and larger trucks mean fewer drivers.

Employers have set up more effective ways of handling labor relations as well. Consider the following description from the 1940s:

Of the approximately 500 Class I Operators in the Central States area, only one very large carrier employs a full-time labor relations executive. Even though most of the Class I operators are involved in negotiating at least four or five contracts annually, as well as handling day-to-day union-management problems and grievances, the operators do not have any effective organization on a company level to cope with these problems. . . .

In most instances the trade associations' bargaining committees or the separate employer collective bargaining organizations function only during a period of contract negotiations and in the interim disintegrate or at best maintain only skeleton organizations. Consequently, prior to the expiration of an area contract, considerable effort must again be expended to revitalize or set up new machinery to represent the employers in negotiations. (Cohen and Lieberman 1949:24)

Since then, things have changed. Companies employ numerous full-time labor personnel, supplemented by labor experts from state employers' associations. In addition, they have set up managerial training programs dealing with labor relations, the contract with the Teamsters, and personnel matters generally. As if this were not enough, many companies call in professional labor relations firms. These firms are often set up by former Teamster business agents who decide to make a better living coaching employers on how to get around the contract than they can defending the interests of the workers. As a result, at a local level the representatives of large employers are now better trained than most union officials and the larger companies have enough continuity of organization to plan and carry out long-term strategies to erode the power of the union and the rights of the workers.

At the national level, too, the companies have developed effective organization. While the national Master Freight Agreement has forced this on them, it has become possible as a result of the other trends discussed in this chapter. The growth of large companies has provided the trucking industry with a "leadership" with enough financial muscle and well-trained personnel to hold the smaller companies in line. This leadership has led to continuous organization and strategic planning instead of the catch-as-catch-can organization of the 1940s. Beyond that, these leaders are well enough organized to have coordinated a lockout in response to selective strikes by the Teamsters during the 1967 and 1979 Master Freight Negotiations. Indeed the employers were well enough organized to ride out the 1970 nationwide wildcat strike with considerable unity.

Government
Attacks
on the IBT

As if the threat posed by changes in the trucking industry were not enough, the leaders of the Teamsters Union also had to deal with attacks from the Federal government. These attacks focused on corruption among the leaders of the union and on the lack of democracy within the International and most Locals, but they clearly threatened to destroy the union: members might disaffiliate their workplaces from the union by going nonunion or joining other unions; the weakening of the union would then let the employers of remaining Teamsters engage in contract violations and let them weaken the contracts in subsequent negotiations; and the creation of an anti-labor climate of public opinion would allow legislative attacks on the unions. In particular, Congress was considering passing legislation to limit Teamster secondary strikes and perhaps even to cripple the bargaining power of all transportation unions. (Eventually, this became the Landrum-Griffin Act.)

From the viewpoint of the union leaders, there was an even greater danger. Rank and filers might become so disgusted with their leaders' corruption, and with the shame of having their union put in such a poor light, that they might attempt to reorganize the union for greater democracy, integrity, and effectiveness against employer and government attacks. That is, there was a threat that the kind of rank-and-file movement that the drivers of Local 208 built might grow into a national movement under the pressure of the various attacks on members' livelihoods, self-esteem, and working conditions; and that the top leadership would be too weakened by the attacks upon themselves by the government and the employers to be able to resist.*

* To be sure, the leaders of the attack on the IBT leaders did not want such an outcome. They aimed at weakening the IBT, not strengthening it. But in their efforts they were running a certain risk of losing control and having the rank-and-file reshape the union into a militant defender of workers' interests.

What was behind all these attacks? Why did the leaders of the United States risk stirring up the ranks of the Teamsters Union? These attacks were a product of business's general opposition to the labor movement, and of long-term policies of both political parties.[4] This opposition was especially pronounced in the late 1950s, because the ability of workers to resist had been weakened by postwar defeats and by the bureaucratization of the labor unions. There was also a desire to weaken the influence of organized crime in the transportation industries. Companies do not like being shaken down for protection money. Further, a lot of their products were being stolen in transit, and business feared that large-scale organized crime could organize this into an unofficial tariff on all goods transported in the U.S. In this regard, the leaders of the IBT and other transportation unions had opened themselves and their unions to attack through their personal greed. Then, too, politicians like the Kennedys saw a chance to further their careers.

All this focused on the Teamsters because of the corruption of the union's leaders and because of the growing importance of trucking in the economy.

The Teamsters faced a crisis in the late 1950s. Trucking companies had grown more powerful and sophisticated, and thus threatened to defeat the union's power and attack the workers' wages and working conditions. Attacks by the government intensified this threat. This crisis also endangered the incomes and other privileges of the Teamsters' leaders.

Jimmy Hoffa emerged from this crisis as the savior of Teamster officialdom, and the respected leader of many rank-and-file Teamsters. He solved many of these problems in spite of the actions of high-ranking Teamster officials.

The Structural Crisis
Within the Union
and the Election
of Hoffa

The Teamsters Union had a long history of local autonomy. In particular, the President of the International had very little power. To quote Leiter's 1957 study of the union (p. 61):

Local leaders of the Teamsters Union have always fought hard to maintain local autonomy. [Daniel J.] Tobin was the undisputed and respected head of the union for nearly half a century, re-elected to the office of president by every convention, without a dissenting vote, yet all his efforts to reduce local control, strengthen the position of the international, or centralize power were stubbornly resisted and vigorously fought. Tobin's desire to set up a national death benefit program was beaten down at every convention. His regular and continual attempts to increase the per capita tax paid by locals made only slow and limited progress. His power to appoint trustees to supervise locals, when in his discretion he thought such action advisable, was used only on rare occasions because he was reluctant to antagonize the locals.

Later, Leiter quotes A. H. Raskin, the labor reporter of the *New York Times*:

When Beck took over the union . . . it was not an international union at all, for all its size, wealth, and strategic position. It was a combination of hundreds of locals, each a law to itself. Daniel J. Tobin, Beck's predecessor, was the most powerful single individual in the A.F.L. He bossed the federation's executive council with shameless arrogance, but he walked softly in the presence of his local leaders. In New York, Chicago, and other big cities, Teamster officials threw their weight around with no regard for the parent organization. On the rare occasions when Tobin sought to blow the whistle, no one listened. (Raskin 1953 in Leiter 1957:61)

Thus in the mid-1950s when Beck had to step down from the presidency of the IBT, the union faced a crisis with no central organization to speak of. The metropolitan barons were each strong, as were the leaders of the Western Conference and of the Central States, within their regions. But the individual baronies were not strong enough to stand alone against the Federal attack, and it was becoming clear that greater unity was needed to meet the trucking industry in negotiations. Further, if a rank-and-file upsurge did develop, it might well triumph within each barony; but a unified officialdom might be able to smother or smash it.

The officials' need was clear: unity. The problem was how to get it. This became the issue during the battle over who would succeed Beck. Most of the candidates were traditional barons, with no real program for change. Their victory would only have prolonged the crisis and led to many defeats. One candidate, Einar Mohn of the Western Conference, may have held out a different possibility. As a "respectable bureaucrat" with a reputation as a "progressive," he seemed to hold out the prospect of turning the Teamsters into a staid, conventionally bureaucratic union, gaining some peace against external opponents by a token housecleaning of corrupt elements in the leadership (Hoffa among them), and developing regional negotiations in freight and, eventually, a national freight contract.[5]

Mohn however was unable to get enough of a following to win, so he made a deal to support Hoffa. The officials preferred Hoffa: Since there was no central power to compel barons to cooperate, it would take a series of fights to force some of them into line.* Such fights could not be won by a "respectable bureaucrat," since he would have no way to force compliance. Hoffa, on the other hand, had already shown, in the Central States, and in his winning control of the New York Joint Council, that he had the necessary strengths; he had been able to appeal to the ranks and to lower officials when barons stood in his way, and to manipulate negotiations in one area so as to pressure other areas' leaders to accept his programs. In addition, the more corrupt officials could not be sure how far Mohn might be forced to go in housecleaning in order to get peace from the government and the media. On the other hand, Hoffa could be trusted; since he was the first target of the attackers, he could not sell the other crooks out.

Hoffa was put into power to carry out a "bonapartist" policy. He had shown how to do so while leading the Teamsters in the Central States, and he formulated his campaign platform on this basis. He proposed to use International Union funds to support strikes over contract terms and organizational strikes; to obtain area-wide and national contracts; to begin a large and well-financed organizing drive to build a 2-million-member union; and to cooperate with other unions in joint campaigns if

* That this is a real problem is shown by Fitzsimmons' effort to organize regional bargaining with UPS in the Eastern and Western Conferences in 1975–76. In both cases, and particularly in the West, he found it very hard to get different cities' leaders to cooperate. And he had a much stronger bureaucracy to support him and with which to threaten "trouble-makers" than Hoffa had.

they would reciprocate. In effect, Hoffa proposed national bargaining and full support of strikes as a way to counter the growing power of the employers, he offered to help other unions if they would stop working with the state and the employers in the attack upon the IBT, and he wanted an expansionist organizing drive to catch the imagination of the members and to appeal to the officials' desire for more dues and initiation fees.

Hoffa gained rank-and-file support through this platform and by using the attacks upon him to fan Teamster chauvinism to new heights. In a typically bonapartist strategy, he used enmity toward outsiders to build support for aggressive expansionist policies, as well as to take the minds of the rank-and-file off continuing scandals in the IBT, off evidence of sweetheart deals, and off the attacks by the leadership on attempts by rank and filers to get more say in the union.

Under the pressure of Federal government attacks, employer gains in strength, and a threat of rank-and-file revolt which was becoming clearer every day, the top leaders of the Teamsters chose Hoffa as their new president. They knew they were giving up much of their baronial power—since this had been the case in the Central States under Hoffa—but their new leader's prior record also made it clear that he would protect the jobs of those barons who did not cross him and would, very likely, be able to defeat the attacks upon the IBT.

Hoffa and
His Presidency

Hoffa himself was in many ways a man of contradiction. He built up the strength and cohesion of the Teamster bureaucracy, yet much of his support came from the rank and file. He attacked the power of the autocratic leaders of many metropolitan joint councils—including Chicago, San Francisco, and New York— yet he retained the support of most Teamster leaders, including some of the barons themselves. His rule meant continued bad publicity for the IBT, and general public dislike for the union, yet it also led to a rapid increase in the size of the union through successful organizing drives, and to a growth of Teamster "team spirit." For the rank-and-file movement in Local 208, Hoffa was a friend and supporter, yet he limited the scope of their activity to their own local and he transformed the Teamsters in ways that smother local activism over the long run.

These contradictions make Hoffa a hard man to understand. Many think of him as only a crook and a dictator—the image the Kennedys and their allies in government and business tried to paint. Yet he was far more than that. He transformed the union from a collection of local baronies, ripe for slaughter by the trucking industry, into a dynamic and unified organization. Some see him as a hero, a man who got good contracts and made the companies live up to them, a man who was available to the rank and file and would either solve a rank and filer's problem or give a straight answer why not. Yet this also misses the point. While he was organizing the Master Freight Agreement, he was also arranging sweetheart deals for some companies. More importantly, at the same time that he was willing to talk with the ordinary member of the union, he was constructing the basis for a bureaucratic power within the union, a power that later turned against the interests of the membership, smashed their strikes, negotiated rotten contracts, and even shut their doors and ears when members came to them with complaints. Hoffa's openness disarmed the ranks, but on many occasions (such as Philadelphia in the mid-1960s) Hoffa smashed rank-and-file organization himself. All this meant he could reorganize the IBT in ways that would preserve the incomes and power of the union's officialdom.

Thus, Hoffa was a union leader who used his power in an unusual and mysterious style. In many ways, he shares this mysteriousness with a number of famous bonapartist leaders in world history—such as Napoleon himself, or Germany's Bismarck, or Cuba's Batista and Castro.[6] In each of these cases, society reached a crisis point, confronting problems which required major social reorganization to avoid a collapse. However, there developed in each case an impasse, as each social class put forward "solutions" to the crisis that would suit its own needs (or, even more strikingly, in which these classes *failed* to put forward such solutions!)—but none was able to organize sufficient power to impose its solution. In such situations of organized stalemate and impending collapse, a bonapartist dictator is often able to gain power using a relatively small group of organized supporters, because of the inability of more powerful groups to find any other solution and the unorganized support of many of society's rank-and-file members, towards whom he directs a propaganda of pride and expansionism.

Such regimes usually share certain additional characteristics with each other and with the Hoffa regime in the IBT. In each case, the leader sets himself up as all-powerful. Usually, he spends a lot of time in contact with the common people—during which, often with lots of publicity, he solves problems on the spot and cuts down Local officials who do injustice. In each case, his power seems to be total, and his discretion absolute. Nevertheless, at the first major setback, the towering edifice collapses and the leader is seen to be without great support—unless he has succeeded in building the power and organization of one of the social classes to the point where it can impose its will on the society. Of course, where this is the case, that class no longer needs the leader. If he loses his power, it does not mourn for a moment, but just puts a new and tamer leader in his place. It should be noted that bonapartist regimes often become very corrupt, as those with money try to buy the favors of the all-powerful leader or his henchmen.

Bonapartist leaders usually have similar policies. On the one hand, they get popular support by a policy of expansionism and empire mixed with demagogic attacks on the nonessential interests of the wealthy. On the other, they do not permit the rank and file to organize any independent power, thus preventing them from attacking the upper classes and increasing their dependence upon the great leader. As a result, the wealthy classes let the ruler wield power, since he is protecting their vital interests from attack from below. They let him reorganize social institutions in ways that attack some of their prerogatives, since the reorganization lets them strengthen their organization as a class and thus establish their ability to reassume direct rule when this becomes necessary.

The peculiarities of Hoffa's leadership of the International Brotherhood of Teamsters are best understood as being a miniature version of bonapartism, created out of the problems facing the IBT in the mid-1950's and the lack of any way to resolve the crisis along "normal" lines.

After the election of Hoffa, government attacks on the IBT increased. A court-appointed Board of Monitors was set up to oversee the union's business, and the full power of the U.S.

Department of Justice was thrown into the effort to convict and imprison Hoffa. Dissident officials, and in some areas rank and filers, tried to secede from the Teamsters Union; their attempts got major support from the mass media and the government. In the face of these events, Hoffa fanned the flames of Teamster chauvinism, organized and negotiated new area-wide contracts (like the first Western Freight Agreement in 1961), and made himself available to rank and filers. He gained massive support among rank and filers and lower-ranking union officials, who found his contracts to be improvements upon the older ones, and among those members who found his accessibility useful or appealing. Hoffa also got ever-increasing support from the barons, as they saw that his policies worked, that the external attacks were being met, and that the rank and file were under control.

It should be understood that the economic security of the Hoffa years was an absolutely necessary foundation for his bonapartism. This prosperity let him negotiate good master contracts without forcing the companies to fight back too strongly—their profits were high. Good contracts, obtained without a fight, let him attain the support of the rank and file without being forced to mobilize and thus organize it. And this atomized support was an effective lever in his battles with the Federal government, the media, and dissident baronies. Take away this prosperity—as the economic crisis of the last decade has done—and you undercut the bases on which Hoffa's regime was built. Thus we can see that Hoffa could not have weathered the storms of the 1970s any better than Fitzsimmons did. Indeed, since he depended on rank-and-file support, he might well have been toppled by now.

In Los Angeles, Hoffa's policies showed an interesting facet of bonapartism. He had little solid support among the Los Angeles officialdom. Beck had directed the basic organizing of the IBT in Southern California from Seattle, and he had made sure no rival had established a firm power base in Los Angeles. This meant that the officialdom there was loosely organized. Confronted by diffuse opposition among union officials in the region, Hoffa used the existence of a rank-and-file movement in Local 208 to get support. He wooed the 208 insurgents, yet he made it clear that he would not let them go too far. Faced with the threat of rank-and-file rebellion, and with the promise of help in containing this insurgency if they supported Hoffa, Los Angeles Teamster officials gave in and supported Hoffa.

Hoffa and
the Bureaucracy

A bonapartist regime that wants to stay in power must develop a stable power base. At first it relies on the power stalemate plus diffuse and unorganized mass support. Mass support can evaporate quickly, however, or it can be replaced by organized radical mass opposition. The stalemate can be broken by rivals who negotiate an alliance among previously contending forces. Thus, bonapartists must develop more organized support quickly. Usually they do so by supporting and reorganizing one of the elite groups among the previously stalemated forces. This was what Hoffa did. He made sure the rank and file stayed unorganized, and he broke the power (but not the privileges or incomes) of the barons. At the same time, he built up a strong, unified, and organized bureaucracy out of the officialdom of the IBT.

Hoffa's development of a nationwide Master Freight Agreement was the basis of his strategy for building a unified bureaucracy. The barons' power had been built around their control of bargaining and grievances in freight. The national contract in freight destroyed this control. The Master Freight Agreement was negotiated all at once in Washington, with regional supplements negotiated at the same time and submitted to the same nationwide ratification vote. Thus, baronial opposition in a given area (such as San Francisco) was crushed by submerging that area's "no" votes with the "yesses" of other areas. Furthermore, the specific mechanisms of the national contract made sure the barons' power was reduced. It put control over grievances in the hands of a pyramid of joint management–union committees. These committees gave Hoffa loyalists a great deal of power over mavericks, particularly since the Hoffa faction, in a fight, could use its whipsaw power over the companies in other geographical areas to get support from management representatives on an area committee. In addition, creation of a nationwide contract and a bureaucratically organized strike-sanctioning procedure meant that legalistic and bureaucratic approaches to unionism came to replace local activism.

Hoffa did not abandon his bonapartism completely as he built up the bureaucracy. He kept several bonapartist mechanisms in force and used them to control the bureaucracy. The grievance procedure is an example: it was set up "open-ended." Thus, where Hoffa had the power to deadlock a case, he could then choose whether to call a strike or to let the matter hang unresolved (which usually meant the company would impose its wishes). He could also use this power to whipsaw companies into cooperating with him, because he could threaten to deadlock minor grievances and then use the deadlock to strike the company in other regions. As another example, Hoffa refused to let the contract establish codification of grievance decisions by using precedents to decide current cases. Such a codified grievance procedure can quickly bureaucratize the grievance process, and this would replace influence peddling (which Hoffa's power thrived on) with legalism.* Finally, as in the case of Local 208, Hoffa set up special grievance panels to protect "maverick" allies against bureaucratic attacks from within the IBT.

Hoffa also controlled the bureaucracy with a special pension fund that he set up for retiring Teamster officials. This pension is awarded in addition to any other pensions due the official. Maverick officials may find that their pensions never materialize upon their retirement; and officials put out of office by a trusteeship before serving three years do not qualify for the pension at all. Thus officials are given a powerful incentive to cooperate with the bureaucracy. The existence of such pensions decreased the officials' concern for the pension funds of the rank and filers; thus, they are less likely to object to the use of these pension funds for investments that enrich the top officers of the IBT or that pay off favors or sellouts.

Hoffa also changed the International Constitution. Before 1961, delegates to the conventions, held every five years, could be elected by the Locals in special elections. If, as with 208 in

---

* Numerous people whom I interviewed told me that under Fitzsimmons this bonapartist trait of the procedures was eroded in practice and that legalism replaced influence peddling, though in ways that aided the employers more than the workers, and only to the extent that there was no bureaucratic interest at stake in a given case.

1961, a rank-and-file upsurge was developing, this let rank and filers elect delegates pledged to change the International. This might become dangerous to the bureaucracy, so Hoffa changed the Constitution. Officers and business agents of the locals would be the delegates in the future. The highest policy-making body of the IBT would henceforth be of the bureaucracy, by the bureaucracy, and (if all went "well") for the bureaucracy.

The organizing drive was set up in ways that would stabilize the bureaucracy. Salaried positions would go to high bureaucrats, their lost power soothed with pay as "organizers." Also, they could give their supporters salaried jobs to do the real work of organizing. And organizing was conducted in ways that would not activate the newly organized—there was minimal consultation of their wishes and negotiations were conducted by "professional" organizers. Bringing in new members therefore did not challenge officials' power. Successes in organizing would show that the bureaucracy was making progress for the union, and that the Teamsters were growing stronger every day. Thus the team spirit of the members could be appealed to, and charges by outsiders discredited, by showing how many people wanted to become Teamsters. Finally, the organizing drive would bring in money for treasuries and pension funds. Every new member meant more dues money, and more initiation fee money. The bureaucracy controlled this money, and could use it to create new jobs for a bureaucrat's supporters, or to buy cars and plush offices for the officials. Hoffa also helped unify the bureaucracy by standing up to the Federal government's attacks on the union's officials. He made himself the number one target, and resisted the attacks for many years. By making himself a heroic unifying symbol, he kept some of the heat off lower officials.

While uniting and organizing the bureaucracy, Hoffa was disorganizing the rank and file. His basic policy was to support bureaucrats who supported him, to disenfranchise the rank and file at conventions, to use International power to defeat rank-and-file movements aimed at his supporters (as in Philadelphia), and to restrain those rank-and-file groups that he did support from becoming a real threat to the bureaucracy. His policy toward Local 208 provides a perfect picture of how he dealt with "friendly" rank and filers—and thus weakened them in the long run.

The Bureaucracy
Triumphant

Hoffa's policy of building up bureaucratic power was a success—such a success that he made himself unnecessary to the
bureaucracy, and indeed became an embarrassment to it. By the
time the Federal government put him in prison in 1967, he had
created a bureaucracy quite able to protect itself. Many now
wanted to end the attacks by the state and employers, and to
become respectable, through political conservatism and alliance
with the Republicans and through letting the companies off easily. They were quite happy to sell out the interests of the rank-
and-file in return for peace and respectability. Hoffa was an
impediment to this détente—as became clear once he was imprisoned. His replacement, Frank Fitzsimmons, had been chosen because he did not seem competent enough to pose any
threat to Hoffa's return to power. The bureaucracy, however,
no longer wanted or needed a bonapartist leader, and found a
nonentity like Fitzsimmons appropriate for a more completely
bureaucratic regime.

    Under Fitzsimmons, bonapartist rule was destroyed. The
International president became inaccessible to the rank and file;
the chain of command replaced personal intervention. To some
observers this has seemed like democratic decentralization—but
it is far more accurate to view it as the replacement of one-man
rule with the rule of a bureaucratic conglomerate similar in some
ways to General Motors (and with as little democracy). The rank
and file of the Teamsters Union suffered one loss after another
under Fitzsimmons; the bureaucracy waxed fat and happy. Indeed, after Hoffa was released from prison, few officials really
rallied behind the movement to reinstate him. In Los Angeles,
with disdain for Fitzsimmons nearly universal among the bureaucracy, only the officals of Local 208 showed any enthusiasm
for returning Hoffa to power. Further, Hoffa's "disappearance"
in 1975 was remarkable for the deafening silence from the bureaucracy. The man who had unified the bureaucracy, saved it
from attack, set up the pillaging of the Central States Pension
Fund for the bureaucrats' use, who created the bureaucracy's
own sacrosanct and rewarding pension fund—this man disappeared. And the bureaucrats showed their gratitude and loyalty

by averting their eyes and doing their best to pretend nothing had happened.

There were a few exceptions, by far the most important of which was the attempt to set up "Action for Hoffa" by Teamsters led by Business Agent John T. Williams and other dissidents from Local 208. However, very few bureaucrats rallied around this effort (even arch-Hoffaite Alex Maheras, Secretary-Treasurer of Local 208, was relatively uninvolved). And the rank and file, in spite of the persistence of some pro-Hoffa feeling, understood that he was not the vehicle to build a rank-and-file movement around. Only 175 Teamsters appeared at the rally.

The bureaucracy had come to power in the Teamsters Union, and used its power to sell out the members in return for respectability, at the very time that hard times were beginning for America, which was to be pounded by ever-worsening waves of inflation and recession. Even under Hoffa, this would have led to bad contracts. The alternative would have been a long and massive national strike of the kind Hoffa had pledged never to engage in—since such a strike would have required sufficient mobilization of the rank and file to disrupt the atomized apathy upon which both bonapartist and bureaucratic rule are based. Under Fitzsimmons' bureaucracy, however, economic hard times meant the systematic and deliberate selling out of the rank and file. In the last few years, under the impact of trucking deregulation and of company demands for concessions on work rules, a further change has occurred in the bureaucracy: its partial disintegration, with a reversion to regional rule under conditions in which national unity is essential. This has led to the gross weakening of the Master Freight Agreement by companies demanding special exceptions, and getting them through their ability to move operations to barns in nearby cities. The bureaucracy has been unable to prevent this, since to do so would require mobilizing the rank and file. This, however, is a recent development. In 1970, the bureaucracy was riding high, and the rank and file was seething at the way they were being treated in the union and by the companies. The result was the 1970 Wildcat.

Chapter 7

Apolitical Activism Ambushed: The 1970 Wildcat

A CRISIS puts human beings under the microscope as well as under the gun. In normal times, their strengths and weaknesses are blurred and little tested. Errors are made, sloppy thinking and routinized activity occur, and nobody pays much attention since the cost is low. However, let a crisis come, and all this changes. Mistakes cost dearly. Sloppy thinking leads to mistaken strategies and disaster. Routine and habit lead to unthinking blunders. Thus, a crisis tests the methods that a group of people have evolved to solve their problems, and indeed tests the foundations of their ideas about their situation in life and the means to cope with it. And a crisis tests people: Those who seemed strong often turn out to be weak, those who seemed wise often are shown to be foolish. Those who had seemed weak or foolish sometimes turn out to be giants.

The 1970 wildcat was such a crisis. It threw great burdens on the Teamsters of Los Angeles. It tested the methods and ideas and organization of the drivers of Local 208, and of many other Teamsters as well. By looking closely at this wildcat, we can see the strengths and weaknesses of what went before and what has followed. In addition, since the 1970 wildcat was a social conflict, a battle between contending classes and organizations, we can learn from it which groups will, in time of conflict, oppose the interests of drivers and other workers, which groups will support them, and which groups become paralyzed and thus irrelevant.

During the strike, there were a great variety of complex events, of which no complete description can be possible. I have been able to touch only upon the high points—those of strategic or analytic interest—and have had to omit many matters that seemed extremely important to participants at the time. For instance, a great many discussions of strikes focus on violence; but I deal with violence only as it relates to important questions of strike organization, strategy, and the development of strikers' ideas.

It is important first to have some idea of the events in general terms.

The National Master Freight Agreement, the contract between the Teamsters Union and freight industry employers, expired at the end of March 1970. Since no agreement had been reached on a new contract (and in 1967 wildcats had led to a renegotiation of the contract and an extra 10 cents an hour in pay) Teamsters walked off their jobs in many areas of the United States on April 1, 1970. However, since a tentative contract agreement had been reached, and since the terms of the contract were to be applied retroactively to April 1, the Acting President of the Teamsters, Frank Fitzsimmons, ordered members back to work on April 2.

In many areas, this ended the wildcat. In others, the wildcat was to last several weeks. In Ohio it led to sniping on the highways and the calling out of the National Guard (the very same units that, a month later, would kill four students at Kent State University who were protesting President Nixon's Cambodian invasion); and in St. Louis it lasted into May and led to the courts' imposing heavy damages on Local 600. In Chicago, where the freight contract is negotiated separately, the Teamsters and the non-Teamster Chicago Truck Drivers Union conducted an authorized strike that lasted into early July. The Chicago settlement increased pay and benefits by $1.65 an hour (over the life of the new contract). The pressure of the national wildcat had forced Fitzsimmons and the employers to agree to reopen negotiations on pay and benefits if Chicago won more than the $1.10 originally agreed upon. These negotiations resulted in a total increase of $1.85 over the life of the National Agreement.

When Fitzsimmons, on April 2, ordered the strikers back

to work after the tentative agreement had been reached, the Los Angeles strikers at first complied. However, the next day, a Friday, Los Angeles Teamsters walked off their jobs at one company after another. Over the weekend, the strikers began to get organized, and on Monday very few trucking companies moved any freight. The wildcatters' demands were based on their view that the IBT was strong enough to get better terms. Most prominently, they demanded that Teamsters in Los Angeles receive sick leave, as do many other Teamsters. They also opposed the new contract's virtual destruction of the clause that allowed 24-hour strikes.

On Monday night, April 6, the leadership of Joint Council 42 stated clear opposition to the wildcat. The trucking companies then seized the opportunity to crush militant unionism among their Los Angeles workers—and that of Local 208 in particular. Most sent telegrams to the strikers informing them they were fired. Somewhere between 10,000 and 14,000 Los Angeles workers were summarily dismissed from their jobs in this manner. The officials of the Joint Council, the Western Conference, and the International Brotherhood of Teamsters did nothing to protect their members, and continued to condemn the wildcats in Los Angeles and elsewhere. The officials of most Los Angeles Locals also condemned the wildcat and did nothing to help the fired workers.

The officials of Local 208 condemned the firings and let it be known that they were in sympathy with the strikers; covertly they gave advice and other aid to the strikers. For the next month, the battle in Los Angeles continued along these lines. On one side were the trucking companies, the Teamster officialdom, the government, and business; on the other were the wildcatters, whose original demands were slowly cut down (as the economic and social pressure against them mounted and as the strikers in the other cities went back to work), to amnesty for the strikers. The employers were holding firm, as was the union officialdom.

Then, the strikers went onto the offensive again. They sent pickets to the San Francisco Bay Area, where they shut down freight movement with the help of sympathetic local Teamsters. Next, they invited college students to join them on the picket lines at freight companies—where the workers had been enjoined from other than token pickets. Hundreds of students, then engaged in protests against the Cambodian invasion, and the Kent State and Jackson State (Mississippi) slayings, picketed over the next few weeks.

These moves dealt powerful blows to the trucking companies, which had already lost many millions of dollars. They were faced with the widening of a strike they had thought all but won, and were leery of what threat might be implicit in the wildcatters' alliance with radical students. Thus, there was a split in the companies' ranks. The interstate carriers and a few of the California carriers agreed to an amnesty, and thereby settled the strike against their companies. However, the bulk of the California carriers, more vulnerable to the militancy of Local 208 and its emulators in other Los Angeles Locals, continued to hold out.

At this point, Blackmarr asked a meeting of the members of Local 208 to declare the California carriers' actions a lockout, thus placing 208's sanction on the strike. The members approved the motion, and the next day business agents were out picketing companies that had not signed the amnesty. A few more companies signed, but within a few days, a court order for 208 to go back to work, and specific orders from Fitzsimmons, led Blackmarr to call off the strike. He signed a compromise pact specifying that about 500 workers would be fired by the California companies (subject to case-by-case appeal before a Blue Ribbon panel of union officials and employers), and that other workers would go back to work, with their seniority rights restored (but only for so long as they obeyed the contract and did not wildcat).

The wildcat's leaders accepted this agreement hoping to keep 208 from trusteeship and in the belief that the particular high union officials specified for the panel would be on their side. They were wrong. Two of the officials refused to sit on the panel, so as not to bloody their hands directly, and their replacements and the employers gave the companies nearly all the firings they wanted in an attempt to terrorize the rank and file. The intimidation was intensified when the employers organized a blacklist of fired workers. In the Fall, 208 was put into trusteeship after all.

The wildcat in Los Angeles was a defeat, kept from disaster

only by the firmness of the strikers and by their reaching out for support to other Teamsters and to students. Nationally, however, the wildcat succeeded in increasing wages, and embarrassed Fitzsimmons as well.

The Strike's
Organization

The strike began under the leadership of stewards from a number of Locals, but with close ties to the Blackmarr administration of Local 208. On the evening after the first, semi-official, strike of April 1 was called off, a group of stewards primarily from PMT and WesCar called stewards from other barns and told them they planned to walk out the next day.[1] Friday morning, two stewards received phone calls at the hiring hall and drove out to PMT to start the picketing. From there, the strike spread across the city. That evening, the stewards rented a hotel room as headquarters. They called a meeting of strikers the next morning in a local park, and spread the word for stewards to come. At the meeting, they told the crowd they were on strike for sick leave, and set up an official strike committee, with Archie Murrietta as spokesman. The Committee was self-appointed, and informed the various yards to send a steward as representative whenever they felt the need for more representative discussions.

As a result, the strike committee was rather chaotic, working on the basis that whoever was present would make decisions. This flowed both from a general desire not to be held legally responsible and from an expectation that the wildcat would be short. The chaos was increased by the constant coming and going at headquarters, the incessant phone calls, the harassment of strike leaders by police, and the exhaustion produced in people who were involved in the strike for days at a time without sleep. The strike leaders' lack of experience also made for chaos, since it meant they had to solve problems they had never thought about before, and led to a general lack of self-confidence among the leadership. The ad hoc nature of decision-making made it difficult to maintain continuity and consistency in strike actions. This problem was met, to an extent, by choosing a few people to stay around headquarters and take part in as many decision-making sessions as possible; this same core of people was to take part in meetings with Joint Council officials to provide some continuity in negotiations. Murrietta, in particular, spent much time at headquarters and in conferences with upper-echelon Teamster officials.

The other side of continuity is breadth of exposure. The strike committee had two reasons to want as many stewards and other rank-and-file leaders as possible involved in decision-making and in conferences with the Teamster bureaucracy. They feared to become isolated from the ranks, and thus wanted a means to spread information and commitment among other Teamsters. They also saw wide involvement as a way to avoid elitism and to maintain rank-and-file control over the strike.

However, the strike committee did become rather distant from the mass of strikers. At mass meetings, the committee members tended to speak down to the strikers; they were, for all intents and purposes, an independent group organized over the heads of the strikers and not really controllable by the strikers; their isolation from the strikers disorganized the strike and prevented serious strategic discussion when it was urgently needed.*

The activist stewards who made up the strike committee belonged to various Locals. Most however, had ties to 208's Blackmarr regime. This greatly influenced the course of the strike. The most important connection between the strike committee and 208's officers was ideological. Thus, Murrietta currently feels he was chosen leader of the strike committee because he was close to Blackmarr and Maheras both personally and in his general views on union matters. In particular, he and most committee members shared the activist but apolitical views that had long typified 208, and thus did not see the need and possi-

---

* For those who took part in the campus strikes during this same period, this probably has a familiar ring. At UCLA, for example, a strike committee made up of representatives of different organizations was set up and proceeded to try to run the strike. It too became isolated from the strikers, and this helped to disorganize the strike. In the case of the Teamster wildcat, this was somewhat mitigated by the fact that the committee was made up of activist stewards with a long and direct experience of leading the workers in their barns in struggles; but the basic similarity is glaring. It shows the need for elected (and recallable) strike committees, and for mass meetings organized in ways that allow serious strategic discussion and democratic decision-making, as the organizational form for mass strikes. This conclusion is reinforced by the successful steelhaulers' strike discussed in chapter 10.

bility for broadening the strike until many crucial weeks had passed. Such an outlook relied on "decent men" within the International bureaucracy. It saw the employer opposition as splintered by internal conflicts, but did not see the need to coerce all employers (including the shippers of freight as well as the truckers themselves). It was so much concerned with staving off a trusteeship of 208, that it never pushed the Local to sanction the strike (as did Locals in those other parts of the U.S.—where no one was fired). Furthermore, it is important that when 208 did, in the end, sanction the strike, this led to a number of employers signing the amnesty. Earlier sanction might have had more powerful results.

The ties to the Blackmarr regime also took more direct forms. In particular, the strike committee accepted advice from Blackmarr and from business agent Alex Maheras on many crucial issues, among them the decision to spread the strike to Oakland and the decision to accept the compromise with the California carriers.[2] Most of the officers of the Blackmarr regime donated part of their salaries to the strike committee, and the committee was allowed to monitor phone calls into the 208 office.

Two Months
on the
Picket Line

The nature of a strike is decisively determined by whether or not the employers try to keep their businesses open. If they shut down for the duration, picketing simply becomes a routinized way of advertising the strike, and many forces tend to make the rank and file inactive. The employers give up some business, but the workers become atomized and demoralized, and the strike simply becomes an endurance contest, unless the workers take the offensive to spread or intensify it. On the other hand, if the employers try to keep their businesses in operation, if they "run scab," picketing becomes a matter of preventing the scabs from working, and the rank and file are involved in a desperate battle to save their jobs. The trucking companies decided to try to break active unionism in Los Angeles by firing the strikers and running scab. As a result, the strike was bitter as well as long, dramatic rather than demoralizingly dull, and unifying rather than atomizing.

When the strike began, many drivers looked on it as a lark. Their experience with 24-hour wildcats and with a brief strike–lockout during the 1967 Master Freight negotiations was that strikes were short, successful, and fun. They saw this one as the same, except larger. Some of the leaders saw it, also, as a way to make names for themselves—a fame which might or might not be put to use in the next Local elections.

The ambush of mass firings during the first week of striking shocked the levity out of the strikers, as did the continued efforts by most employers to run scab. As Eddie McKiernan, one of the strike leaders, put it (interview of March 11, 1974):

> We never realized the full blunt of the thing until four or five days after it started because it was a hit and miss thing. A lot of it was curiosity, and also we were fed up with BS about "the big strike in '29" [*sic*] and none of us realized what it would come down to. It frightened a lot of us. We had underestimated the guys we were protesting against. And we found out how deep the [expletive deleted] were [in the Joint Council] too late. . . . There was an enormous number of rumors. . . . Every barn had such a different experience, no two were the same.
>
> What came out of it, with the number of injuries and so forth, we did remarkably well. The employers, the International, and sheriffs were our enemy. The sheriffs trained, using us to train on. . . . The reality came down in terms of the number of scabs they could put together, and the sheriff's armor they brought down.

To some extent, the full realization of their situation was postponed even when the employers fired the strikers, since they received two weeks' severance pay. However, by the end of the third week of the strike-lockout, the money was running out, and mortgage and installment payments still had to be paid. In the following weeks, the economic pressure became overwhelming. Some strikers lost their homes; some families split up; everyone underwent considerable hardship.

In this context, every striker had to live on hope. They had been fired; victory was needed to get their jobs back. Every rumor was heard with bated breath; every action or initiative became magnified. A desire built up to take drastic action to resolve the situation. Thus, there arose sporadic incidents of violence against company property: one terminal burned to the ground; another partly burned; a demolition bomb was planted at yet another terminal; grenades were thrown at one barn (by someone who failed to pull the pins); innumerable acts of small-scale sabotage, such as pulling the airhoses on semis or breaking windshields, took place.

When the situation is desperate, and morale crumbling, leadership inadequacies become devastating. According to Ray Smith, a black steward at Western Gillette (March 22, 1975): "The strike was very demoralizing. The leaders never came down to the lines. And the strike committee was far from the people. At meetings they talked to us like children." The failure of the strike committee to put out information sheets meant that every rumor seemed real. Leaders of the wildcat had anticipated neither the lockout nor the International's siding with the employers. Coupled with the leaders' failure to put forward any strategy for ending the strike, this weakened morale and eroded strength. It would have meant rout for the strikers but for the fact that the employers had given the workers no out.

In this tense situation, employers—with the assistance of the union's Teamsters' Opportunity Program, which trained poor and minority men in truck driving—began to hire blacks to replace strikers. In the social climate of 1970, this threatened to provoke racial conflict among the strikers, and thus to break their unity. It also could enlist allies for the employers among blacks.

This was dangerous to the strike only because of the long-standing refusal of the Teamsters Union to confront and defeat the racism of employers, of many white workers, and of the union itself. Only the history of 208, which had stood up for its black members, and the ability of black strikers to deal with the situation prevented a disaster. The existence of racism always weakens a union; moreover this weakening just becomes more evident during strikes and other crises. Consider the words of Vance Scott, a black union activist and a member of the strike committee (interview of July 14, 1974):

Blacks participated more on the union side than I've seen in the past. At [one company] all but one black scabbed. At [another company] only three or four of the 30 scabs were black, and then they hired some.

I had to talk like hell to get blacks out at the start of the strike; most weren't enthusiastic. The second or third night I had a real hard time convincing some of the people at [one company]. At [another company], they had _____in there drinking beer with them. Management had .45's in there. I pulled him and the line drivers out to picket.

Thus, racism weakened the strike from the start. When management began to hire black scabs, the results were even worse. In the words of Scott, "If a white scab came in, there was only a little hostility. But if a black scab came in, there was huge hostility; maybe it was fear of blacks taking their jobs."

According to Ray Smith, whose actions in dealing with the problem were crucial in preventing a disaster (interview of March 22, 1975):

The first two weeks, no freight was being moved and we had all gotten our severance checks. On the third week, the California Trucking Association advertised in five or six black community papers for help. They brought blacks in to seek jobs at all the companies. . . . Black people came in to get jobs as drivers, and I was told by a black driver that they were being given applications for permanent jobs as they came in. The air hoses were being cut, and so forth, so it was dangerous. [One company] was scabbing with shotgunners next to the drivers.

Me and _____ [a white driver] were at the gates one day, and he said to me, "They're bringing niggers in to take our jobs." I pointed out that he and people like him were the cause of the problem. Most blacks in LA had been making $1.35 an hour, and wanted to be able to get jobs paying at $4.85. So I don't like the word "scabs" in all cases, though most people in the Teamsters don't see it this way.

They hired *lots* of blacks; all the companies had fifteen to twenty drivers; they were running without freight in the trucks to hurt our morale.

We filed with EOP [Equal Opportunity Program] against the CTA [California Trucking Association] for trying to create a riot. A very quick hearing was called. The CTA brought their attorneys; me and _____ handled it for our side. We pointed out that 97 percent of the industry was non-black, and then when a strike came with everyone on the street, the CTA starts advertising for blacks for the first time. Of course they were trying to start a riot.

The referee said, "I've never thought of it like that before but you're right." One day later, Western Gillette's Public Relations guy calls me and says the injunction against me being near the gates was lifted.

[I was asked] after the strike to withdraw the charge against the

CTA for racism. I said no, and it almost led to a fight. . . . But the charge has never been heard.

In general, then, black strikers had to deal both with the black scabs and with white strikers who tended to make a racial issue of their presence. They were fairly successful in this, preventing the strikers from splitting along racial lines any further, and convincing a number of blacks not to break the strike. As previously noted, the strike committee was not itself capable of handling the problem.

The employers attempted to crush the strike by intimidating its leadership—by lawsuits, public insults, and redbaiting. To quote Scott once again, one company "had a half million dollar and $15,000 a day suit against me, and issued letters in Los Angeles calling me a Black Muslim Communist rebel and in San Francisco calling me a Black Panther Communist rebel. They also named _____ a neurotic and _____ a wino." The CTA sought injunctions and damage suits against the strikers, and subpoenaed strike leaders to testify on their activities. The risk of legal action was thus kept constantly before the eyes of the leadership. Similarly, Murrietta reports daily frisks by police, and tells of being taken for a "ride" by police on several occasions when leaving strike headquarters. All this, of course, tended to disorganize the leaders' work as well as frighten them.

Meanwhile, the *Southern California Teamster* carried reports that the strikers were reds, which angered many war veterans, and upset many strikers' families. Against these pressures, the strikers had to rely on their solidarity, their tactical wisdom, and their strategic insights. They were greatly aided by the experience that members of 208 had built up in the preceding 15 years of rank-and-file struggle and militancy.

Solidarity, in fact, was strong. There was, considering the intense pressure upon the strikers, relatively little strikebreaking by those who had once gone out. In this regard, we should consider the case of women. Many people of both sexes incorrectly think that women are less militant and the first to collapse in a long struggle. However, when women are organized into a union, they do their full part. Consider the following statement by Archie Murrietta (March 25, 1975):

[Women Teamsters] struck as well as men. Some were *much better*. Western Gillette women used two-by-fours on trucks. And at other barns like IML, Acme Fast Freight, and Consolidated Freightways, women certainly held their own.

At PMT the girls [*sic*] were not Teamsters, and were thus laid off as a result of the strike. They gave us a hard time.

Tactics

The basic strike tactic is of course the picket line. Picketing in hot, dusty Los Angeles put the drivers and other workers out in full view of management, subject to taunts and insults. It is no wonder that, once the employers began to run freight with scabs, the strikers sometimes attacked the scabs and the trucks.

They often used roving pickets, a traditional Teamster tactic developed by revolutionary socialist Teamsters in the Minneapolis strikes of 1934.[3] Trucks, of course, are most vulnerable when they go out in the streets. In the past, roving pickets would follow a truck to its destination and then picket the company where it was delivering or picking up freight. This could cause strikes or slowdowns at the customers' operations. Since, however, the Taft-Hartley and Landrum-Griffin Acts outlaw such "secondary" strikes and slowdowns, the 1970 wildcat relied on more direct forms of the roving picket. Sometimes they would stop a truck and force its driver to abandon it. Sometimes they would follow a scab truck and beat the driver up. Sometimes guns were fired at trucks, particularly on freeways, where there were no red lights to stop the truck and make it vulnerable to bodily attack. Similarly, rocks were often thrown through the windshields of trucks. In the words of Archie Murrietta, "there were roving teams on freeways with blank guns to shoot at drivers. Or they would use flare guns, which looked like bazookas. This would also be used sometimes to decoy the cops, if we wanted to get something else." Scabs would also be attacked on their way home from work.

Sometimes, in spite of these tactics, a company would succeed in building its operations back to a fairly high level. In such cases, a large number of strikers from different barns would get together, carrying baseball bats and other weapons and, invading the yard, drive the scabs off.

As mentioned before, a certain amount of bombing and arson occurred. The strike committee decided not to organize such sporadic violence, and indeed to oppose it. They were under considerable pressure to set up demolition squads made up of war veterans, but, aside from feeling the publicity would hurt them, they did not want people to get killed. A related problem was to keep drunks, or other strikers who were incompetent to deal with explosives, from trying to bomb their terminals and getting arrested or blown up in the process.

Strikers must also develop tactics to obtain needed information. They must be able to determine how successfully the employers are maintaining their operations, so that they can deal with employers' propaganda and plan how and when to shut down which terminals by force. Some of this information was easy to come by—the strikers would see how many trucks were moving, and by the way they rode determine how many of these were empties being run to hurt morale. They would also count the number of scabs' cars in the parking lots—which required a calm head, and perhaps such subterfuge as sending a couple on a lovers' stroll through the area. The strike committee also received some information from employers who went to CTA meetings, did not like what they heard about the success of one or more competitors, and leaked information to the strikers. In this regard, the strike committee sometimes deliberately played the companies against each other. In the words of Murrietta, "We would let some companies put on a few scabs, and the CTA would brag about how the companies were doing business again. So the companies that weren't running would get jealous, and would report to us about what was going on. Then we would try to verify the information."

The strikers' approach to the police was mild. They usually obeyed injunctions, and in other ways tried to avoid direct confrontations. Sometimes, they would distract the police, organizing a brawl to get their attention while other strikers burned a scab's car or beat up a scab. However, they were not always able to avoid confrontation. Sometimes the police would take the initiative and "use us to train on." But confrontation with the police was sometimes avoided very successfully by massing so many strikers at one place that the police did not dare intervene. In one case, hundreds of strikers gathered in front of PMT to prevent any scab freight from being moved; the police took one look and went about their business. (And, of course, no freight was moved and many strikebreakers were convinced never to come back.) Naturally, much time and energy went into organizing bail. Some of the stronger yards were able to bail out their own workers, but much of this job fell on the strike committee.

A central strategic problem facing the strike was how to deal with the union bureaucracy. A number of mistakes were made in this regard, but first let us look at some of the tactics the strikers used. Their problem was straightforward—the officials of the Joint Council were openly siding with the employers, with the support of the head of the IBT, Frank Fitzsimmons. The question was how to try to change this. Complicating the problem was the fact that many Teamsters officials gave the appearance of supporting the strikers. Thus, in the words of one member of the strike committee:

We were in contact with several officials, whom I can't name, while the wildcat was going on. They were sympathetic and surprised that LA could have a militant, controlled, all-pulling-together strike. Almost all the officers of Local 357, though not Secretary-Treasurer Volkoff, and of other locals were sympathetic.

In six to nine cities, well-established old secretary-treasurers I talked to were shocked we could do it, and sympathetic.

Jim Harding, a close associate of Hoffa's and high official, was sympathetic, since he knew us. We hoped to get him involved in negotiating for us with the employers and with the union. [We had] known Harding eight years, very closely for six years.

In the East, we wanted Roy Williams [then head of IBT's freight division; now, President of the IBT] to help, but they wouldn't let him intervene.

Faced with this apparent sympathy, the strikers actively sought to get union officials to intervene in their behalf. They sent a delegation to the Washington headquarters of the IBT, but this and similar attempts had no success. The only near-success came when the strikers were trying to shut down the San Francisco Bay area near the end of the strike, when, in the words of one strike leader,

We were in San Francisco to talk to Roy Williams to get him to intervene with the International in our behalf. [An official of Joint Council 42] called him from an employer's home phone and Williams blew up that he was *there*. So Williams called the San Jose Local and told them to shut down San Jose. And we shut down Frisco Airport, too. But this didn't lead to much, so we saw that even though Williams [disliked the official's action], he'd back him. And we decided to try to put as many back to work as possible.

Thus, the strikers found that the Teamster bureaucracy supported the employers rather than the rank-and-file when the chips were down.

The strikers did not rely only on diplomacy in their dealings with the bureaucracy. They also organized mass rallies in front of the Los Angeles Teamster offices, at which some of the demonstrators hanged its chief in effigy. This, however, was not enough to sway the bureaucracy.

Decisions

A few decisions made by the strike committee show some of the problems the strikers faced. One decision, which always comes up in a mass Teamsters strike, was what, if anything, to let operate. In 1970, the strikers decided to let military and hospital supplies move, some small companies operate, and grocery deliveries continue. Vance Scott, a member of the strike committee, remembers what was not shut down (interview of July 14, 1974):

Small yards were not [shut down], so they could survive, medical supplies were let run, and national defense supplies. Five or six of us would sit down and kick it around.
(*How did you decide criteria on this?*)
We didn't want bad publicity, for example, if someone died in a hospital. Or, if a barn went out of business, others in similar barns would get worried. . . .
I made a 4 A.M. decision to let Brake-Meier run, since it handled medical supplies and was not in our local. Four or five of us would sit down and kick it around, or lots was done by independent decisions by people in a place to give it. . . .
In prior strikes, we always let perishables be unloaded, and military and medical supplies run OK, and vehicles brought back to the yard.

Or, in the words of Murrietta (and note here that the committee adopted the viewpoint of 208's officialdom):

On the question of who *not* to shut down, we relied on the BAs, and they gave us good information. For example, at the three-man Sumner operation, the guys gave us $50 per week [as a donation to the strike funds], and did night strike work, and we didn't close them down. . . . We shut down the food industry a few times, but it didn't stay shut. The Local pointed out that if the guys were fired, they didn't have a grievance system, just arbitration, so they would lose (interview of April 4, 1974).

Lack of information and communication among the strikers was a major problem. It is hard to know what is happening at a terminal 10 miles away from where one is picketing. Without effective communication, demoralizing rumors often arose. Thus, a strike paper was critical, but none was ever set up. Murrietta remarked on this (interview of March 25, 1975):

No, there was a hassle about who would do it. _____ 's paper got him roughed up a little when he handed it out.* People told him if he were to do it, he better clear it through strike headquarters first. This gave us a sour taste on the question. Some members have access to presses through moonlighting jobs, so we could have put one out; and four or five mimeo sheets *were* put out. We just weren't geared to it. Eddie McKiernan talked about it several times, but the question was who would do it and who would decide what it said.

Now we see the need. We were all green then. We'd no real experience. And for the first two or three weeks we had no leader or spokesman.

One of the most important decisions during the strike was to accept the offer of amnesty by the transcontinental carriers, even though the California carriers were still holding out. The practical consequence of this decision was to undermine the morale of the remaining strikers, thus setting them up to gamble with the firing of 500 strikers. There is still much bitterness about this decision. It was reached at a meeting composed of one steward from each yard, at which the representatives were told that the transcontinental and some California carriers would give amnesty. The stewards from the nonamnestied carriers then voted to approve the return to work of the amnestied strikers.

* This was a series of mimeographed leaflets put out by a couple of drivers who were trying to establish a political presence in the strike.

When the California carriers and the strikers reached agreement two weeks later, the terms were that 530 strikers would be fired, pending decision by a special panel. Since this procedure led to the firing of virtually all the strikers subjected to it (including some who had been sick throughout the strike) it is odd that the strike committee agreed to it. In part, this came from having been worn down by a long strike—yet union and management sources I interviewed had doubts about how much longer the California carriers could have held out. The crux of the matter, then, was that the strike committee, in spite of their experiences during the strike, still hoped that some high union officials would act decently. In the words of Murrietta (April 14, 1974): "We had hopes if the panel was made up of trustworthy people. Representatives from all the locals met with Blackmarr and asked if Roy Williams, [Bill] McCarthy, and [Harold] Gibbons would be part of it. He made a call, and said McCarthy and Williams would." These illusions cost 500 jobs.

Reaching Out

The Los Angeles Teamsters were in many ways captives of their own localism. For a long time Local 208 had stayed reasonably successful by playing it safe and not really reaching out to other Locals. When the wildcat came, the strikers largely let other areas take care of themselves. They never made a sustained effort to shut down trucking operations in Orange County, and they let a show of force by the bureaucracy of Long Beach Local 692 keep them from shutting down freight operations in the Harbor. (The lack of spontaneous action by Teamsters in these areas can be traced to 208's earlier failure to try to reach their members in the 1960s.)

The leaders of the wildcat did maintain some contact with wildcatters in other cities, however. They did give advice to would-be wildcatters from Las Vegas and Denver. But they did not see such action as essential early in the wildcat—when the strikers in many other areas returned to work, with no organized attempts by Los Angeles strikers to sustain the strike nationally until all could be assured of amnesty.

It was not until early May—when the St. Louis strikers went back to work—that the pressures of the situation made it clear that local militancy was not enough. The strikers made contact with Local 70, in the Oakland area, and arranged to house pickets in that Local's hiring hall. The Oakland Teamsters, who had a long tradition of militancy, wanted to bust the contract that had been negotiated, but had let themselves be driven back to work by a no-picketing injunction. Thus, they welcomed the Los Angeles strikers. Within a couple of days, there were no trucks moving anywhere in the Bay Area. This put strong pressure on the companies, which now had to deal with the shutdown of the two major ports, and of the two major areas, of West Coast trucking. As Murrietta said wistfully—"If we had done this from the start . . ."

The strikers at Western Carloading then took another initiative to reach out to new allies. WesCar contacted striking students at Los Angeles area colleges, asking them to picket. Hundreds responded. The strike committee soon became involved, largely over the question of which barns had drivers who would react too negatively to radical students and which did not. (The black caucus advised black strikers not to be present when students came, because the police might get involved and blacks would be most likely to be shot.)

The effect of these two forms of outreach was decisive, within a few days, in obtaining the transcontinental carriers' agreement to amnesty. The strike in the San Francisco area made it too expensive for them to hold out longer, and the alliance with student radicals had too serious long-term implications to be allowed to continue.

Unfortunately, when the transcontinentals (and some California) carriers went back to work, pickets were withdrawn from the Bay Area, weakening the pressure on the California carriers. Students continued to picket, but their effect was comparatively minor—although, as Eddie McKiernan makes clear, they did succeed in saving some jobs (interview of March 11, 1974):

Bringing in students helped us settle things at WesCar. At Coast Cartage, I *know* students were responsible for getting people rehired. They had people inside and people outside refusing to work with each other. We had students there, and the Southern Pacific police department ordered the students off, saying nonemployees would have to leave. I told the lieutenant of those police that the students were employees' relatives, and the drivers and students started behaving that way, and this broke their backs.

Reasons for
Success
and Failure

In many ways, the wildcat was a remarkable achievement—the strikers held out against the combined attacks of employers, police, courts, newspapers, T.V., and the bureaucracy of their own union, and weathered many errors arising from their inexperience and their misconceptions about the nature of the contending social forces. They held out, and got back all but 500 of 14,000 lost jobs. Of course, the employers' actions had left them no choice once they had been locked out, but the role of 208's past experience was also important. The Local had developed a tradition of struggle and solidarity largely lacking in American labor today. And they had created organization centered around the stewards in many barns. Their stewards had become leaders of 24-hour wildcats, and had usually won concessions in doing so. Further, the drivers had learned how to maintain barn unity while fighting the company. Those barn organizations became mainsprings of the strike, providing both example and material support to the drivers of less organized barns. Further, strikers from other Locals, in most cases working at the same terminals as the 208 drivers, could gain strength from the drivers' organization.

The stewards of 208 provided the nucleus around which the strikers organized their central leadership. It was no accident that most leaders of the wildcat were 208 stewards; the stewards' meetings and organizing drives brought barn leaders in 208 together.

The social atmosphere of 1970 aided the strikers. It was a year of rebellion. Student insurgency was at its height; the struggles of blacks were still going strong; the Chicano movement was gaining momentum in Southern California. And postal workers had just completed a reasonably successful wildcat strike. All of this strengthened the Teamsters' sense of combativity and hope of victory.

In the end, though, the basic source of strength was the courage, determination, and intelligence of the rank-and-file strikers. They held out without income for two months; they took risks when necessary; they avoided provocation; they worked out successful tactics—and, ultimately, by their strength, they averted the disaster that was in the cards and fought their way out of the employers' ambush—though with 500 casualties.

However, there was no serious preparation for the strike.[4] Many of its other failures flow from this, as it is hard to improvise once the action has started. Of course, to the extent that the strike was completely unexpected, no preparations could have been made. While many workers anticipated a strike—and many persons I interviewed told me they did, and spoke of taking specific precautions (like saving money)—these tended to be inadequate, since they expected the strike to be short.

In any strike, a spouse—if left uninvolved—can be a restraint on the striker's militancy. According to Vance Scott (interview of July 14, 1974):

The big problem was wives dictating to their husbands. People who wouldn't come out and actively participate in the strike—I credit that to wives. . . . I went on a panel show at Channel 11, and they broke up my comments with comments and with commercials, and wives called in on that program a lot. I influenced a lot of wives; lots of marriages were on the rocks due to the hardship. Lots of people would bring their wives to hear me at rallies, too.

(How did you try to reach wives?)

Wives want security. That's the only reason they got married. So I'd talk about security—for example, about scabs taking our jobs away. And about the need for sick leave. Therefore, we need to stop the scabs to keep our jobs and to get sick leave.

I'd take one of my daughters along to show we had hardships, too. My wife wasn't working, then.

Murrietta described it as follows (interview of April 4, 1974):

Wives would get upset and call in to headquarters. And at twenty minutes per wife, this is *lots* of time. Most weekends I spent there at headquarters, and I told my wife she could bring the kids and come there to see me. Some wives came to headquarters. We tried to discourage women from being there because of how it might look, and I set a rule of no women. But it was a mistake.

Contrast this to the strike by Minneapolis Teamsters in 1934:

Another step in preparations was . . . that a women's auxiliary be formed. The aim would be to draw in wives, girl friends, sisters, and mothers of union members. Instead of having their morale corroded by financial difficulties they would face during the strike . . . they should be drawn into the thick of the battle where they could learn unionism through first hand participation. . . .
    [The leaders of the womens' auxiliary] began by speaking at meetings of various sections of the union where demands upon the bosses were being drawn up. At first they were received with an air of courteous toleration. Then some men began to ask questions about the project, wanting to know what the women could do in a strike. [It was] explained that staffing a union commissary, handling telephones, helping in a first-aid station, were only a few of the many things women could find to do during a strike. After a time the men began to talk to their wives about it, and to the surprise of some, they found the women were interested. (Dobbs 1972:68–69)

Similarly, in the 1937 Flint strike, which established unionism at General Motors, a Womens' Brigade was one of the main forces.[5] This Brigade went far beyond an "auxiliary." It became involved in picketing and in winning major battles with police.
    By failing to involve spouses, the wildcatters seemed to feel the union was the business only of the workers involved. This weakened the strike, limited the forces involved, and caused strikers' wives (most of the strikers, of course, were men) to become a restraint on involvement and militancy—even though women strikers are able to take their full share of the burdens and the risks. As Eddie McKiernan noted: "A driver at Garrett was cooking some dynamite in the kitchen and it blew and wrecked the house. His wife got so mad she took a ball bat and went out and beat up some scabs with it."
    Another weakness of the strike was its failure to dramatize the issues. As Steuben points out in *Strike Strategy* (1950):

Skillful dramatization is an important part of fighting on the offensive because human beings respond so readily to drama. When the human character of the strike is pointed up, it catches the imagination of the strikers. The public, too, gets the workers' version of the struggle, is moved by it, and often, as a result, ignores company propaganda. (p. 160)

Parades of wives pushing their babies in carriages, the establishing of army tents in front of a mill, airplane distribution of union leaflets, a nice picket line at the homes of the scabs and even the boss—it is this kind of ingenuity and technique that dramatizes a strike, wins sympathy and becomes "the talk of the town." (p. 163)

The wildcatters could easily have dramatized their cause. Members who had been visibly maimed on the job could have leafleted and picketed in front of hospitals. The refusal to pay unemployment compensation to fired strikers could have been dramatized by, for instance, a "50¢ budget meal" Eat-In in front of a local restaurant frequented by city officials and reporters.

Similarly, the strikers failed to try for public sympathy or the active support of other workers. With 14,000 people fired, they could have mobilized hundreds to go to factory gates, union meetings, and shopping centers with leaflets and appeals for donations. The experience would have helped to keep up morale and, if successful, would have put the strikers in a position to defy the injunctions against mass picketing. But they passed up the opportunity. As one worker said in a newspaper interview (*People's World,* July 18, 1970, p. 8): "A militant in General Motors' Southgate plant, and himself a member of an insurgent caucus, told me, 'Twice, I got the local executive board to the point of passing a resolution in support of the Teamsters. Both times nobody from Teamsters came out to talk to the Board.'"

One of the most serious failures of the strikers was that they had no strategy of how to win. Thus, John Butler, who had been President of 208 from 1962–65, told me, "After a month, I met with a member of the Hyatt House strike committee, and asked if there was a plan. They didn't have one, they were just hoping it would work out." Murrietta told me, "For the first one and a half weeks, the committee was lost. We didn't know how to run an organization." Or, in the words of one rank-and-file striker from a different local, "Instead of the stewards' providing coherent leadership, there were two or three cliques. There was no immediately visible and responsible leadership, nor any clear game plan." Contrast this with the following discussion by Steuben:

To maintain the offensive is the core of correct strike strategy. On the basis of his experiences in the great 1919 steel strike, William Z. Foster writes on this subject as follows: "We must attack always, or at the worst be preparing to attack. . . . The workers, like soldiers (and they are the same human beings and subject to the same psychological laws), fight best on the offensive. They are then fired with a sense of power and victory; defensive fighting demoralizes them and fills them with defeatism. Every good strike leader, like every good general, must take this basic fact into consideration."

What does this theory of offensive imply in a practical sense?

It means first of all to spread the struggle. The greater the number involved in the strike, the stronger the feeling and confidence of the workers. . . . When it becomes obvious that the struggle will be sharp and protracted, additional forces must be thrown into battle (if possible) and the strike spread further to render the companies involved additional hard blows. (1950: 148–49)

Instead of taking the offensive, the wildcatters stagnated. Soon after the strike began, thousands were fired; the leaders' response was to talk to the union bureaucracy, to hold out hopes that perhaps one or another Teamster Vice President would speak up in their behalf. They also let small companies start up again, and allowed specified kinds of freight to move. Thus, instead of bringing in new forces, they let some of their forces leave the battlefield. Further, their lack of plans was obvious to the strikers, and devastating to morale. My own experience in the 1974 New Jersey strike showed the same thing; when it is clear that the leaders have no plan to break a deadlock, strikers become demoralized and start to talk about going back to work.

Desperation, however, is sometimes a good teacher. Under the pressure of events, with defeat possible, the leaders of the wildcat finally shut down the Bay Area, and invited students to help them in Los Angeles. This double offensive somewhat restored morale, and demoralized the companies to the point, in many cases, of signing the amnesty. Of course, the strikers' decisive action points up their early failure to develop strategy.

Another serious error was the strikers' decision not to pressure 208 into endorsing the strike soon after it began. This decision had important consequences; it meant that some workers crossed the picket lines who would not have scabbed on a strike sanctioned by a Local (even if the sanction were itself illegal or in violation of Teamster rules), and it meant that the strikers became more vulnerable to firing. The major drawback, in the

strikers' view, to a sanction was that this would make Fitzsimmons almost certain to carry out his threats to put 208 under
trusteeship. Had 208 sanctioned the strike, the Local's officers
would probably have taken over its direction. This would have
meant that the instigators of the strike could not have used it to
build their prestige for the coming union elections, and, that the
Local's officers could have called off the strike when it suited
them. (In fact, precisely this had happened in a 1965 strike in
Philadelphia, reported in McBride [1966]. That strike started
when a company's drivers walked out over the firing of some
co-workers. Hoffa gave the company a free hand to fire the
strikers, so the drivers forced the Local to sanction an area-wide
strike against the company and against Hoffa, leading to a bitter
strike and a court injunction against the Local. At that point,
the Local's officers called off the strike—and, indeed, broke it.
Hence, those who say that Hoffa would never have let the companies fire the Los Angeles wildcatters should consider that in
Philadelphia he did precisely that.)

Thus, while the decision not to obtain 208's sanction for the
strike had dire results, the alternative might have been no better.
As it happened, Local 208 did, when the California carriers refused to sign the amnesty, ultimately sanction the strike; the
courts and Fitzsimmons did order 208 to call off the strike; and
this maneuver was indeed what finally brought the strike to an
end.*

It is very hard to win a battle if one does not understand
who one's enemy is, or what are his chief characteristics. I was
quite surprised at the strikers' limited conceptions about their
enemies. They saw the problem in terms of individual employers
aided by "whores" in high Teamster offices. In my opinion, this
is wrong. Rather than individual trucking companies, their
enemy was every company and industry in the country, supported by Federal, State, and Municipal governments. Rather
than individual Teamster officers, their enemy was the entire
Teamster officaldom. Therefore, the strategies they relied on—
the search for friendly Teamster Vice Presidents and the at-

* During the Trusteeship Hearings Pat Patton testified that he believed Blackmarr had
deliberately sanctioned the strike as a way of ending it. There is some support for this
view among others in 208 as well. It should be added that, although he was a BA at the
time, Patton was not in Blackmarr's confidence. (See Teamsters, 1970: 2961.)

tempts to pit the trucking companies against each other—were totally unsuited for the battle they were involved in. The situation required them, instead, to form an alliance with rank-and-file Teamsters, and indeed with other workers as well, wherever possible, and to shut down the whole country until they got their jobs back (and perhaps won their other demands as well). Only when they moved in this direction, by shutting down the Bay Area and allying with radical students, did they crack their opponents' stand on amnesty.

The nature of the employers' coalition must be clear. The 1970 wildcat was an attempt to upset a national contract in freight. Many other national contracts follow the wage settlements reached in the freight industry. Thus, the wildcatters were trying, in effect, to raise the wages and shipping costs of every manufacturing corporation in the United States. Even more, coming on the heels of a successful Postal wildcat, a totally successful Teamster wildcat might have sparked off a long period of worker militancy throughout the country. It is no surprise, then, that the opposition to the wildcat took on a class character, with all employers and all governmental bodies against the strikers. Injunctions, police attacks, financial arrangements among trucking companies to subsidize those that might crack under the strain—all this was to be expected. And, just as the battles between Local 208 and their employers in the early 1900s were really battles with the entire strength of the Merchants and Manufacturers Association, so, in 1970, businesses outside of trucking, such as "Cleveland Businessmen Against the Teamsters' Strike," gave financial assistance to the companies.

When the IBT bureaucracy printed a justification for its role during this period, it in effect pointed out the nature of the enemy that Teamsters face. In the *International Teamster* of July 1970, an article on page 10 entitled "National Freight Negotiations (An Analysis)" argued that:

Because of the nature of the industry, with the public highly dependent upon the delivery of freight, both the White House and the Congress view these negotiations with much concern and are ready to move in more quickly than would be the case in negotiations where a work stoppage would have less immediate impact on the general public.

The article elaborated on this point, but its implication is clear—rank-and-file Teamsters were forced to confront the entire employing class to obtain such necessities as sick leave and a livable wage increase, and to try to maintain their right to 24-hour strikes. When, in the course of this struggle, their employers fired them, they had to take on all of these enemies simply to keep their jobs.

The Los Angeles wildcatters also made the mistake of placing their hope in some International officials, and found that, in their moment of crisis, the entire officialdom of the Teamsters Union was willing to let them lose their jobs. The strikers found that most officials would sympathize with them verbally—when confident that the conversation would remain private—and found, indeed, that at one point one high officer of the union, Roy Williams, briefly helped them to shut down San Jose; but they discovered that even the so-called friendly officers were willing to let 14,000 Teamsters be fired without openly opposing Fitzsimmons. Indeed, when the special panel was convened to consider the question of 500 workers' jobs, Harold Gibbons and Roy Williams stood aside and let the jobs be lost.

Archie Murrietta, in an interview on April 4, 1974, told me of his trip, with several other strike leaders, to Washington to ask help from the International. He described their futile attempt to see Fitzsimmons, and the runaround they received in trying to get Roy Williams to come to Los Angeles to help them. "We were being jacked off," Murrietta concluded; "nothing came of it in action. So we lost hope in the International."

The leadership of Local 208 itself does not come off entirely well either. The leaders started the 1960s as rank-and-file militants, but by 1970 their institutional loyalty to Local 208, and thus their fear of trusteeship and of lawsuits against the Local's treasury, led them to play a vacillating and indeed harmful role. Rather than place themselves on the line in support of the membership, they claimed to be uninvolved in, and opposed to, the strike. Behind the scenes, Blackmarr and Maheras gave advice, but they refused to interpose the Local between the employers and the members. Further, after the strikers had extended the strike to the Bay Area and brought in the students, and the Transcontinental carriers and some California carriers had signed the amnesty, Blackmarr apparently played an unfortunate role.[6] He called Oakland and told the pickets there to return to Los Angeles—which meant the strikers who had been fired by the remaining California carriers lost their major weapon!

Shortly thereafter, he sanctioned the strike against the remaining companies, through the Local's declaration of a lockout—only to call off the strike when the inevitable court injunction was issued and the inevitable telegram from Fitzsimmons arrived telling him to put the strikers back to work.*

The weaknesses of the strike, as so far discussed, were due in part to the nature of the strike committee, its beliefs, and its relationship to the rank-and-file strikers. The strike committee was composed of stewards elected for their ability to file and win grievances, for their capabilities as leaders of barn organizations, and for their capacity to lead 24-hour strikes. They all knew one another, and tended to form cliques who would cooperate on most matters and work together in Local elections. Their experiences rather distanced them from the rank and file; in particular, they were acquainted with Teamster officials whom they had met at grievance hearings, and had somewhat come to trust because, on specific matters relating to grievances, they were sometimes reliable.

Further, many of the stewards were satellites of the officers of Local 208, and thus had been part of discussions about the "good" and "bad" officers in the union—where "good" and "bad" behavior was understood in terms of grievances, favors, or internal maneuvering within the bureaucracy. As a consequence, stewards who became strike leaders saw their salvation through maneuvers in the bureaucracy, and tended to trust the higher officials of the union. By and large, the rank-and-file strikers had no such illusions. According to Murrietta, "Stewards, as opposed to the rank and file, had hopes in the International. We were always hoping they would give us their word; in the past it had been good." And it should be remembered that the decision to let the Transcontinental carriers go back to work was made by a vote of California carrier *stewards*, not by the rank and file.

A related weakness of the strike organization was that the leaders were not only stewards, but usually had close ties to Blackmarr. They went out of their way to protect the Blackmarr regime, and saw its preservation as essential for their own fu-

---

* He also pointed to a Supreme Court decision that had just been issued that held that a Federal Court can issue injunctions against strikes called in violation of union contracts.

tures, even though the Local's officers were standing on the sidelines while 14,000 Teamsters had been fired. The stewards also tended to share Blackmarr's basic approach to unionism—militant but seeking an umbrella of the type provided by Hoffa rather than seeking to spread and deepen the strike. Their ties to Blackmarr may be gleaned from the following comments of members of the strike committee. Murrietta notes (interview of April 4, 1974):

I was connected with the Blackmarr regime. PMT caucused with him, and as long as he gave an explanation we would support him. When it came to the wildcat, my ties with him led to my becoming the leader.

And, in the words of Scott (interview of July 14, 1974):

Eight or nine of us were on a policy level. . . .
(How did the group get there?)
They had been organizing it. Some didn't want exposure this way and so didn't make decisions. And the others on the committee, except for me, were followers of Blackmarr.

As a result, they made a number of mistakes, many derived from their views on who their enemies were. Thus, they agreed to the Blue Ribbon panel that approved the firing of 500 strikers, and during the strike they allowed many freight companies to operate.

Perhaps even more important, the committee's maneuverist views on how to win the strike and its members' view that, as stewards, they knew what was best, led to a very demoralizing relationship to the rank-and-file strikers: A striker, who prefers to remain anonymous, on what the strike committee was like:

A bummer. It wasn't putting out news to the people on strike. There was no information going out on the phone, just "Hold the line." I manned the phone one day, it was just "Tell everyone to hold the line." I was there 12 hours before I could get someone else to man the phone.

Ray Smith:

We had a meeting at the Shrine when some of them came back from D.C. There was very little information; they told the members almost nothing. . . . After the Shrine meeting where they reported on it, Vance said to me that some Vice President was in their corner (but they wouldn't say who) and I said there was no one in the IBT who understands our situation, and he said I was right. . . . The strike was very demoralizing. For example, the leaders never came to see us. And the strike committee was far from the people. And at meetings they talked to us like children.

A rank-and-file member from a small barn:

There was no leadership. I don't know how these guys became leaders. The strike had the ingredients in rank-and-file militance and so forth to win, but when they started to follow injunctions, what can you do? There were no regular meetings. And when people did get together the meetings were very unstructured. Archie would stand up and report on the latest scuttlebutt about "sympathetic Vice Presidents." Even Blackmarr was said to be a good guy.

The strike's organization also contributed to the failure to devise a winning strategy. Thus, a strike committee of inexperienced cliques of stewards, taking advice from a Local regime of relatively narrow vision, could not see the need to go on the offensive—at least not until pushed. This would not have been so harmful had there been regular meetings of the strikers at which the general direction of the strike was discussed, and had the strike committee been elected by the membership. Under such circumstances, other strikes have, in fact, been able to keep a clear view of strategic necessities. The 1934 Minneapolis Teamster strikes, the 1937 General Motors strike, and the Coal miners' 1969 Black Lung wildcat are cases in point. In the 1970 wildcat, however, the meetings were not places for decision-making, or even for debate, but rather for hearing "scuttlebutt." Thus, for most strikers, the strike became a long vigil at their own barn, plus occasional forays in a roving picket against scabs with perhaps a short stint picketing at a friend's barn, where the heat and dust would be the same but the faces different. In this situation, strikers tended to focus on the tactics of keeping their own barn shut down—and thus on how to get back at scabs or even burn buildings—rather than on how to extend the strike or in other ways take the offensive. This was particularly true since the successful 24-hour wildcats had led drivers to see their barns as the places where victories were won. There was relatively less pressure on the leadership to take the offensive, since the members were thinking on a tactical level and, in any event, saw no way to get their strategic ideas put into practice. Thus, many weeks went by before the first moves to spread the strike were taken, and the strike was greatly weakened.

Why Did
the Strike
Happen?

There is still much curiosity among the Teamsters of Los Angeles about how and why the strike started, since enough information has come out to make clear that the strike was not simply the result of two men spontaneously deciding to picket PMT. I will not pursue this in any depth since it is not of central importance to this study. However, it is worth a brief speculation—with the warning that I do not attest to the truth of this speculation but simply raise it as a hypothesis.

It is possible that the wildcat may have been initiated by high-up Teamster officials who were unhappy with the way Fitzsimmons was running the IBT. Thus, some of the early centers of the wildcat were cities whose top leaders were widely considered to be anti-Fitzsimmons. Furthermore, Los Angeles strike leaders were given verbal encouragement by a number of high Teamster officials. Perhaps most interesting is the negative evidence of what did *not* happen: Namely, that rank-and-file strike leaders did *not* see the need to coordinate across cities.

If the strike was begun by dissident higher-ups, the firing of thousands of strikers in Los Angeles created a problem for these officials—how to save as many jobs as possible without letting the Los Angeles strike spark a nationwide rank and file rebellion that might attack the *entire* bureaucracy and not just Fitzsimmons. This was solved for them by the Los Angeles strikers: by their failure to set up national rank and file leadership or coordinating bodies for the strike but also by their ability to force through an amnesty for most of the strikers.

If this speculation has any truth to it, then the Special Panel (which okayed 500 firings) and the 208 trusteeship should be seen as ways by which Fitzsimmons and his supporters not only struck back at the rank and file but also mortified dissident officials by publicizing their inability to protect their supporters and even their unwillingness to defend them in administrative hearings. In putting 208 under trusteeship, Fitzsimmons did so on pretexts which made clear that he was not planning a general purge of the dissidents but just using 208 (which, isolated in its Joint Council, was particularly vulnerable) as an object lesson against crossing his power.

As I said, this is just informed speculation. However, it is important to note that this is *not* a crucial question from the viewpoint of rank and file workers. It is true that opportunist bureaucrats can spark wildcats when it is in their interest, and that workers must be aware of this. However, such maneuvers can be turned into a two-edged sword, for such a strike can become a weapon in the hands of the rank and file, leading to substantive victories such as sick leave and the restoration of the 24-hour strike clause and to the organization of the rank and file on a nationwide basis. Thus, had the leadership of the Los Angeles strike been more democratic, had it known enough of the lessons of other strikes to avoid certain mistakes—had it, above all, reached out to the wildcatters in other cities at the beginning of the strike, and made firm agreements that no one would go back until everyone went back, and that there would be coordinated action on a nationwide scale to win the strike— then no jobs would have been lost, sick leave and much more could have been gained, and the seeds of an effective Teamster opposition would have been planted.

Effects of the Strike on Strikers' Worldviews

An experience like the 1970 wildcat can change a person. Two months of picketing, of daily decisions about whether to go without pay a little longer or to scab, and of trying constantly to determine how to deal with one's employer and one's union's leadership, is two months of searing one's soul. One comes to new realizations about oneself and about the world, and is slow to forget them. Indeed, the 1970 wildcat is still frequently a subject of intense conversation, and people are still judged by their conduct during those two months.

Some of the effects were small scale, though important. Thus, before the wildcat, the Teamsters locals in many barns were feuding and divided. At PMT, for example, the drivers in 208 and the dockworkers and clerical employees in 357 had feuded bitterly. People were even bringing guns to work, and one worker was shot in the stomach. However, during the wildcat, they learned how to work together, and even established firm friendships. In other barns as well, the Teamsters learned that to let jurisdictional disputes divide them would help only their employers.

The desperation of being slowly ground down in a struggle also had effects on strikers' beliefs. When they came into the strike, many active unionists had a narrow, parochial view of unionism. They saw it in terms of their own employer and those Local members in their own barn. Some looked beyond—but only to the Local as a whole, and to its situation in Los Angeles. However, the strike taught them that the struggle was far wider—that their opponents were organized nationwide and that both the state and the bureaucrats running the Teamsters Union supported the employers. They also learned that they could unite with Teamsters in other Locals, and even in other cities, and that this was sometimes necessary. Further, they learned that even student radicals could be useful allies—as shown by the following statements made by three Teamsters who talked to reporters during the strike:

This was like a shot in the arm for the workers when the students came—seeing that someone thinks what we are fighting for is important.

As long as the students and working people stay together, you're going to see some changes in this country. Maybe we should have done this years ago.

Regardless of what the students do in college, this is the greatest thing they ever did.

Of course, a number of strikers wanted no part of the students; yet the core of militants, by and large, found their views on this issue changed. Indeed, when a few months later some student supporters started a newspaper about rank-and-file struggles, *Picket Line,* there was active cooperation between Teamster militants and the avowedly socialist newspaper.

Effects
of the Wildcat
on the Active
Unionists

The key to understanding the wildcat lies in understanding its effects on the union activists, the core of successful unionism. In many ways, the wildcat had grown out of their experiences. They were weary of the International's failures, and bitter over the failure to get sick leave in the new contract. They saw the union as moving backwards—for instance, in allowing the gutting of the 24-hour strike clause that legitimated their strength and activity in the barns. They wanted to show what they could do when they had the chance. The younger members had stirrings of discontent at hearing tales of the long PFL strike of 1937 and of the rank-and-file takeover struggle of the 1950s; and many activists felt stirrings of political ambition to run for Local office on the basis of the leadership of a great and historic action. And the activists also wanted to fight the pressures of inflation, recession, and productivity drives.

The strike's effects on the local activists went deep. They discovered that the International bureaucracy was even worse than expected, particularly in letting over 10,000 members be fired. They learned that, when the chips are down, all the established institutions of society are against the striking worker. Many activists found that they had unexpectedly much in common with student activists. And a certain number—though far less than had the wildcat been more democratically organized—came to the conclusion that a systematic, political, radical response would be needed to deal with the problems facing them.

On the critical issue of the effect of the wildcat on the morale and combativity of the local's activists, however, the picture is mixed. Almost every activist was angered by the events, and in this sense a basis for increased struggle was created. Unfortunately, many activists were also demoralized by the outcome of the strike and by the fact that 500 persons lost their jobs. Yet many others were determined to continue the struggle and to find and correct the errors made in the past.

But at this point, the International put Local 208 into trusteeship, in the hopes that the morale and influence of militant local activists could finally be broken.

Chapter 8

Trusteeship

DURING THE four months between the end of the wildcat and the imposition of the trusteeship, the morale of Los Angeles Teamsters, and of Local 208 in particular, was further weakened: 500 strikers had been fired; the leaders of 208 and of the wildcat took no significant steps to oppose this action. Heavy layoffs, caused by the general economic downturn and the slow recovery of freight after the strike, also lowered morale and combativity.

When the Special Panel began to hear the cases of the 500, it quickly became evident that it would fire almost everyone. However, many of the 500 thought that they would get justice, since their firing was so clearly unjust, and wanted no part of any mass action on their behalf.* Further, the workers had just been through a long strike and wanted to earn money. Thus, response to the hearings tended to be low-key. Several dozen Teamsters, however, did drive to the La Costa Country Club during the Frank Fitzsimmons Open Golf Tournament to complain about how the hearings were being run. There, they had a brief talk with Fitzsimmons, while his bodyguards pointed shotguns and other weapons at them. They then called the press and held a news conference on the hearings' injustices—running up a huge bar bill (which they charged to Fitzsimmons) while they waited for the reporters. Nothing real came of this episode.

During the hearings, a number of employers' cars were vandalized, and at the barns freight was stolen and there was minor sabotage. Such actions are normal after a defeated strike move-

---

* The 500 were supposed to be those who had been most aggressive during the strike and worked for companies that had not signed amnesty. However, I am told that this is only partly so. Many militants kept their jobs. The companies had a tendency to victimize workers with high seniority (and thus longer vacations) and Chicanos. Strategically, it was probably an attempt to undercut the base of support for the militants by making the point that others, too, would suffer. To put it bluntly, the companies tried to terrorize and to divide the workers.

ment, as workers vent their anger by attacking the employers' equipment.

Once the Special Panel made its report, confirming nearly all of the firings, numerous picket lines were set up around trucking terminals. However, they had no effect—morale was too low, too much time had gone by with no action taken, and the heavy layoffs spread even more gloom. Further, the split between those who had struck the transcontinental carriers and those who had struck the California carriers had become embittered. Demonstrations at the Teamster Building also had no effect.

Meanwhile, the fired 500 were also blacklisted. (Blacklists are illegal, but this does not stop companies from using them.) Thus, one task facing the Teamsters of Los Angeles was to obtain new jobs for the 500. They met with some success, especially since, even under the trusteeship, the more strongly organized barns could exert enough pressure to have new openings filled with wildcat victims. However, some of the victims still had not found steady jobs five years later, and all lost years of seniority.

Trusteeships in Theory And Practice

On October 1, 1970, the officers and members of Local 208 were informed by a letter from General Vice President Frank Fitzsimmons of the IBT that Pete Kurbatoff, President of Joint Council 42, had been appointed as Trustee over their Local. This meant that the elected officers and business agents of the Local had been removed from their offices and that the affairs of the Local were to be run by Kurbatoff and those he appointed. James Easley was appointed Administrator, with the power to appoint business agents, to call meetings of the Local (or, as it happened, not to call meetings), to decide which grievances would be processed by the Local and which would not, and to spend the treasury as he saw fit. Before the arrangement would become final, a hearing would determine whether or not the temporary Trusteeship should be maintained; pending the hearing, of course, Easley would run the show, and the elected business agents and salaried officers would receive no paychecks. Further, the hearing, conducted by union officials loyal to Fitzsimmons, would simply make recommendations; Fitzsimmons would then take whatever final action he felt like. Trusteeship meant dictatorship.

Although it may be argued that a trusteeship allows, for example, the International to step in and clean up a crime-ridden Local, usually, trusteeships are a weapon of the union bureaucracy to keep the rank and file in line. The United Mine Workers once had so many Locals under trusteeship that it appointed a majority of delegates to union conventions. Teamsters trusteeships are similar. Sometimes they are used to shore up the regime of a loyalist whose position is shaky. An example is the trusteeship imposed on Local 436 in 1974. In that case, the long-time head of the Local, "Babe" Triscaro, died, leaving his son-in-law, Sam Busacca, as acting president. However, as rank-and-file unrest threatened to unseat Busacca, the Local's executive board and officers asked Fitzsimmons to put the Local under trusteeship. Busacca, as the administrator of the trusteeship, was then able to rule the Local for 18 months (the maximum duration of a trusteeship under the Landrum-Griffin Act).

Local officers use the fear of trusteeship to keep the membership in line. Sometimes they warn that, if members organize to take over the Local, the resulting unrest will lead to trusteeship. Even more insidiously, they use this fear to justify not taking action against employers. In 1974, there was a long, bitter strike, sanctioned by Local 804, against United Parcel Service (UPS) in New York. It could have been won only if 804 carried the strike to other UPS operations—in particular to New Jersey. Early in the strike, some workers went to picket the Secaucus, New Jersey, Terminal. However, a driver ran a truck across a picket line and killed one of the business agents. Subsequently, 804 never returned to picket in New Jersey, even though the ranks wanted to. Ron Carey, leader of the Local, continued to talk about "going back to Jersey," but he also continually pointed out that such action might lead to trusteeship—and he never did lead them "back to Jersey." Instead, he accepted a contract that was in many ways a defeat.

A few months later, members of New Jersey's UPS Local 177 wildcatted. Their strike was supported "unofficially" by

newly elected officers of the Local, at least one of whom was
arrested for pulling the airhose of a scab truck. However, within
a few days, the ranks were forced back to work by the threat
that their Local would be put under trusteeship.[1]

Thus, trusteeships serve the interests of the bureaucracy.
And since that bureaucracy and the employers both gain from
a docile rank and file, the employers' interests are also well
served by a trusteeship. The problem facing the members of
Local 208, in October 1970, was what to do about this.

Trusteeship
Hearings

The membership's first step to fight the trusteeship was to go
to court. They claimed that most reasons given for imposing the
trusteeship were false (the reasons included such gems as a
"wildcat" during the summer that had really been a sanctioned
strike), and asked that the court cancel it. However, while agree-
ing that the grounds for the trusteeship were indeed flimsy, the
court did not order its cancellation. It did order the International
to allow the Local's elected officers representation at the hearings by an attorney whose fee (up to $2,000) would be paid by
the Local, and it ordered that the officers continue to receive
their salaries until the final decision by Fitzsimmons.

It was a precedent-setting case that seemed to offer the
Local a fighting chance to stave off trusteeship and made it
possible for the Local to obtain hearings that were procedurally
fair and balanced (even though not substantively fair and balanced—a fair hearing before a stacked court being less than
fairness). But these legal victories and precedents made no difference; the Local ended up in trusteeship in any case.

Upon the failure to win quick victory through court action,
the drivers of 208 had to work out further strategy. They chose
to treat the hearings as a fair tribunal, and to prepare and argue
a case aimed at convincing high Teamster officials that the Local
had done little wrong. If this move failed, they would appeal the
verdict to the International Executive Board, and from there to
the International Convention the following summer, and from
there to the courts. They did this—and lost all along the line.

They had two other options. One was to treat the hearings
as a propaganda platform, to speak not to the hearing officers

but rather to the rank and file. Had they done this, instead of denying their role in the 24-hour walkouts of the preceding years, they would have said that they had indeed been involved in them, and that 24-hour strikes were an excellent weapon of self-defense; they would have exposed the bureaucracy's sellouts; they would have sought generally to build a rank-and-file movement against the bureaucracy, using the hearings as one vehicle of organization while also organizing in the barns and coffee-shops. They would have ended up under trusteeship—as it was clear that they would in any case—but they could have begun a rank-and-file movement that, building on the distrust of Fitz-simmons and the momentum of the wildcat (viewed as a success by many Teamsters outside of Los Angeles) might have become a major force in the next few years.

Their other option, which could have complemented that of speaking to the ranks, was to try to prevent trusteeship through mass action. They considered this. In the words of Archie Murrietta, the spokesman for the wildcat but also a confidant of Blackmarr (interview of March 25, 1975):

There was no mass action at the Trusteeship Hearings. We decided it would have hurt us. This was discussed at several meetings of 50 or 60 people. We felt we had a legitimate fight, with a chance of winning. Now, I think a *controlled* demonstration would have helped, with people seeming to be violent but not really doing anything. We were sure we could get four to five hundred people here but we feared how the judges would react. This was a mistake.

We discussed and nixed the idea of pulling people off the job to go to the trusteeship hearing. It would maybe have hurt us, and I still wouldn't do it.

John T. Williams, who had been a BA and Vice President of 208 before the trusteeship was imposed, saw it as follows (interview of March 29, 1975):

The trusteeship itself destroyed what possibilities of mass action were left. Members felt the Local had been captured, by the International and by the Joint Council. Some of us, like me and Alex Maheras, didn't *want* mass action, figuring we had to have 18 months of good behavior or else they would use it as an excuse to prolong the trusteeship.

As it was, the closest they came to mass action was to collect thousands of signatures on a petition opposing the trusteeship.

Thus, after all they had been through, many of 208's leading activists—such as Murrietta—still had a residue of hope in the fairness of the International. Beyond that, even those—like Williams—who saw they had no chance of avoiding trusteeship still adopted a parochial strategy. Rather than reach out to Teamsters in other locals to build a rank-and-file movement at a time apparently ripe for it, as was confirmed by the growth of TURF in the following months (see below) they chose to undergo a period of good behavior and then regain their own Local under conditions that, as it turned out, would hamstring the new administration.

The hearings lasted a long time; there are 26 volumes of testimony from 26 different sessions of hearings.[2] Testimony in favor of the trusteeship came almost exclusively from employers and union bureaucrats; testimony from rank and filers and 208 officers was almost entirely against it. John T. Williams, backed by the lawyers, acted as defense attorney, and often cut the other side's testimony to shreds. The prosecution often did not even bother to cross-examine hostile witnesses.

The Hearing Panel recommended that the trusteeship be continued, and on February 9, 1971, Fitzsimmons made it official. None of the subsequent appeals or legalistic maneuvering reversed this decision.

The Trusteeship Period

The Trusteeship was in office for 21 months (three months more than the legal limit), from October 1970, through June 1972. At that time, elections were finally scheduled—after a lawsuit was threatened. For the members it was a time of demoralization but also of fighting back. Consider the words of Vance Scott, a black member of the strike committee and active in the rank-and-file resistance to the Easley trusteeship until, shortly before its end, he went onto its payroll as a business agent (interview of July 14, 1974):

(*What was the trusteeship like?*)
Plundering of the local; reversal of decisions (in grievance hearings); weakening of contracts; penalties for the strike after it was over; employer had his way.

Toward the end, they started a play for members' votes. So they took me into the administration.

Contrast this with the words of another black activist:

I've been in this Local since 1959. I saw the Cohen Administration, Blackmarr, Easley, and Maheras. I saw no difference. In the Easley administration, there were more black people than before appointed to office.

Or consider the views of John Franklin, a steward at TIME-DC for a number of years (interview of March 18, 1974):

Some trusteeship BAs knew nought about contracts. . . .
A lot of yards felt we slipped back in the trusteeship, but *we* didn't very much. During Blackmarr's administration, and the trusteeship, and Alex's administration there's not a nickel's worth of difference. We've been just as successful in each case.
(*Why?*)
I use the same tactics in each case; we have our meetings and we'd tell the BA how we wanted it. We wouldn't go into management without knowing the minimum we'd accept, and having the BA know it. We'd maybe ask for more, and negotiate for what we wanted in the first place.
(*Where is there a difference?*)
Only one I've seen is that during Alex's administration we've had membership and steward's meetings.

(*What about weaker yards?*)
Weaker ones sank during the trusteeship and sank fast. Some, like CF, that we thought were strong went way down.

Finally, consider Alex Maheras's views; Maheras, a BA under Blackmarr, was one of the leaders of the opposition to Easley, and is currently Secretary-Treasurer of 208:

First off, Easley seemed like a nice guy. We knew little about him. He seemed such that we could have had a worse person, so we gave him *some* cooperation, but it didn't last long. His policy, and the people he hired, were unacceptable. Rank and filers were not allowed in the office, and the shades on the windows were always drawn (they were, here in Ed's office, under Blackmarr too, but now we keep them all open). There was a screening committee, with two BAs as head BAs. And business agents had to get an OK to make decisions, for example if they went into a yard. And grievances would be screened by two BAs to decide if they should be filed or not.

The hiring hall was in chaotic condition. . . .

They were meeting with employers without stewards present. In or out of the yard, without the members knowing.

The picture seems contradictory at first sight, and to some extent it probably was. As I was never able to interview Easley, much of the following is speculation; however, his actions seem to indicate a certain contradiction in his policy. To some extent, he was trying to run a good Local, according to his own bureaucratic conception of what a good Local is. But it appears as if he was also supposed to punish the militants for the wildcat and for their antibureaucratic stance. In addition, particularly near the end of the trusteeship, he had to try to develop some sources of votes if he wished to stay in office. Thus, he took advantage of the preexisting racism of the Local, and bid for black support by appointing a number of them as Local officials.

Further, in some barns, he made a sincere effort to give good representation. In other barns, some of the strongholds of the wildcatters, he seems to have given management a green light to break the barn organization. He would even sometimes help them, as in trying to oust wildcat leaders from stewardships. He took these actions during a period when the employers, seeing a chance to bust the strength of the Local, were harassing stewards and other activists. Thus, at some barns the employers apparently laid off more drivers than necessary, which caused those drivers immediately below the activist stewards on the seniority list to blame those stewards for the extent of the layoffs. At another company, management seized upon an incident and fired six stewards; the six got their jobs back, but the intimidation led a few of them to cast their lot with Easley.

Because the pressures to which the drivers were subjected, and their ability to resist, varied among barns, the drivers currently have a wide variety of views as to what the trusteeship was like. In those barns where the drivers were well-organized, the attack on them not too strong, and the trusteeship helped neither management nor drivers, they found the trusteeship bearable. In those barns which were weak to begin with and most reliant on support from the Local, the trusteeship was a time of setbacks, particularly in working conditions. And in barns like

WesCar, and PMT, where the employer and the trusteeship seem to have worked together against the drivers, while the drivers managed to maintain their organizations, the trusteeship is remembered with pride as a time of great bitterness and hard struggle—which was survived.

The Fight Against the Trusteeship

Trusteeships can be defeated—but only with much difficulty: Union officialdom and employers can manipulate the grievance procedure to make the trusteeship look good; union officialdom can finance the trusteeship, give it good coverage in the Joint Council newspaper, and bring in important union officers to speak for it; a trusteeship can hire "goons" to deal with opponents, see that oppositionists are fired, and issue withdrawal cards to out-of-work opponents so that they are in effect no longer in the union. Nevertheless, Local 208 defeated the trusteeship imposed upon it. It did so in a way that shows the importance of barn organization, and in a way that was to influence events thereafter.

When the International imposes a trusteeship, its opponents have two major tasks. They must prevent the trusteeship from getting roots within the Local—and do so without helping the employers. They cannot simply sabotage the workings of the union, but rather must work out means of self-defense that protect the workers while discrediting the trusteeship. They must also organize the opposition's strength to take the offensive in ousting the trusteeship. When such organization is tied into the process of fighting the employers, and when large numbers of workers participate, it can strengthen the ability of the post-trusteeship regime to fight against both management and the International bureaucracy. But when the offensive, in ousting the trusteeship, remains legalistic and electoral—and thus fails to develop the independent power of the rank and file—it will create a post-trusteeship regime that owes its power to state intervention (via the courts), and will also have a less activist rank-and-file base.

Local 208 was put into trusteeship in a time of demoralization—the wildcat had been defeated and there were economic hard times. For months, too, the leadership of the Local had been telling the members not to engage in mass action or even in short strikes. As a result, many drivers were discouraged at the failures the previous leadership had brought them, and the trusteeship had a better chance to establish itself.

A key question for Easley, then, was whether or not he could assemble a competent staff of BAs. If he could, he might be able to gain adequate representation for the membership, while keeping it disorganized and passive, and establish a base of support. To find such BAs, and at the same time to neutralize the militants by coopting their leaders, he offered jobs to Archie Murrietta, Alex Maheras, and other BAs and leading stewards of the Blackmarr regime. For similar reasons, the companies offered management jobs to some of the militants. However, by and large, they refused to go along, although Murrietta did suggest the names of several possible business agents. Easley, however, did not act on his suggestions, thus ending up with less competent BAs and also confirming to the militants that he was not serious about good representation.

Growing more and more convinced that Easley would not adequately help the membership, the militants adopted several tactics to weaken him. One tactic was simply not to offer corrective criticism, and to pass the word to other active unionists not to do so. One barn leader told me what happened to the BA assigned to his barn:

He was a nice guy, but he didn't have a chance. He didn't have the time to learn the job and that was no fault of his own. You just don't put a green guy in that position. He had come down to the yard and he knew one man there. Management always tries to buy people off, not necessarily with money but often dinner, drinks, coffee, this type of thing. So when this guy, this agent, came around, we saw it happening. Management would give him coffee and tell him what a fantastic agent he was, and the guy went for it. We could have keyed him into what was happening, but we didn't want to do that. We wanted to see just what he was made of. He went for it. And the next thing we knew The Man was having coffee with him every time he came into the yard, and all we did was point out to the men that this was happening.

People would talk to the trusteeship officials as little as possible. Stewards tried to handle the problems by action within the yards; they made sure that only as little information as possible reached the officials, and they would cooperate with the business agents only if an important case had to go to grievance. In such cases, the stewards sometimes even set the trusteeship up—a sort of "fair turnabout" since, near the end of the trusteeship, management and the International were cooperating on the grievance boards to ensure that the Easley administration looked good. Murrietta gives some examples of "set-ups" (interview of March 25, 1975)*:

(*Were they being given good decisions to strengthen them?*)
One driver was fired after being caught stealing. He was a pro-company guy, and was given a choice of resigning or being fired. He came to me for advice and I told him to go to the Local and tell them Archie told him to fuck off. And he did. At Long Beach it was deadlocked. He got his job back at the hearings in Frisco.

Near the time of the elections, they got lots of non-precedent-setting decisions. [One company] okayed having six stewards at meetings with management to build up [the BA] and we've been able to stick them with it since.

[A leading militant] beat up a supervisor. We arranged to let Easley think they would get support at [his barn] if they saved [him]; people were calling in to the office all day to ask them to save him. And it worked, he got his job back.

One of the most effective ways developed to prevent the Trusteeship from establishing a base was a series of leaflets entitled *Rape of the Membership*. The administration was doing a poor job, and was undemocratic and spendthrift. The well-organized and humorous leaflet campaign therefore helped to destroy any remaining illusions and to build up drivers' morale. The following remarks are from an interview I had with the person who put out *Rape of the Membership*, who wants to remain anonymous even now.

Then *Rape of the Membership* came out. It really, as it grew, the people took notice of it. It was encouraging. And it had the facts.

* They also show that PMT activists did their best to defend all members against being fired.

(*How did you get the facts?*)

Certain documents; some people who worked under the trustee gave us information, and we'd check it out and it was facts. It shook them up.

There was no schedule on it; it was put out when. . . . Distribution was by mailing a packet of 50 to fifteen or twenty different barns, to the houses of guys from these barns. One packet per barn; then they'd split it among themselves. Some were hand-delivered. Twenty-five people would get a packet.

(*How many people knew who put it out?*)

Maybe five people knew it for a fact. There were lots of rumors. That's a key, keep your enemies guessing. Once they know, they can concentrate on it.

(*How many people were involved in getting and checking facts?*)

One—one person put it together. The facts would come in. Other people—25 roughly—were involved, but a lot didn't even know where it was coming from. You'd hear through the grapevine who wanted to get a packet, and we'd check with drivers to see if they had gotten out. If not, the receiver of the packet would be scratched off the list.

I could at any given time ask five guys what I wanted to know, and they'd keep their ears open, and find out what's happening all over. And I could pick different sets of guys, too, since there are so many different networks.

(*And check it out?*)

Some, though more so on more important items. Though if it's 75 percent true, it's a winner.

(*When did it come out?*)

They were never dated, weren't over a dozen of them. In '71 they started, in March or April, before the July Convention. About one every 45 or 50 days. They were on different color paper to differentiate them.

At first, some good guys didn't take it seriously. But it bugged the hell out of Easley and the Joint Council, and it perked up the members, it encouraged them.

There was suspicion on a lot of guys. [Here he discussed some of the ways he kept his identity secret, such as having three different people unconnected with the industry sign "Brotherhood" at the bottom.]

The Easley guys put out "The Real Rape of the Membership" to show the other side.

One of the wildcat leaders described the reaction of the

drivers, and the use to which *Rape of a Membership* was put, as follows:

All of a sudden a leaflet came in the mail and it hit in the yards. You should have seen a copy of it. Well, those were all facts and the funniest thing in the world, no one ever really knew who put it out. I got accused many times. I'll tell you what, if I dotted an ''i'' I would take credit for it. It was a fantastic thing. . . .
     The funny part of it is, whenever we had a yard meeting and the Administrator would come down, or a business agent would come down, they would challenge what it said to the membership. We would always say, well, good, let's take incident for incident, let's prove it or disprove it. And there were eyewitnesses for everything. Every time we got a leaflet we also got some additional information behind it to back up the incident. Naturally, because you can't put everything in that one little sheet of paper. . . .
And the guys would go, like this [where we were talking] is a truck stop. In the afternoon you come here and you find maybe 15 or 20 truck drivers. Well, it would be taped to the wall here. So if you didn't see it in the yard, you saw it in the coffee shop. It was a hell of a conversation piece.

Of course, to get inside information was not easy. One way was by befriending one of the BAs who felt unappreciated by the administrator and shunned by the drivers. The activists took him out drinking and soon he was regularly giving them information.

Ultimately, the strongest force preventing the trusteeship from developing a base was its own actions, which flowed from its basic nature. As an institution created to suppress rank-and-file action and to encourage cooperation, rather than confrontation, with the employers' attacks, the trusteeship had to behave in ways that would lose support. Thus, it had to be undemocratic to keep the ranks in line. It had to go along with many employer demands to fit Fitzsimmons' (and, indeed, officialdom's) policy of encouraging profits. (As an example, it agreed to employers' requests to exclude drivers absent on layoff or long-term illness from participation in annual bids and thus from establishing steady runs in set areas of the city upon their return to work.) The trustees could hardly hide the fact of such cooperation with the membership's opponents.

How, then, did the activists of Local 208 try to organize to oust the trusteeship? In almost every barn the active unionists, who had developed out of the rank-and-file movement of the 1950s and during the Blackmarr years, continued to defend themselves against management with little help, and sometimes outright opposition, from the Easley forces. To the extent that they could maintain their barn organizations and their combativity, there was a natural base from which to launch attacks at the trusteeship. There were also attempts to unite broader groupings to take on the entire International bureaucracy, and Fitzsimmons in particular. Three major channels developed through which one grouping or another tried to gather forces to oppose the administration: A series of rank-and-file committees; TURF (Teamsters United Rank-and-File); and, finally, a legal electoral campaign.

Attempts to organize rank-and-file committees were numerous. This was to be expected, if only because Local 208 had found the rank-and-file committee useful in establishing the drivers' power and activism a decade earlier. This time, the rank-and-file committees were less successful, although they did chalk up some accomplishments. They held stewards' meetings (since Easley did not), which helped to keep the stewards united and to limit "barn feudalism." This was necessary since it would have been difficult to develop rank-and-file coordination had most of the barn organizations completely lost contact with each other. (Contact was of course also maintained through informal discussions at coffeeshops. Indeed, such informal discussion of how to deal with problems happened more often than it had when the Local had had formal ways to win grievances.) The rank-and-file committees also developed mechanisms to prevent Easley from establishing a base. Further, they exerted pressure upon barn leaders opportunistically tempted to ally with the trusteeship in order to become BAs, and in the case of Consolidated Freightways, delayed the defection of several talented opportunists for many weeks.

However, the rank-and-file committees were never able to develop an offensive strategy until they allied with the electoralists. This is not surprising, given the limited options open to such committees. One option, successfully used in the late 1950s, is to intervene in union meetings to pass resolutions, set up action committees, and so forth. Such actions make it possible to lead the struggle against the employers while, at the same time, building forces to attack the regime. However, during the trusteeship there were neither membership nor official stewards' meetings.

Another option for such a committee is to take the lead in organizing action: Picket lines or mass demonstrations against the trusteeship or against the International bureaucracy; slow-downs, sabotage campaigns or wildcats against the employers; even, if these actions are successful and the movement increases, actions against the employers to try to force the International to end the trusteeship. This last course is dangerous, akin to the 1970 wildcat in its potential to bring down the forces of the state, the employers, and the union officialdom against the movement. Thus, it was ruled out by the defeat of the wildcat, since few drivers wanted to go through such a battle again without many allies. (The failure of TURF—described later in this chapter—also made it impractical.)

The committees also might have issued a newspaper to co-ordinate rank-and-file resistance to the employers, to muckrake the Easley regime while proposing ways to fight it, and generally to organize a powerful, activist drivers' group ready to take over the Local—whether via mass action or via elections—when the time became ripe. In this way, the drivers could establish dem-ocratic and activist control over the post-trusteeship regime. The committees' failure to do this left *Rape of a Membership*, with its essentially passive opposition (that is, criticism without action and with minimal organization for future action), as the only significant anti-trusteeship voice.*

Many problems prevented the rank-and-file groups from taking some of these options. Their members tended to be heav-ily recruited from the strike committee of the 1970 wildcat, thus mistrusted by those who blamed them for the wildcat or its defeat. Also, many of them were barn leaders, too busy with their barns' day-to-day struggles against management and the Administration to spend much time organizing local-wide actions or putting out a newspaper. Further, most were still apolitical

---

* To some extent the drivers relied upon *Picket Line*, the student-based paper that grew out of the support group for the wildcat, as a publicizer of their views and activities. However, an "outside" paper cannot do this unless it becomes so incorporated as to be "inside."

militants of the Blackmarr-regime stamp, who did not think in terms of reaching out to other rank-and-file groups to establish a power adequate to defeat their enemies, but, instead, aimed simply for the restoration of the days of the Blackmarr regime; in this, they failed to see that the end of the 24-hour strike clause, with increased support by union officialdom of the employers' interests, had made the old way of struggle obsolete. Thus, the rank-and-file committees could not find a way to cut through the obstacles and oust the trusteeship.

Another avenue some 208 activists explored was TURF, a nationwide attempt to find solutions to such problems as beset 208. Teamsters United Rank and File (TURF) was formed in July 1971 by representatives of 11 locals and of the "Teamsters International Committee for 500 at 50."* By the time of its first convention that September, representatives from at least 34 locals attended. TURF aimed at democratizing the Teamsters. In its newspaper, it opposed the structure that allowed a group of high-paid officials to run the union and, in particular, to have almost unchallenged power within the union. TURF also took up the issue of pension reform, and tried to mobilize Teamsters to fight for a better 1973 Master Freight Agreement than appeared likely.

TURF chapters were constantly harassed by Teamster officials and their supporters. In a number of instances, armed "goons" tried to disrupt their meetings. Clearly, the officialdom was worried by TURF—a reasonable fear given the massive discontent at how the union was run and given the later successes of PROD and TDU.

Unfortunately, TURF did not succeed in democratizing the IBT, and indeed fell apart after a year or so (although, in Los Angeles, a hollow shell existed for years). In large part, TURF's failure came of its inability to find a mode of action that would hold it together, let the members learn to trust each other, and give members a way to sort out their leadership. TURF did initiate some lawsuits, but these did not accomplish much—nor could they provide an activity around which to organize a na-

---

* A group that had been formed to fight for improved pensions of $500 a month at 50 years of age, and had gathered over 200,000 Teamster signatures on a petition calling for such improvements. 500 at 50 was centered in Los Angeles, with its officers being members of Local 208.

tionwide rank-and-file movement. TURF did put out a newspaper, a sounding board for discontent, but this alone could not build an organization in the absence of real struggles that would involve the members.

In particular, TURF did not get involved either in the daily struggles of workers on the job, or, in most cases, in the fights for more democratic and active locals. Potentially, of course, it could have done so; it could have served as an umbrella under which to organize support for the many groups around the country who were trying to transform their own locals; it could have made this the major focus of its activity, putting only secondary emphasis on the confrontation with the bureaucracy over issues of national Teamster democracy, and even of national contract contents, until its forces were gathered through fights at a local level. Thus, TURF could have provided an organizational vehicle for such local groups in their Joint Council and region of the country; the TURF paper could have brought the news of successes attained in various Locals, and discussion of how they had been attained, to other groups who might have found them useful.

However, none of this occurred. A national organization is very hard to set up; some leaders were opportunists seeking to use TURF as a road to official status; and (for it is far easier to see what will work after the fact) it was somewhat unclear as to what TURF should do.

The experience of some 208 members with TURF will help clarify why TURF failed nationally. In particular, the failure of TURF to find ways to intervene in 208's fight against the trusteeship both epitomized its failure nationally and figured in the inability of 208 members to find an activist solution to the trusteeship.

Most of 208's activists joined TURF. In particular, delegates from the rank-and-file committees and "500 at 50" went to the TURF founding meetings. Alex Maheras was one of the first to join. With members, then, from all of the various groups of activists in the local, TURF could have tried to unify them and to develop its own action program in 208. TURF could have pushed those barn organizations whose leaders were members to integrate their day-to-day defensive operations with TURF activities. It could have put out a special Los Angeles TURF paper or even a 208 TURF paper to pull together and organize activities. It could have tried to organize a nationwide TURF petition and a campaign to demand that the International release 208 from trusteeship. But it did not.

This was quite unlike the situation more than a decade earlier, when the rank-and-file activists of 208 built a strong movement that succeeded in ousting Filipoff and then Cohen, and built an organizational base and solidarity in the Local that still exists. They did this through uniting barn organizations and through local-wide activity. TURF, given its membership and the widespread discontent, had the potential to unite the struggle in the barns, the struggle in the Local, and the struggle against the IBT bureaucracy. It did not do so, and in reality did not even attempt to do so; thus, it failed. Further, its failure meant that the rank-and-file activists in 208 were unable to organize a national opposition or to rely on others for support; thus, they felt unable to develop an activist struggle against the trusteeship and, often, against the attacks on their jobs and working conditions by their employers. Only a passive, legalistic path was left them with which to try to free the Local.

The legal-electoral attempt to end the trusteeship was organized by Alex Maheras and Archie Murrietta. When Blackmarr retired, on the basis that this would make it easier to free the Local from trusteeship, Maheras was his obvious successor, long groomed by Blackmarr for the Secretary-Treasurer post. Maheras believed that the way to survive the trusteeship was to endure it, fighting on the barn level to maintain some organization and to protect the members, but taking no actions that would give the International an excuse for prolonging the trusteeship. While he took part reluctantly in rank-and-file committees, he did not see them as a solution, although he initially saw TURF as a possible way to deal with problems on the International level (although not as a way to rally the Local).

When 208 had been in receivership for the legal limit of 18 months, and no change was in sight, Maheras and Murrietta organized a lawsuit to force some action. The IBT then set an election for June 1972. The Local held its first meeting in almost two years so that nominations could be made.

Maheras organized the elections so that no one ran for two posts—under Blackmarr, many candidates had run for both BA and Executive Board posts. Maheras was responding to the strong current of opinion in 208 that BAs were hired employees who should not run the decision-making Executive Board; rather the officers composing the board were to be working drivers whose interests and experiences would be those of the membership. The separation of officers and business agents would also lessen tendencies for the BAs to form cliques and prepare, behind the Secretary-Treasurer's back, to run for his office, maneuvering which Maheras felt had resulted in less effective representation for the membership during the Blackmarr days.

Maheras' slate won 10 of the 14 positions in the election. Two BA positions were won by John T. Williams and Carlos Valdez, also running as oppositionists but too far to the political left to be included on the slate. Two members of Easley's slate won, but one of them resigned. Thus, the elections put rank-and-file oppositionists in 13 of the 14 positions, and put the remaining spot in the hands of a newcomer to union politics who had supported Easley out of a mixture of opportunism and ignorance. It would seem that the trusteeship had been decisively repudiated, and that rank-and-file militant activism would again be the practice in Local 208. However, this did not happen. Instead, what 208 got was the Maheras regime, much more legalistic and much less activist than the 208 of the 1960s.

The nature of that regime flowed from the end of the 24-hour strike clause, the defeat of the wildcat, and the fear of another trusteeship—reinforced by the effects of the fall of the trusteeship having been accomplished through a legal-electoral path, rather than through activism.

However, any reservations about the nature of the post-trusteeship regime and the nature of the Local since 1972 should not obscure something very important: Local 208 had been put into trusteeship but came out of it intact, with the membership electing oppositionists and kicking out the administrator and his allies. This is of great importance for activists in other Locals who fear trusteeship; it can be beaten.

The ingredients to beat a trusteeship should also be clear: Rank-and-file organization at the workplace that, defending the members to some degree even in the face of a union administration in league with the employer, helps maintain worker morale, communication among barn organizations, and solidarity to isolate supporters of the trusteeship and to support those who are casualties of the struggle (such as the finding of jobs for many of the 500 wildcat victims).

The barn organization, communication, and solidarity of the drivers of Local 208 came out of the earlier struggles against union bureaucracy and the employers. These struggles produced practitioners of activist, democratic unionism who, by their large numbers, were able to survive the demoralization resulting from the wildcat's defeat and the attacks upon the drivers during the trusteeship.

Thus, we find that active struggle for decent unionism is itself what lays the basis to survive trusteeships. Passivity and legalism leaves one always at the mercy of the courts and of those who control the union bureaucracy.

Chapter 9

Militants
Enchained

WHEN THE Maheras slate defeated Easley and the Trusteeship, and came into office as the elected representatives of the drivers of Local 208, many members expected a return to the best days of the Blackmarr regime. After all, Maheras had been the BA who had supported the wildcat, and ran on a slate with such leaders of the wildcat as Archie Murrietta, the new Local President. Thus, many drivers hoped for a regime in which the Local administration would encourage direct action against employers' attacks.

Such hopes were mistaken. As one steward put it much later, during a discussion at a coffeeshop of this lack of direct action "We thought we were voting for tigers, but we got pussycats." At the level of the leadership, 208 has abandoned the activist but apolitical unionism that once made it successful in favor of a "play it by the book" mode of operation.

Where's
the Action?

Had the new Maheras regime restored activist, democratic unionism, it would have set out to build and support organization for rank-and-file action as the Blackmarr regime had done when it first came to office, and as many drivers expected it would. It would have passed the word to militants to rebuild barn organizations shattered by the trusteeship, to draw up a list of demands for each company to undo the losses suffered during the trusteeship, to work out a plan of action to win these demands, and—perhaps—to force, on a company-by-company, whipsawing basis, the rehiring (with seniority) of the 500 workers who lost their jobs during the wildcat. A knotty problem would, however, have had to be solved. The elimination of the 24-hour strike clause in the 1970 contract made it much harder and more dangerous to use a favorite and successful tactic. However, many other effective tactics could be used. For example, in the mid-1950s some barns had won the stewardship system by a sabotage campaign. Slowdowns, while hard to organize in trucking (where neither management nor fellow workers can observe a driver's actions while making pickups and deliveries), could succeed on issues important enough to create sufficient voluntary solidarity. Numerous other tactics are available and known to drivers everywhere. If such militant actions were taken too openly, however, the International might use them as a pretext for another Trusteeship. A new Blackmarr-type regime would have met this danger by pretending that these events were simply part of a campaign to organize the Local to process grievances combined with a period of low driver morale (and thus poor workmanship). A regime of activists who had learned the lessons of the wildcat would also have launched an outreach campaign, unleashing and coordinating the energies of activist drivers to help other Teamsters make their own locals activist and democratic.

The Maheras regime took no such actions. Instead, it organized the business agents to process grievances, and trained them to help stewards deal with grievances through the grievance procedure. After Maheras had been in office for a year, the Master Freight Agreement came up for negotiation. He urged a "no" vote, but warned members that the MFA would be ratified and that they should not wildcat. At the barn level, the Maheras regime was equally sophisticated: it would urge use of the grievance machinery and warn against direct action, while bemoaning the need to play it safe.

Why was the Maheras regime so legalistic and conservative? Was it an about-face due to overwhelming forces of the opposition? Not in the case of Alex Maheras, whose policy represents what he has stood for during most of his career as an active unionist. As Murrietta notes: "He always felt the 24-hour clause was unnecessary except in the very last resort." According to my own observations, Maheras tends to be cautious and legalistic for as long as possible.

In this context, Maheras' actions in the part of the struggle against the trusteeship which he led is deeply symptomatic. He tried to restrain the ranks from action, to avoid giving a pretext for prolonging the trusteeship; when he chose a slate, he was careful to keep the radicals off of it, and he organized his own slate (rather than calling a large meeting to choose nominees by voting) which restricted membership involvement and thus retarded the growth of activism.

As a result, it should have surprised no one that Maheras has attempted to encourage legalism rather than activism. Similarly, Murrietta's views also show a conservative strain. He told me—and observers confirm it—that, although he became the leader of the 1970 wildcat, he did not do so out of strong belief in the wildcat itself, but because the workers at his barn wanted the wildcat and thought he should help to lead it. As a leader, he tended to trust the bureaucracy (which, he admits, hurt the wildcat). Even as the wildcat was ending, he believed the bureaucracy could be trusted on the question of the Special Panel and, during the trusteeship hearings and the fight against the trustee administration, he respected the advice of higher-up Teamsters. Thus, although a confirmed 24-hour wildcatter, who still will say that he believes in wildcats in some instances, he has tended to support bureaucratic procedures. And the Maheras regime has given him a chance to try out his trust. The result is that he has become a confirmed practitioner of legalism.

Legalism
Rampant

In practice, there has been a strong push by the highly respected (and indeed in many ways very impressive and upright) leadership of Local 208 to solve problems with employers by the grievance procedure and problems with the International bureaucracy by diplomacy. This policy was so shaky at the beginning of their administration that the IBT officialdom nearly drove them into activism. When they first came into office they found that the grievance procedure was not working well for them— a difficulty widely believed to have been the bureaucracy's retaliation for the defeat of the trusteeship. However, as it became clear that the new regime was going to be legalist rather than activist, this was reversed. The period of adverse grievance decisions now stands as a reminder of one way the bureaucracy can punish activism.

In striking contrast to how the drivers in 208 functioned before the trusteeship, under the Maheras regime there have been neither 24-hour wildcats nor other unsanctioned strikes. The literature produced during the 1974 election campaign for Local offices gives a further idea of Maheras' approach. A brochure in behalf of the Maheras slate for business agents includes the following introduction:

ACTION Speaks Louder . . . and the action of the above incumbent business agents not only speaks loud—and clear, but their record has been one of experienced representation on behalf of our membership. . . .

The issue in this election is "representation"—and not the comedy act which some of our opposition have attempted to project. However, their comedy is not the solution for protecting our contract and when a brother member is fired—"This is not a laughing matter." It was "representation" which resulted in the successful processing of over 1,800 grievances during the past 30 months; grievances involving seniority disputes, improper layoffs, subcontracting, change of operations, medical leave, protection of casuals, working conditions, house accounts, interpretations, warning notices, suspensions, and discharges. These grievances resulted in over $95,000 being received in back pay, with forty-two members returned to work following their termination.

The focus is on grievance-processing and representation. No mention is made of leadership in direct action, or of help from BAs to barns needing to set up tight operations to deal with their employers.

Similarly, in a brochure in behalf of the Administration slate for Executive Board positions, Maheras focuses on both the post-trusteeship rebuilding of the Local's finances, and the following specifics:

YOUR EXECUTIVE BOARD:
—Has established an Open Door Policy for the Membership.
—Has provided FREE information regarding the Local Union, including copies of the International Constitution, Local 208's By-Laws, Labor Agreements, and other materials requested by members.
—Has established a Shop Stewards Program with Professional Lectures on the Labor Movement.

—Has provided that your Shop Stewards receive copies of decisions and interpretations of the Labor Agreement.
—Took the initiative to seek legal action for a Health and Welfare for Casuals, as provided under the Agreement.
—Has established a continuous Watch Program in recognition of the Membership.

The latter point refers to a program under which members of long standing receive wrist watches. Further, this brochure points with pride to positions within the bureaucracy to which Maheras has been appointed:

In 1973, he became a member of the Local P.U.D. Negotiating Committee in Washington, D.C., Co-Chairman of the Joint Western Area Grievance Committee, and appointed as a Trustee of Health and Welfare.

The tone is consistent, the ideas are coherent, and the direction is fixed. Maheras is leading the Local into a unionism different from that of its past. Reliance upon diplomacy with the rest of the bureaucracy, court action to pressure the bureaucracy when necessary, and the grievance procedure is the new mode. Action is out. In return, the bureaucracy appoints Maheras to important committees and posts, so that he has a degree of influence over matters important to the membership, and gives the Local a fair deal in the grievance committees. Given the enormous personal integrity of Maheras, such a path seems effective—at first glance, anyway. However, in a period when the International is giving employers a free hand to rewrite important rules through contract "interpretations" and to shuffle their operations every which way without regard for their workers' interests, and in a period when, every time it is negotiated, the contract becomes worse for the workers—in such a time, legalism is, at best, a holding action against a powerful tide. It does not help to organize resistance to these attacks; it weakens such resistance. The legalism of the Maheras regime has led it to oppose many proposals and actions that seek to develop a strategy to oppose employers' attacks and to defend the drivers against IBT collaboration with employers.

For example, in 1975, 208 BA John T. Williams ran for the Presidency of Joint Council 42, largely to draw together active unionists throughout Southern California and to develop and propagate a rank-and-file program for improving the Joint Council. The nature of the campaign (which I shall discuss further below) should be stated: Williams had no chance of being elected, and in fact his candidacy was ruled out of order because, not being an officer of his Local, he was not an official delegate to the Joint Council. However, the campaign had potential as a propaganda and organizing device, especially to reach out and organize the militant Teamsters in other Locals as a step toward breaking the isolation of 208. The reaction of Maheras and his forces to this campaign was to try to ignore it. They did not want to antagonize the head of the Joint Council by supporting Williams' candidacy, even though they despised the incumbent President and most of what he represented. However, an open repudiation of the Williams candidacy would have looked bad to the activists in 208, who supported many of Williams' ideas (as did Maheras, too—in the abstract). Maheras therefore tried to remain uninvolved in the issue, a position made easier for him because Williams, who did not want to provoke a fight within the Local, did not push him. Further, Maheras' basically apolitical approach to union affairs made his stance easier, since he viewed a campaign with no hope of winning as a nonevent and could discount its possible long-run advantages.

In addition, some members, active in various leftish activities, proposed in 1974 that the Local set up a newspaper. Maheras and Murrietta called this a good idea, but infeasible. They termed it too expensive and time-consuming, and raised the issue of who would decide what was to be printed, claiming that the proposers were maneuvering to get control of such a newspaper to push their own ideas. I believe their reasons, while sincere, did not get to the core of Maheras' and Murrietta's uneasiness with the proposal. Committed to a legalistic strategy, which requires relatively little strategic discussion but simply a case-by-case defense of members, they could see as relevant only discussion about how to make information on precedents more available to stewards, and perhaps a discussion of how to use the courts to try to clean up the International. Further, genuine strategic discussion might endanger their plans and ideas. In particular, it might show that a legal strategy cannot deal with the problems drivers face; it might lead to the development of concrete and feasible activist approaches for change; and it might mobilize the drivers to act on such approaches. This would both discredit the legalists in the eyes of the membership and anger the IBT bureaucracy. Since the Maheras regime feared a new trusteeship, it thus feared to risk strategic discussion—even though any strategic discussion would probably have led to organizing outreach campaigns to discontented members of other Locals and thus made possible an attempt to displace the bureaucracy throughout the Joint Council.

The potential of the Stewards' Council has been watered down by the way the Maheras regime has led it. In the stewards' meetings, the real problems facing the Local and the drivers could be discussed, much as in a newspaper,* but without the problems involved in putting out a paper or the composition of an editorial board. However, under Maheras these monthly meetings have focused very narrowly on the issues raised by legal-bureaucratic techniques. Many of the meetings have been straightforward educational programs on the meaning of the national contract and the winning of specific sorts of grievances. Others have involved lectures by police speakers on highway safety, laws involving truck operation, and means of gaining police support when demanding that an employer fix safety problems. They also ran a series of lectures by professors on topics such as labor law, the history of the labor movement, and economics. Notably absent have been discussions among the stewards on responses to the steady deterioration of contracts, the reinterpretation of contract language in committees, or the IBT bureaucracy. Indeed, when it was proposed at a stewards' council meeting I attended that the stewards themselves, rather than the Local President, set the agenda, Murrieta successfully opposed this.

---

* There are some important differences. These discussions would be restricted to stewards, who are active unionists but thoroughly permeated by the legalism of the grievance procedure. Thus, much of the activism of the rank-and-file might be absent, though this tendency is counteracted by the fact that many of the most activist rank-and-file gravitate towards stewardship. Another difference between stewards' meetings and a newspaper is that the discussion at a meeting is more of a give and take than that in a newspaper. New ideas can develop in such a meeting, and those who have ideas already are more likely to be able to convince others in a face-to-face setting. On the other hand, a newspaper reaches more members, and is more useful as a way to reach out to involve previously inactive members on the basis of a new program they think might work.

Hard Times

In the recession of late 1974, hard times hit the Los Angeles trucking industry. Hundreds of drivers were laid off, and many companies closed. With employers pressuring the officialdom to protect the companies' profitability, grievances began to be lost on a wholesale basis. These problems still continue.

The response of the Maheras regime was to downplay the problems, to oppose action, to blame the members for bringing "frivolous" grievances that were sure to be lost, and to play up to the IBT bureaucracy.

Here are some of the problems which have arisen since 1974, some ways rank-and-filers have suggested they be dealt with, and some responses of the Maheras regime:

Unemployment increased due to layoffs. The February 1975 meeting of 208 unanimously called for 32 hours work for 40 hours pay, in order to spread available work, and for immediate organization of an overtime ban, so that laid-off drivers would be called in to do the work. However, the union officials did nothing to implement this motion, and reported at the next meeting that an overtime ban would violate the contract. Under prodding, Maheras said that if there were absolutely 100 percent support for an overtime ban at a given workplace, he would back it.

Employers have increasingly used "changes of operations" to attack workers in freight. Mergers or the creation of new terminals in outlying areas are used to increase productivity and to lay workers off; new terminals are also used to move as many operations as possible into the jurisdiction of malleable Locals. Under recent conditions, such attacks have taken particularly nasty forms. Mergers often lead to layoffs. In times of high unemployment, the rules governing who gets laid off become crucial. The companies prefer to terminate all the workers at a bought-out company, thus avoiding the longer vacations that high-seniority workers have earned, and allowing them to hire new workers who will be grateful for any job. The national contract calls for dovetailing of seniority lists, in which seniority is retained for all time worked at either of the merged companies; however, as the IBT bureaucracy has moved more and more into alliance with the employers, special committees set up in the Master Freight Agreement to oversee changes of operations have reduced the rights of the bought-out company's employees. Maheras has verbally attacked this practice, but has taken no action. At one stewards' council, changes of operations were discussed, but no plans for action were raised by the officers. In particular, no discussion occurred on how to force union members of the special committees to stop betraying the membership.

The economic crisis has meant that trucking companies, to keep their profits up, cut corners on the contract, maneuver to force drivers to work harder, and use the drivers' fear of losing their jobs during hard times to deter them from fighting back. Furthermore, increased collaboration between union bureaucrats and employers in defense of employers' profits has caused the grievance committees to make more pro-company decisions. One might have anticipated that in this kind of situation, 208's officials would use the grievance procedure very actively to find legal ways for drivers to protect themselves, and would search for ways to pressure the committees to cease favoring the companies. However, this did not occur. Instead, some BAs tried to discourage members from filing grievances.

When Teamster rank and filers organized nationally in Teamsters for a Democratic Union (TDU), the Maheras regime failed to support them. Although most of 208's officers have not been outwardly hostile toward TDU, they have stated their belief that TDU cannot change the IBT and that maneuvering within the bureaucracy is a more effective strategy (see chapter 10).

Dynamics of Reversal

The experiences of Local 208 support one long-standing analysis of workers' struggles: either they keep making gains and extend their support, or they are rolled back. In a conflict as intense and hard-fought as that between employers and workers, there is no such thing as a standoff.

In the case of 208, the rank-and-file movement started, won some victories, and went on to take over the Local. It used the mechanism of the 24-hour wildcat to deepen the struggle and to turn it into an attack upon harmful employer practices. This led to the growth of powerful barn organizations and retarded the bureaucratization of the Local's leadership. However, within a few years, the reliance of Blackmarr upon the umbrella provided by Hoffa blunted the forward thrust; even those sporadic attempts by a few of 208's leaders to reach out to help the ranks in other Locals became fewer. Local 208 remained isolated, the only militant and democratic local in Joint Council 42.

Hoffa's jailing sped up the reversal. Fitzsimmons removed the umbrella. As Fitzsimmons and the employers tightened relations and Fitzsimmons sold out more and more of the Teamsters' past gains, employers in Los Angeles increased their pressure on 208. The wildcat was the climax. And the employers took this opportunity to break the Local. A heroic effort by the drivers saved them from destruction, but their morale was battered. Then came the trusteeship.

Under this attack, the legalistic mode of operation came to the fore. Maheras used it to lead the fight against the trusteeship, and then to deal with employers' attacks. His hope, and that of his supporters, was that legalism would let them defend themselves without further confrontations, and that conformity to the rules would let them lobby within the International bureaucracy to win a change of policy from collaboration (i.e., giving the employers what they want) to militant business unionism. This has failed.

One reason it has failed is that the International bureaucracy is a stratum with interests and world views generally opposed to those of the rank-and-file.

Legalism is at best a long-term strategy, even in prosperous periods. It was not designed to deal with hard times. Amidst an unending and worsening series of flipflops between recessions and massive inflation, legalism provides no means of defense. The IBT bureaucracy supports the companies and goes along with employers' arguments that, in hard times, the workers must tighten their belts (and forget about "frills" like safety and seniority) so that the companies can stay afloat. Thus, contracts get worse, and are rewritten by special committees when the companies wish. Meanwhile, grievances are lost as grievance committees allow the companies great leeway to improve productivity. The legal strategy can deal with this only with hopes that, in 20 years or so, lobbying may put a ''good'' leader into office; meantime, drivers are urged to suffer in silence.

Even if economic crisis had not hit, however, the legalist strategy would have led to the reversal of all that made 208 great, as well as to worsened working conditions and other hardships for the drivers. After all, the driving force and mainstay of 208 was the large number of activist unionists formed through the struggles of the 1950s and 1960s. These activists became leaders in the barns where they worked, and it was through the joint actions of the drivers in any barn that solidarity and aggressiveness developed and victories were won. *The legalistic strategy meant the decline of this activist core and of solidarity among the drivers in each barn; thus, 208's success would be turned to ashes by legalism, even in the absence of hard times.*

During the 1960s, activism led to high morale and interest among the members, as Mannie Labastida, a BA elected on the Maheras slate in 1972, notes:

Then [during the Blackmarr era] managers weren't so educated, so we could holler, and thump the desk, and threaten, and use 24-hour work stoppages as a club. Now, the managers know the contract better. The CTA has taught them. And the 24-hour stoppage has been taken away.

The basis of the activism of the Blackmarr era was that members could be active in their own defense, and the rank-and-file thus could develop their own leaders, with whom they could share ideas and discuss strategies and tactics. These discussions were significant, since they related to joint action by the drivers. Reliance upon the grievance procedure, however, has a very different dynamic. It develops a stratum of barracks-room lawyers, skilled in tortuous arguments about contract language and in organizing evidence for presentation to a hearing panel, but in no way trained in workplace struggles. Further, these contractual legalists come to view their successes as due to their own skills as grievers, and to view the membership as uneducated, as unable to understand the limits of what can and cannot be won for them, and thus as ungrateful. The rank and file reacts in kind, and begins to view stewards as people who *do things for* the membership, and the Local as a service organization rather than as the fighting unity of the drivers against the employers. Business Agents change from organizers and supporters of barn struggles to grievance handlers—and since they spend their full time on contractual legalism and do not drive, they have a tendency to see themselves as a race apart.

During the Summer of 1974, for example, Local 208 was asked by the employees of Western Truck to help them to organize themselves into the union. I observed negotiations, a vote by the workers on whether to accept an offer from the company (they voted "yes"), and then a strike when the company went back on its offer. On several occasions I was at the picket line at the same time that several BAs were there; and in each such instance the BAs stood aside and talked among themselves rather than to the Teamsters of Western Truck. In contrast, Local 208's Vice President, George Brightwell, and other working drivers mingled with and talked with the Western Truck workers as equals.

The end result of the legal-contractual strategy is to drain the blood of the democratic activism that made 208 strong, to make active unionism a thankless task, and ultimately to reduce the involvement and activism of the Local's members to a faded memory. Indeed, many of 208's active unionists have complained to me of the lack of interest in the Local among the membership, contrasting this to the Blackmarr days. This was not the "good old days" nostalgia endemic among unionists in the United States; it was much more specific and much more recent.

However, while legalism may pose a threat to union activism, it does not necessarily kill it off. Drivers are human beings, and thus can react to such threats. Local 208's drivers are more experienced in social conflict than are most workers, and are not likely to sit back and watch as their Local is weakened and their conditions deteriorate.

Oppositionist
Stirrings

There were several attempts to build an oppositionist current within Local 208 or the Southern California Joint Council 42 of Teamsters. Some of these were formally organized around programs, meetings, and so forth. Others were more amorphous. None were very successful.

THE JOINT COUNCIL 42 CAMPAIGN

Of all the oppositionist efforts, the one I observed most closely was John T. Williams' campaign for the Presidency of the Joint Council. This was because Williams, a major organizer of the rank-and-file movement two decades earlier, asked me to observe the campaign, and indeed to assist in it. Instead of simply recording how the organization of the campaign held it back, I was able to experience the frustrations of seeing good ideas and initiatives ignored.

The campaign began when Williams spoke with a few long-time militants in 208 and other Locals about the idea of his running a propaganda candidacy. This was followed by a series of planning meetings, a large breakfast gathering of his supporters, and a picket line outside the Joint Council meeting at which the election was held. Literature was produced, and to some extent distributed. A legal appeal was organized in anticipation that the Joint Council would rule that Williams was ineligible to run for the Council Presidency because, as a business agent rather than an Executive Board member, he was not a member of the Council.

What is most interesting about this campaign is that it amounted to very little. Many of 208's and other Locals' most prominent oppositionists took part, and there was widespread hatred of the policies and leaders of the Joint Council among Southern California Teamsters. Nevertheless, the ideas of the campaign struck no sparks, its literature was sparsely distributed, and it spawned no lasting organization. The campaign was marked by several highly related weaknesses: Undemocratic organization; conservatism, with ideas for strengthening it and for spreading the program widely among Teamsters never carried out, and with a challenge to the officers never organized by the membership; disorganization and organizational mistakes, and confusion rather than a focus on a strategy. In addition Williams kept a tight leash on the campaign.

There were about a dozen Teamsters at the initial meeting of the campaign. Most had been active in the Teamster support group for the United Farmworkers, all were competent union activists, some had had experience as political organizers as well; thus, the group had the talent to put together a strong campaign.

The meeting was called by Williams and his campaign manager, Carlos Valdez (who had been elected BA of 208 on a slate, with Williams, as leftist opponents of the Maheras slate). It began with people introducing themselves and giving ideas about the prospective campaign. Unfortunately, instead of a free discussion about basic campaign strategy and tactics, Williams organized the meeting so that, once others had said their piece, he presented his own program as the tentative one for the campaign. The discussion which followed was disorganized; Williams and Valdez failed to focus it. As a result, discussion wandered, and one or two persons' long-windedness ensured that no decision would be reached. For example, a couple of participants proposed a petition campaign. However, their proposal was ignored in spite of their best efforts to get a decision on the issue. Other proposals died in similar fashion. A number of those present therefore neither came to later meetings nor helped to organize the campaign, even though they continued to support it in principle.

Subsequent planning meetings were similarly disorganized. This was pointed out to Williams repeatedly, but he blocked all attempts at structure. Proposals aimed at organizing an effective propaganda campaign would be raised (and on some occasions would seem to be accepted by the meeting) but the organizational machinery to make them real was never set up. Thus, it was ''agreed'' that motions to support the Williams candidacy would be raised, and the campaign program would be distributed, at Local meetings. Neither happened. Williams would say that he and Valdez would organize them, but then would do nothing, as the days slid by.

A basic strategic rift existed within the committee from the beginning: activists saw the campaign as a way to get ideas out to rank-and-file Teamsters preparatory to organizing further activities to change the union; legalists saw it primarily in terms of setting the stage for a challenge to the rule that only Joint Council members could be elected Council officers. The activists greatly outnumbered the legalists, but one legalist had an amazing ability to take the floor amidst a discussion of how to reach other Teamsters and talk for 10 minutes about the legal strategy. Given the absence of effective chairing—indeed, the absence of any real commitment that the meetings make decisions and plan a campaign—there was no way to set and enforce agendas, and no way to decide which aspect of the campaign should be given priority.

Along with this disorganization went a lack of committee structure. To organize any campaign requires committees to produce and distribute literature, to set up meetings at a grass-roots level, and to plan activities such as breakfast meetings and the picket line. Planning meeting members knew this and frequently proposed such committees. However, Williams and Valdez let such proposals die. The result was that the campaign remained disorganized; power over what did and did not happen remained firmly in Williams' hands.

The confusion carried over to the breakfast meeting. Much had been planned for this meeting. The speeches, particularly one in which Williams outlined his program, did take place as scheduled, and were quite effective. But money was to be collected for the campaign, and here the inadequate planning led to a mistake. The man who made the pitch for funds did so by holding up a dollar bill, talking about how inflation was eating away at it, and warning that a lot of money must be given to make the union more effective. Then he announced he was giving $20. But all the time he had been talking, the collection was going on; people had been donating one dollar each. People approached after he said he was giving $20, however, gave several dollars each. Prior discussion would have prevented this error. At a planning meeting a few days earlier, it had been decided that the breakfast meeting would be used to organize the picket line at the Joint Council meeting. As it turned out, there were merely a couple of brief announcements made that it would take place, and so a chance was missed to set up a barn-by-barn organization to mobilize the rank and file for the action. No one at the planning meeting had proposed a democratic discussion and vote on the issue. Finally, one purpose of the meeting was to distribute the basic program document presenting Williams' ideas, but this would have been forgotten entirely if I had not reminded one committee member that the document had not been distributed. By that time, many people had gone home.

As it worked out, the program leaflets went primarily to the officers of the Joint Council rather than to rank-and-file workers. Williams made sure that a group spent several hours mailing a copy of his program to each Executive Board member of every Local in the Joint Council.

Nor did the campaign lead to further rank-and-file organization. The plan had been for Williams to call the planning committee back into session to decide what to do next—but he never did so. A number of planning committee members were quite disappointed, but the organization had been so Williams-centered that no one felt it appropriate for anyone but Williams to try to organize the group.

A campaign to lay the groundwork for rank-and-file organization through a rank-and-file-oriented educational campaign turned into something quite different. Much of the campaign went into attempts to convince union officers rather than rank-and-filers. The other chief result was to prepare the ground for a legal challenge that never came off. The hope and time that active rank-and-filers put into the campaign led to no lasting organization.

This transformation in the campaign indicates the role that business agents and other paid staff can play in organizing a rank-and-file movement. On the one hand, BAs are too busy processing grievances to be able to lead such a campaign; a major reason why Williams did not call a followup meeting was that he found himself swamped by unprocessed grievances after the campaign. On the other hand, a BA has a problem of job security that tends to be conservatizing. Had Williams mobilized rank-and-file activity in behalf of his campaign, and organized motions at Local union meetings in support of his candidacy and its program, he would have brought the wrath of officers in every other Local down on 208. He would also have put Maheras in the tight spot of having to choose between attacking or supporting Williams' candidacy—in a context where Maheras might interpret the campaign as a dry run for fielding a slate against himself in the upcoming Local elections. Thus, although an oppositionist business agent may be able to mobilize support for a rank-and-file movement, problems develop if he leads it.

Further, the lack of democracy and consequent disorganization of the campaign flowed directly out of the bind Williams found himself in. Had the campaign been organized democratically, the rank and filers might have turned it into a mobilization to transform the bureaucracy of the Joint Council—a mobilization that would create problems for Williams. That is, Williams found himself riding a potential tiger, so it is no surprise that his actions disorganized his own campaign and restricted its use by rank and filers as a vehicle to promote the very changes Williams desired.*

OPPOSITION AT LOCAL MEETINGS

Discontent with the direction that 208 was taking came out at union meetings and at the stewards' council. Often it would be amorphous, taking the form of hostile remarks about what the officers or the companies were doing. On a number of occasions, however—usually when one or another current of the "208 left" decided to raise and fight for an issue—it took more specific form.

At the meeting of March 27, 1974, oppositionists based around the remnant of TURF proposed that 208 set up a Local newspaper. The President of the Local opposed this, on the basis of cost, and asked backers of the idea to attend the following Executive Board meeting to discuss it further; but it was voted down there.

These same oppositionists fought my being allowed to study the Local. At the meeting in January 1974, they presented their case against letting outsiders into their affairs; they did so quite well, but were voted down, 105 to 42. At the same meeting, one oppositionist attacked the officers for the cost of the popular stewards' jackets. Major oppositionist spokesmen then recurrently raised points of order over minor issues, leading to pro-

---

* From a cynical point of view, this whole campaign might be seen as a maneuver by Williams to corral the oppositionists in his own camp and to show Maheras that he had too much support to be left off the Maheras slate in the Local election, and also that he was able to control the troublemakers while using them. This seems to me both to miss the main point—that these pressures work to limit what sincere reformers can do while they are BAs—and to be mistaken. Williams was aware that Maheras had no intention of dropping *any* incumbents from his slate, since he did not want to split the leadership at a time when this might lead to real opposition getting started.

longed procedural hassles. In short, they managed to convince many members that they hassle for the love of hassling. Thus, one steward assured me, I should not let their attack on me get me down: they were always "disrupting meetings with their b.s."

Another incident, at the June 1974 stewards' meeting, involved the TURF clique and another oppositionist. The latter requested that the question of harassment of stewards be the subject of the next stewards' meeting. A TURF diehard then jumped up and said that the stewards themselves should be able to decide their own agenda. Murrietta responded that if a subject does not interest people in terms of their own jobs, they will not attend the meetings—but that he appreciated suggestions and, it being his job to set meeting agendas, appreciated this suggestion . . .

This incident points up, once again, the need for tactical precision in raising opposition at union meetings—a point the rank and filers of the late 1950s had learned well. By attacking Murrietta's power to set agendas before he had replied to the substance of the original proposal, the TURF member made sure the proposal would be buried, and also let Murrietta off the hook. Four leading stewards in different major barns had recently been fired. Thus, discussion of how to defeat this was clearly an appropriate topic for stewards' meetings, and would also have set the stage for discussion of activist versus legalist approaches to grievances and driver defense. It was clearly a discussion crucial both to the average steward and to those who wanted to make 208 more activist. Had Murietta rejected the proposal, the question of who set agendas could have been raised effectively. As it was, one oppositionist saw his proposal ignored because of another oppositionist's blunder—hardly a way to build a united force to change the Local. (Control over the agenda at stewards' meetings was democratized several years later, at TDU initiative.)

As with Williams' Joint Council campaign, a basic lesson of these incidents is that union officials' ability to keep the lid on activism thrives when meetings are confused. Indeed, a major problem with union meetings is that they tend to wander, to be filled with procedural wrangling, and not to get down to business—which means that officials get to make the decisions and members regard the meetings as a waste of time. A major task of any opposition is to cut through this fog by putting forward clear proposals and organizing to ensure that their proposals are taken seriously and discussed coherently. Support must be lined up before the meeting, and tactics for presenting proposals worked out. Further, *serious* oppositionists—those who really want to transform their union into a fighting union—must discipline themselves. If they spend all their efforts on correcting minor points of order (such as whether the Local President should discuss a minor item under New Business or under Good and Welfare) they will not only get a reputation as jerks but will add to the confusion and rambling that protects the power of the officials.

MEANWHILE, BACK AT THE BARNS

The problems of the 1950s sparked barns to organize for their own defense, and to make their weight felt in the Local. It should be no surprise that, as 208 turned to legalism instead of activism and as conditions deteriorated for the drivers, there would be a resurgence of barn organization, particularly in those barns that had not had to organize once the Blackmarr regime had come to power. Precisely this was beginning to happen late in 1974. As one example, Hall drivers had again organized to the extent of winning the right to stewards of their own.

Another example occurred at one terminal. My first awareness that things were beginning to happen there came in the course of a conversation with one of its stewards at the breakfast meeting in support of the Williams candidacy. That steward told me that this particular terminal was "a loose barn where the Terminal Manager and Assistant Terminal Manager used to go drinking with the guys. But now there is a new Terminal Manager who is setting all sorts of rules, and a lot of the guys are beginning to get more union-minded. A meeting has been called at the hall for the drivers."

There were a series of such meetings. At the first, a list of outstanding grievances was drawn up, and most, if not all of the approximately 80 drivers working at the company signed it as a petition to management. The first meeting also set up a committee to police the way casuals were hired—in particular, to pressure the company to hire casuals as regular drivers and to pressure nonunion casuals to go to the hiring hall to be dispatched, rather than taking "temporary" work directly from the company.

These actions did not change company policies. An activist describes what happened:

> Last meeting, we discussed how the company hires 15 casuals a day, and how to deal with this. I proposed a bunch of us to go in and tell the manager to hire hall guys. We agreed to go to the hall and have the hall drivers set up picket lines. *We* would go to work, punch in, check the vehicles, and then be unable to get them out across the picket lines.
>
> [The hiring hall dispatcher] agreed, but the hall people wouldn't go along with it. There is a lot of fear there.

Thus, we see that worsening working conditions and the inability of the Local to deal with them led the drivers to begin organizing themselves for direct action. They also began attending union meetings, where they sat together and supported each others' statements and proposals. This is reminiscent of the 1950s and impressive since this unity developed in the face of a severe problem—about half the drivers at this terminal were first hired as scabs during the 1970 wildcat. However, the existence of common problems created by the company, and the active fight by some who did not cross the picket lines in 1970 to end harassment of scabs by other strong unionists, created the possibilities of organizing both a united fight against the company and a barn presence at Local meetings.

Summary

Battered by the wildcat and the trusteeship, the drivers of 208 elected the Maheras slate in 1972 to bring back the activist business unionism of the Blackmarr era, but found that you "can't go home again." Rather than being Blackmarr's heir, the Maheras regime turned out to be his negation. From activism, the Local moved to legalism, then began to slip even farther. However, in the rebirth of barn organization, and in other oppositionist activity, the negation of Blackmarr is facing its own negation. Teamsters in 208 and elsewhere are organizing to develop a fighting union.

Chapter 10

Teamsters Rank-And-File Organize Nationwide

AMERICA'S STEELHAULERS won a wildcat contract strike in 1979.* During the negotiations for a new Master Freight Agreement, steelhauler members of Teamsters for a Democratic Union (TDU) formulated demands for their part of the contract—a "Special Supplement"—and organized support among other steelhaulers. When the Master Freight Agreement expired, Fitzsimmons called a strike against selected freight companies, but "made it clear the Union wasn't serious about steel since very few steel carriers were struck."[1] Steelhaulers then wildcatted in Canton and Youngstown, Ohio. They held regular meetings that not only heard reports but also discussed and decided on tactics and strategy for the strike. After solidifying the strike in Canton and Youngstown, they—aided by other TDU activists—distributed leaflets and organized roving pickets throughout the key steelhauling regions of Michigan, Ohio, and Pennsylvania. This shut steelhauling down.

The officers of several Locals backed the strike, and ultimately got verbal support (but not formal sanction) from the International. Further, the strikers understood their need to organize independently—rather than relying on "good" union officers—and they had superior sources of information and gen-

---

* Some steelhaulers, particularly owner-operators, have been much in the news since the late 1960's when the Fraternal Order of Steelhaulers (FASH) was formed to force the IBT to negotiate better terms for them. FASH has conducted several shutdowns since then, including one early in 1979—but it has won little, particularly since their frustrations with the Teamsters led them to pull out of the union to try to organize as a separate union. Some FASH activists were heavily involved in the 1979 TDU wildcat and in the new TDU Steel Haulers Organizing Committee.

eral organizational strength. The local officials were therefore unable to take control of the strike after they endorsed it. In the midst of the strike, TDU steelhaulers called a meeting of strikers from different cities to organize themselves to keep control after the strike: to make sure that their gains were not lost in grievance procedure "reinterpretations," to use their power on the job to win fresh gains, and to coordinate steelhaulers' efforts to change the IBT with those of other parts of TDU. They ended the wildcat successfully, having won most of their demands, organized for future battles, and, crucially, prevented any reprisals against individual strikers or Locals.

The contrast with the 1970 strike in Los Angeles is clear, and shows the potential importance of national rank-and-file organizations like TDU.

First, this chapter presents the history of TDU. Then, it compares TDU chapters in Detroit, Los Angeles, and New Jersey; discusses the conditions and strategies that let TDU establish itself; and considers the nature of the struggle for power in which TDU is engaged. The chapter concludes with brief discussions of the meaning of TDU for Local 208 and for Teamsters generally.*

Taken as a whole, this chapter presents evidence that the general analysis of rank-and-file movements presented in this book is valid beyond Local 208, and that the power of the Teamster officialdom may indeed be vulnerable to challenge by rank and filers.

Brief
History
of TDU

TDU began with a nationwide campaign to organize rank-and-file pressure for a better Master Freight Agreement in the 1976

* This is by no means a complete analysis of TDU. Thus, I do not discuss TDU's attempts to find successful ways to fight racism, nor do I discuss the general political questions raised by TDU, such as how it is forced to relate both to broad political issues and to governmental intervention in the trucking industry and the Teamsters. However, the alternatives to ignoring these matters are either to treat them superficially or to add 100 pages to the length of this book. Similarly, reasons of space as well as its lack of presence in Los Angeles lead me to mention another Teamster opposition group, PROD, only in passing. PROD and TDU merged in November 1979. The merged organization chose TDU for its name.

negotiations. A socialist group, the International Socialists (IS), was the catalyst in bringing together Teamster activists with a broad range of views and experiences. Some had been involved in several Teamster rank-and-file newspapers around the country, including *From the Horse's Mouth* in Pittsburgh and the *Fifth Wheel* in the San Francisco Bay area.

The initiators were in touch with numerous rank-and-file activists, including PROD, a legal self-help organization for truck drivers with loose ties to Ralph Nader. It was proposed that a coalition, including IS members, PROD, and other activists combine efforts to organize a petition campaign to pressure the Teamster bureaucracy into negotiating a good contract in the 1976 freight negotiations. Many of those involved hoped that this activity would start a permanent rank-and-file group, but they also realized that this would require building trust and solidarity through a period of effective cooperation.

Approximately forty Teamsters came to the meeting called to set up the proposed campaign, which they named Teamsters for a Decent Contract (TDC). They wrote up a petition with a long list of demands defining a contract they could vote for, since they reasoned that a large number of contract demands would appeal to the particular interests of a wide range of different workers covered by the Freight Agreement. Thus, workers with a burning interest in one or two specifics would take part in a campaign around the united needs of all the workers. Since a petition campaign is relatively safe, they thought many workers would be willing to sign, particularly if other people were doing so in large numbers. TDC's initiators hoped that some of these workers would themselves solicit signatures and call meetings in their cities. By and large, this logic worked. Thousands of Teamsters signed and many wrote in for petitions to pass around.

Further, the logic of the campaign, given this success, was toward further organization. No one could realistically believe that the entrenched officialdom of the IBT would fight the employers just because 20,000 or 30,000 workers wanted a decent contract. Thus, when TDC activists saw there was a good response among other freight workers, TDC leaders broadened the effort. They set up a newspaper, *Convoy*, started a campaign for Local union endorsements of TDC's demands, and held demonstrations around the country. These efforts were successful, and TDU grew apace. As a result, the Teamster bureaucracy began to redbait TDC. A few PROD officers saw the possible emergence of TDC into a national organization as competition for PROD and thus dropped out of TDC. In spite of these attacks, support for TDC grew. A number of locals endorsed the TDC contract demands and the demonstrations attracted a total of thousands of Teamsters. This pressure from the ranks led Fitzsimmons to increase his demands on the companies, ultimately settling for more than he had originally planned to ask for (*Business Week*, December 15, 1975 and April 19, 1976).

When the contract expired, and the bureaucracy saw that TDC was prepared to coordinate a national wildcat, Fitzsimmons seized the initiative by calling the first national freight strike in history. TDC leaders believe this was done to disorganize the rank and file and to establish Fitzsimmons' ability to end the strike. They note that many officials confused the members about which companies were being struck and which ones were being allowed to operate; that some Locals didn't even join in the strike; and that rumors were floated every few hours that an agreement had been reached.

However, in the Midwest (particularly in Detroit, where TDC was strongest), Teamster officials were not able to control and demoralize the strike. Indeed, a wildcat for a better contract developed in Detroit when the official strike ended. This wildcat was ended without victimization after TDC leaders, who knew that Los Angeles had been isolated and picked off in 1970, saw that there was no way to spread it significantly beyond Detroit.

To build a successful TDC chapter, the first requirement was the creation of a serious leadership core in a given city. This was difficult and required going beyond "old time" leaders. Often, these veterans of past struggles had developed approaches that would no longer work. For instance, in some areas they considered it a waste of time to leaflet every worker in the major barns, since "there are only a few who will be interested and we already know them." To succeed, TDC needed to involve new people who had not developed routinized ways of organizing the ranks, and who would see TDC as their own organization and thus feel a responsibility to carry out its decisions and ensure the success of its actions. Sharon Cotrell, a key organizer of Los Angeles TDC, which built one of the most successful steering committees, described how she went about this (interview of August 26, 1976):

At each meeting, we got a list of names of those attending. I spent hours and hours on the phone with them. And I spent hours following up people who came to my attention at the meeting. . . . At the end of December and in early January, it seemed to be falling apart. We didn't have the people on the steering committee we needed. Then the first issue of *CONVOY* came, and I went out with it and spent the whole weekend going to selected people's houses under the auspices of delivering *CONVOY*, and I talked them onto the steering committee. . . .

We had a problem, that people such as Doug Allan [who has since become a national TDU co-chairman] who have ideas often don't see themselves as leaders and thus don't volunteer for the steering committee. Doug had collected $70 at his barn. . . .

_____at Yellow was like that. He had ideas about what the steering committee should do, and would pull me aside to tell me, but he wouldn't volunteer. He had to be talked onto it.

_____ and _____were recruited to the steering committee that same weekend. . . . They came to the second meeting. After meetings, I'm swamped with people who come up with ideas or want help in their barns. _____and _____came up after the second meeting, and talked nonstop. They wanted this done, and that done, and the other thing done. I told them to write *Grapevine* articles. I asked them to steering committee meetings but they didn't come. Then, I went to their house with *CONVOY* . . . and we spent all night arguing and insulting each other. . . . I put to them the problems with the steering committee as being people who wouldn't *organize*, even though they had good intentions—so they had to join the steering committee. They had not wanted to "fight again." And they came to the next steering committee meeting and are invaluable.

Successful chapters needed TDC activity in the barns. This became both possible and necessary in the fight for Local endorsements of the national TDC contract demands, which made it seem reasonable to set up yard meetings for every shift at every possible barn. TDC activists spoke at these meetings about what they were doing and about upcoming attempts to have the contract demands endorsed at Local meetings. The workers at the barns were asked to attend their Local meeting to vote for endorsement, to become active in TDC, and to set up TDC organization within their barn.

TDC groups were most successfully built in areas where TDC meetings were thoroughly democratic. Successful groups had meetings where issues were discussed, where proposals were put forward in clear ways that got at the core of the issues without hiding real differences, and where votes were taken. Equally important, the members then *did* what was decided on— in contrast to the John T. Williams campaign for Joint Council 42 presidency, in which "decisions" would be only vaguely arrived at, and after the meeting nothing would be done. Demoralization rapidly developed in such cases. In TDC chapters such as that in Los Angeles, where democracy prevailed, solidarity and trust resulted. Since they themselves would carry out decisions and take risks, TDC activists discussed their tactics and strategies very seriously—and learned much in the process that has helped in building a lasting rank-and-file organization.

The end of the freight contract campaign could have meant the end of TDC. However, most activists wanted the organization to continue as a national opposition group. Working out the details took time, so several months elapsed between the Master Freight Agreement and the formation of Teamsters for a Democratic Union (TDU) in September, 1976. During this time, TDC continued to function, and relationships among the activists solidified. TDC was involved in contract fights in jurisdictions like carhauling that tend to follow the lead of the Master Freight Agreement, as well as in strikes at freight companies trying to get easier terms. Union officials usually provided little support to the strikers, and tried to localize the strikes and run them bureaucratically. TDC activists built support in other barns, worked to help spread the strikes, and pushed for democratic strike committees among the strikers. TDC also coordinated a rank-and-file challenge in the election of delegates to the 1976 IBT convention that summer in Las Vegas—which was a very limited activity since, in most Locals, only officers could be delegates. Pete Camarata, a leader in the Detroit freight wildcat, was elected as one of the TDC delegates from Fitzsimmons' own Local. At the convention itself, TDC held a demonstration, and Camarata tried to have officials' salaries cut down to less unreasonable levels. He and another TDC activist were beaten up after the convention.

Then, in September 1976, a meeting of 200 Teamster activists from all over the country, including many previously involved in TDC, created Teamsters for a Democratic Union. They worked out its organizational structure and its preliminary policies and plans at this first meeting, which involved very open and upbeat discussion and resolution of different conceptions of its constitution and approach.

In the years since then, TDU has been very active, and has grown considerably. By November 1979, TDU had approximately 5,000 members, and at least 35 active chapters. It then merged with PROD, which had a similar number of members (Will 1980:31). TDU Chapters have run bylaws campaigns in attempts to democratize their Locals; run slates in local union elections, some of which have won office; organized fights around shop-floor issues; organized a contract coalition around the 1979 Master Freight Agreement; and supported the Miners' strike in 1978. At least twenty chapters put out regular local newspapers (Paff 1980), and TDU publishes its own newspaper, *Convoy-Dispatch*.

TDU has reached beyond the trucking trades to organize Teamsters in canneries, breweries, factories, and warehousing. Nationally, TDU has established a network of lawyers who intervene when TDU members or other rank and filers are attacked and help TDU when it files suits against the companies or the union. TDU ran two members—Camarata and Vlahovic—for International offices at the 1981 IBT Convention. Although they got few votes, TDU won respect for daring to run. It also won respect by proposing resolutions that aimed at improving the union's ability to fight employers' demands. The defeat of these resolutions is a sign that the bureaucracy's interests differ from those of the rank and file. TDU has actively attempted to get Teamster pension funds into the hands of trustees elected by the rank-and-file.

TDU has also developed strength in jurisdictions such as carhauling and steelhauling, and among workers in such companies as the Kroger grocery chain and in Roadway, a giant trucking company. Thus, it intervened forcefully in Kroger contract negotiations in 1979: It kept Kroger workers better informed about the negotiations than their local officials; helped them organize a contract rejection (by 706 to 1988) vote; set up TDU groups among Kroger workers; and established a Kroger rank-and-file newsletter, *The Kroger Connection*.

TDU: Comparison of 3 Regions

TDU has been diverse. One way to understand its dynamics is to look at it in three different regions in which TDU has had very different degrees of success. These areas are Northern New Jersey, where TDU never really got started; Detroit, where the TDU movement is a *movement* and a *pole of attraction* that poses a real threat to continued bureaucratic functioning of the Teamsters union; and Los Angeles, where TDU has had moderate success, and can best be characterized as a *service organization*, able to offer aid to rank-and-file Teamsters in Southern California (including Local 208), and strong enough to organize and coordinate such outbursts of militancy as do occur.

NEW JERSEY[2]

Rank-and-file activity among New Jersey Teamsters has been relatively weak, since the Teamsters in New Jersey are dominated by the Provenzano family.* At least one Teamster dissident in the area has been murdered, and many others beaten. Most New Jersey Teamsters are scared. The results of efforts to build TDC and then TDU were thus very limited. At the peak, a small number of old-time activists from scattered Locals were involved, together with a few activists who work for United Parcel Service (UPS). Most of the UPS activists were part-time workers, which made their working conditions worse and their combativity higher, but also made it more difficult for them to involve full-time UPS workers.† Since the Northern New Jersey

---

* Tony Provenzano has been imprisoned for murdering a union rival and for labor racketeering; his brother Nunzio has been convicted on labor corruption charges.

† The UPS workers were able to do somewhat more than this. For awhile, they had a small chapter of UPSurge functioning, and put out a newspaper of their own as well. However, they have as yet been unable to develop any size or momentum. UPSurge was begun by I.S. and a few others at about the same time as TDC, but continues primarily as an occasional national UPS rank-and-file newspaper and a weak rank-and-file organization.

grouping was too small and too scattered to have enough strength in any one local or workplace to be able to *do* anything, it collapsed. The merger of TDU and PROD revived New Jersey TDU by bringing the New Jersey PROD chapter into TDU. This, however, was also weak, due to the repressive atmosphere among New Jersey Teamsters, and the chapter remains weak.

DETROIT[3]

TDU in Detroit resembles the movement that took power in Local 208. Detroit TDU, however, is active in many Locals and is part of a national movement. Thus it will be much harder to isolate or to localize. This is particularly true given that Detroit TDU's leadership sees the dangers of being boxed in and understands that the Teamster officialdom is an institutionalized bureaucracy rather than just individuals who have "gone wrong."

When I first interviewed Camarata (January 1979), Detroit TDU had several hundred members. Quite a few of these were "very active." They were involved in some TDU activity every week, were widely viewed as TDU activists, and were active in their barns or talked about TDU with acquaintances fairly aggressively. Scores more were "steadily involved," attending meetings regularly, and helping to distribute TDU literature twice a month. Looked at in another way, Detroit TDU had members in about one-third of the freight barns in the area, as well as in almost every carhaul barn in Detroit. Further, TDU had enough strength in Locals covering grocery, United Parcel, cement and construction, and various small shops and auto dealers to run candidates in these Locals' elections with a respectable amount of success.

By April 1981, Detroit TDU had extended its strength. In Camarata's own Local 299, it had gone beyond the freight and other trucking industries to develop support among small-warehouse workers. Similarly, TDU in Local 337 had moved beyond the large grocery companies to recruit workers in meatpacking and in small food-delivery companies. One result was that minority-group Teamsters became more represented and more active in Detroit TDU. It began to have a limited degree of electoral success. In the October 1980 elections in Local 337, TDU candidates won the Secretary-Treasurer spot and a trustee position, and came close to defeating IBT International Vice President

Bobby Holmes for the Local Presidency, in spite of numerous irregularities in election procedures. A few months later, Camarata won election as a delegate to the 1981 IBT Convention from Local 299 and two TDU members were elected as Local 337 delegates as well.*

It is the activity of Detroit TDU that is its real strength. Its chapter steering committee meets at least once a month. There are other meetings in between. For instance, members from each Local will meet to discuss their strategy, and in barns where TDU is fairly strong, there are frequent meetings to discuss barn issues. These barn meetings consider how the workers in the barn can be mobilized for Local elections or Local meetings, or for city-wide demonstrations, and also deal with the day-to-day struggles in the barn. These sometimes spark refusals to work overtime or slowdowns over company actions. On at least one occasion, a successful two week strike (with local sanction) prevented give-aways a company was demanding. Thus, Detroit TDU is establishing the same kind of organic linkage between the struggle in the barns and the struggle in the Locals that produced victory for the rank-and-file movement in Local 208.

In addition, Detroit TDU puts out a newspaper of its own, *The Rank and File Speaks*.

The Detroit TDU office is a center of activity. If the workers at a company have a problem, they call the TDU office, and an activist (or even a small committee) is sent to help them. For example, when the contract at Leaseway was to be renegotiated, its workers contacted TDU. With a TDU activist advising them, the workers were able to organize themselves and affect negotiations that in the past had been conducted by officials without much regard for what the workers might want. Similarly, TDU gets calls to help out with grievances. As a result of these efforts, TDU gains in reputation, experience, and membership.

* The two TDU officers of 337 were delegates *ex officio*. Locals 299 and 337 are among the relative handful that get to elect any delegates to the convention. Any Local with less than 5,876 members has some of its officers automatically delegates under the IBT constitutional provisions which Hoffa sponsored (see chapter 6). As of April 30, 1981, Camarata knew of approximately 30 TDU members who would be delegates: 9 from Michigan, 6 from Vancouver, 4 from Spokane, 6 or 7 from California (including Doug Allan of Local 208), and 4 others. Most of these were local union officers. Some TDU members are officers in locals with small memberships, and thus do not become delegates.

Much of Detroit TDU's strength comes from its success in involving wives of Teamster men in its activities. They are active in virtually every TDU project, and have taken full part in its steering committee. Further, they have carried out actions on their own, such as demonstrations at the Detroit Teamster Union office building during several bylaws campaigns and during the 1979 carhaulers' contract campaign.

LOS ANGELES[4]

Los Angeles TDU had a couple hundred members (as of March 1981), which would seem to make its strength comparable to that of the Detroit chapter. However, Los Angeles TDU has fewer very active members, plus a smaller circle of members committed enough to attend occasional meetings and help distribute newspapers. However, it would be inaccurate to see Los Angeles TDU as feeble, merely because it has not yet become a movement. As a service organization for rank-and-file unrest, and as an organizer when struggle does break out, it has considerable influence; and it stands ready to become a movement when and if a reasonably widespread activism should again develop in some Los Angeles industry under Teamster jurisdiction. This latent strength will become clearer as we look at some of what Los Angeles TDU is doing and at some events in which it has taken part.

First, the chapter puts out a newspaper, *The Grapevine*, which has a press run of 10,000 copies. The paper comes out erratically, a flaw that stems from the lack of a well-organized core group to put it out, and from a related lack of money. At any rate, Los Angeles TDU is not currently involved in the flood of activity that could provide constant copy for a newspaper. Nevertheless, *The Grapevine* is widely respected among rank-and-file Teamsters, which gives it a certain power to intervene.

Further, Los Angeles TDU has been involved in a number of struggles, largely over the renegotiation of contracts. One such struggle shows both the potential and the limits of the chapter. Consider what happened when one company hired a leasing company to handle its freight and fired several dozen workers. The leasing company paid dock workers approximately half what the former company had paid and used brokers to haul the freight rather than hiring drivers or owning trucks of its own.

The leasing company claimed their workers were under contract to another Teamster Local, and thus already union. Local officials confirmed the claim.

Under normal circumstances, this would have been the whole story. However, half a dozen of the fired workers were TDU members. These activists decided to strike—and they got the other fired workers to go along with them. The ensuing strike lasted many months: it forced the other Teamster Local to renounce its claim that the leasing company had a legitimate union contract that covered the jobs in question, and won support from Teamsters throughout Southern California. The strikers accomplished this by having a democratically elected strike committee, putting out a regular strike bulletin distributed throughout Southern California, and spreading the strike to company terminals in other cities. Their roving pickets followed trucks carrying company freight, and picketed them wherever they stopped off—so that, in some cases, all work stopped at the terminals involved. Resolutions were brought to several Locals, including 208, for financial aid, and passed.

However, this was not enough. Rank-and-file solidarity was not sufficient, given the weakness of TDU and the strength of the companies and the Teamster bureaucracy, to shut down the parent company altogether. Thus, a combination of grievance hearing decisions against the strikers and court decisions that levied fines against them and threatened more to come, forced them to give up the strike. And yet, the defeat was not total. The company had been hurt by the strike, and workers had seen that resistance to closings is possible. Thus, other companies were, to some extent, deterred from trying the same maneuver. In addition, the reputation of TDU as fighters and militants, competent and ready to wage a good fight, was considerably enhanced.

Since then, Los Angeles TDU has intervened with some success in a number of other contract fights. For example, during the 1979 strike over the Master Freight Agreement, it set up a 24-hour-a-day communications center to answer questions and to mobilize pickets. However, it has been unable to use these activities to build its strength. In particular, it has been unable to establish a large number of active members, of committees actively intervening within locals, or of its own barn organizations. These failings both cause and result from its inability to link barn struggles with the struggle within the union. Thus, when a fairly large freight company, Garrett, disciplined a dock worker, and the other dock workers responded with a sabotage campaign, TDU was not involved. Nor did it find itself able to become involved when Garrett retaliated by laying off 29 dock workers and changing work rules to force drivers to unload their own trucks. In this case, TDU *could* have linked up the barn struggle with the joint efforts of dock workers (in 357) and drivers (in 208) to resist and to force the union to resist. However, TDU was not asked to intervene, and members were not strongly enough placed to intervene without invitation. As a result, Garrett won; in addition, Teamster officials got off with some embarrassment but with no increase in the ability of the rank-and-file to organize their own struggles through TDU. Nevertheless, TDU is well placed to grow. It has developed an experienced core of leaders for future actions.

The Social Context of Rank-and-File Organization

Most attempts to set up enduring rank-and-file organizations in the Teamsters and in other unions, have failed. Why has TDU become as strong as it has? TDU was formed at a time when conditions were ripe for Teamster revolt. There was a substantial ''push'' in the economic hard times of the previous ten years, which translated into increased demands by employers for greater productivity, into instability of employment as companies folded or merged, and into an increased willingness of union officials to heed companies' pleas for lower pay scales or, in grievance hearings, for weaker protection of workers. These forces were felt even in relatively good Locals like 208; in weaker Locals they often were felt even more. Such pressures made many Teamsters willing to take action to change things—at least, if the risks did not seem too great.

Risks were reduced by the disorganization of those forces that tend to keep the rank and file intimidated. The economic crisis led to differences between small and large trucking companies; between trucking companies and the manufacturers, wholesalers, and retailers who rely on trucking and demand lower freight costs; and, perhaps as a consequence, between governmental bodies and top Teamster officials. This disorganization and factionalization showed up in the temporary split, after the 1976 Master Freight Agreement, of the bargaining agent for the employers into small versus large company agents; in the increasing discussion of trucking industry deregulation as a way to reduce freight rates and to weaken the Teamsters Union; and in attacks on corruption in the IBT. Such attacks on corruption sprang up anew after the disappearance of Hoffa and remain a standing threat to Fitzsimmons and other top union officials. These disagreements among the powerful reduced their ability to repress the rank and file, and thus created elbow room for the rank and file to organize. The dynamic is similar to that of the late 1950s, when government pressure on IBT officials helped 208's rank-and-file movement to survive and grow.

Thus, economic hard times provided a push toward rank-and-file organization, while disorganization at the top reduced the constraints on organizing. In addition, questions of milieu, consciousness, and strategy can affect the outcome of attempts to organize, and did so in the case of TDU. Looking briefly at two other recent attempts to organize rank-and-file movements will gain us a better understanding of these latter forces.

Consider the automobile industry, and the attempt initiated by auto activists, including some socialists, to build a Coalition for a Good Contract (CGC) in 1976. The pressures of hard times were heavier on auto workers than on Teamsters, since the auto companies have developed very effective "speedup" programs, and since the industry was very hard hit by the energy crisis. Questions of milieu and consciousness shaped what happened. The same general strategy that worked in freight to build TDC and then TDU led in auto to very feeble results in spite of the greater economic push. First, consider consciousness. The auto shops were a center of rank-and-file unrest from the late 1960s until 1973 (Serrin 1974; Geschwender 1977; Weinberg n.d.). However, this unrest remained localized and was greatly weakened by racial splits among the workers. The unrest was therefore repressed, and many workers fired. Thus, in 1976, when

CGC was organized, many auto workers were still demoralized and thought CGC would gain nothing but risk much.*

Paradoxically, this demoralization was increased by the heavy layoffs in the industry in 1974–75, showing that economic difficulties can either lead to a fight or to a demoralization that holds workers back. In addition, the milieu in auto, as contrasted with that in freight, also weakened CGC. In freight, workers are able to talk outside of the sight and hearing of company or union officials. In auto, this is only possible after work; and overtime reduces workers' time and energy for such discussions. In freight, fired workers can often get new jobs with a different company that keeps them in the same Local and, in the case of drivers, lets them maintain many old friendships through meetings at loading docks and restaurants. In auto, firings remove activists from their Locals and from worktime contact with those they are trying to organize. In freight, the large number of barns allows stewards much autonomy and the chance to develop into leaders independent of the officials. In auto, committeemen are full-timers, and all union organization is easily overseen by local officials. Such differences in milieu weakened the ability of CGC to reach out to other workers, and also meant that relatively fewer grievance handlers would help CGC than TDC. This, given the low morale of auto activists, meant that CGC had little effect and did not lead to the establishment of a lasting rank-and-file group.

Now, let us compare TDU with TURF. This will show that strategy is indeed an important shaper of movements. TURF, an attempt to organize a national Teamster opposition group in the early 1970s, was organized during poor economic conditions; and at a time when Teamster combativity was still high from the effects of the 1970 wildcat (which was viewed as a success in most areas other than Los Angeles, for the simple reason that

---

* The ability of the union and the companies to repress rank-and-file organization was not weakened by anything like the splits that beset the freight industry's leaders. Nevertheless, the rank-and-file response to CGC was too small for this to have been *directly* decisive in influencing the fate of CGC. We can see, though, that this relative unity of corporate officials, auto union leaders, and government officials in suppressing auto workers' activism at an earlier time may indeed have had an effect on CGC—but indirectly, by affecting workers' morale.

only in Los Angeles had there been heavy costs for the workers involved). The split at the top was less pronounced than in 1976, but it *was* there, in the Hoffa vs. Fitzsimmons feud. Thus, the major difference between TDU and TURF was strategic. TURF looked to elections, and to a lesser extent to court action, as a means of fighting the union bureaucracy and democratizing the union. It did not get heavily involved with barn struggles or contract campaigns. Thus, TURF started strong, but rapidly fell apart since it did not tap workplace struggles for energy, membership, and activities with which to keep itself as a thriving organization rather than a mere talk shop. TDU, on the other hand, had a strategy of uniting the fights at work with those to reshape the union—and has continued and grown.

Looking again at the differences among Detroit, Los Angeles, and New Jersey, we note that by and large, these three areas were subjected to similar economic pressures, so that the "push" factor caused by poor economic conditions cannot explain the differences in TDU in these areas. Also, the social organization of driving (the "milieu") is similar in each of the three areas. In Northern New Jersey, the TDC/TDU failure seems to be due to the heavily repressive nature of the union leadership. As Pete Camarata expressed it to me, "The repression is greater in New Jersey than in Detroit. We have it relatively tame in Detroit."

Looking at Los Angeles, Teamster bureaucracy in Southern California was too weak, and the history of rank-and-file struggles in 208 and in other locals too strong, to prevent TDC from organizing fairly strongly at the beginning. Indeed, TDC developed some strength even in Long Beach Local 692, then perhaps the most repressive Local in the region. However, TDU did not develop into a movement as it did in Detroit, probably due to the workers' consciousness. In Los Angeles, the memory of 1970 hung over the Teamster rank-and-file and the organizers of TDC like the smog; and it has continued to ever since. Simply put, many of the older activists are scared of undergoing another ambush, and feel in addition that they "have done their share—it's other people's turn now." This state of mind has retarded the growth of Los Angeles TDU, and has hindered its ability to obtain support for such actions as the leasing company strike discussed above and a widespread strike against Safeway in 1978.

With respect to repression, Detroit's Teamster bureaucracy was the spawning ground for both Hoffa and Fitzsimmons, but the fight between Hoffa and Fitzsimmons in 1973 and 1974 (best described in Moldea [1978]) weakened their ability to suppress the rank-and-file. Further, Detroit's freight workers had not gone through a brutal strike. Thus, when TDC began to develop strength, it sparked a mass movement leading to the brief 1976 wildcat (after Fitzsimmons terminated the official freight strike) and, in turn, to continued growth in TDC/TDU, and the election of oppositionists as delegates from Detroit Local 299 to the 1976 Teamster Convention.

The wildcat carhaulers' strikes later in 1976 gave a crucial boost in transforming Detroit TDU. Detroit's position as the center of the auto industry meant that these wildcats over the terms of the carhaulers' contract involved hundreds of Detroit Teamsters. TDC activists did what they could to help out, and recruited a large number of members. Many of these became very involved in TDU, and carhauling has been a center of ferment and a source of TDU activity ever since.

Thus, on the one hand, the success in Detroit depended on the spontaneous mass movements that developed first in freight and then in carhauling. TDC helped set the stage for this—but the volatility of the freight milieu, the weakening of repression caused by the split in the bureaucracy, and the extra push due to the craft pride of carhaulers and to the extreme difficulty of their work (which the 1976 contract was seen as worsening) were also essential causes.

Leadership also played a part. It is not easy to organize such a lasting, strong organization as Detroit TDU out of the relatively brief, spontaneous movements involved in the 1976 strikes. This is evidenced by the failure of the steelhaulers to develop an effective leadership, which caused the collapse of the organization they built in the 1979 strike. To do so requires considerable leadership abilities among a group's core organizers. They must be able to involve others in the core, and then to help the new leaders develop their own capacities as organizers and strategists. Also, they must develop democratic modes of functioning within the group—which as we have seen is not easy. Further, the organizers must find meaningful activities for the organization—so that members will see the group's relevance to needed change, and their sacrifices as worthwhile, and so that rank and filers outside the organization will approach it for help with their problems.

Detroit TDU's leaders found important ways to involve TDU in workplace and union reform struggles, which in turn led other people to bring more such struggles to its attention—and a spiral of deepening involvement developed that created a movement.*

Problems
TDU
Faces

TDU is engaged in a struggle for power. On the one side, there stand the employers, the union bureaucracy, and the State, each with a vested interest in a quiescent rank-and-file. On the other side, there is TDU—attempting to organize the rank-and-file; to fight over wages, conditions, and control of work; and trying to take over the Teamsters Union and reshape it into an organization run with democratic rank-and-file involvement. If it is to do so, TDU must build more support, reach out to prevent its being boxed in, avoid its own bureaucratization, deal with the dilemmas of taking office, prevent rebureaucratization after Locals or the International are taken over, and use the power that is won. In discussing these issues, we shall consider the experience of TDU so far, as well as what can be inferred from the analysis of Local 208. However, much of this discussion will of necessity be theoretical and speculative.

---

* Two of my informants argue that the development of *The Rank and File Speaks* newspaper was particularly important both in cohering a leadership core and in getting them involved in strategic discussion. I am not in a position to assess the accuracy of this claim, although it parallels the experience in Los Angeles and in several other cities where TDU newspapers have led to the development of leadership cores. In Detroit, however, the presence of a mass movement may have rendered the newspaper less important.

BUILDING SUPPORT

Although TDU has grown far larger than anyone predicted, it is still far too small to reshape the union or to force its will upon the employers. Even in jurisdictions like steelhauling and car-hauling, it requires situations like contract campaigns or burning issues to be effective.

Worker apathy is a term often heard. Many Teamsters are unwilling to spend the time and take the risks required to change things. If asked, they claim not to care about the issues, or say they are satisfied with the way things are. Such workers, it would seem, can realistically be characterized as having an apathetic attitude. However, such a characterization ignores other reasons for such responses, such as fear. And it misses something fundamental in the social psychology of conflict: almost everybody is torn by inner conflicts paralleling the social conflicts that have direct impact on their daily lives. Thus, even "company men" whom I talked to in Local 208 are often angry at the company and simply suppress their desire to strike back. Conversely, most militant activists often feel a desire to avoid strife or fear the consequences of activism. Thus, in the interview presented in chapter 3, John Franklin both described his work as having no problems and expressed gratitude that there was no battle going on at his barn—and he is a staunch unionist.

Apathy, then, is the result of the interplay of contradictory forces—and therefore subject to change if these forces change. Pressures toward cynicism, fear, and contentment meet those toward anger, militancy, and commitment.

But are there social dynamics at work in the Teamsters and in TDU that will lead workers to organize around and act on their combativity rather than being paralyzed by their doubts? I believe so. The dynamics that once mobilized the rank and file of 208 are taking place now throughout much of the Teamsters Union. TDU is linking barn struggles with efforts to reform the union. The unified movement that results is changing some workers from passive sideliners into activist militant leaders, and creating the same kind of layer of activists that energized and organized 208. And it is doing so nationally. Of course, there are no guarantees that this process will succeed. It could be derailed by strategic errors—for instance, if its leadership opted to pursue only electoral paths, to the exclusion of direct action. Likewise, although the rough economic conditions of the late 1970s fueled TDU, massive layoffs since then have disorganized and deterred TDU activities in some chapters. Furthermore, the mobilization process goes on at different rates and intensities in different areas, depending on the local strength of the union bureaucracy and on the extent to which the workers are exposed to the general conservatism of American society. In jurisdictions like freight, carhauling, and steelhauling, the workers have an occupational isolation from the mainstream, and a culture of their own, that let them organize more readily than in less isolated parts of the union.

"Apathy," therefore, is a problem to which the solution may already exist. The rank-and-file mobilization process that once cut through the apathy of 208 should work just as well for TDU today.

Dave Wolfinsohn, a socialist TDU activist, describes a second problem TDU faces in building support—an erosion of militant *activity*. This is *not* just the absence of apathy, since apathy is an attitude rather than a (lack of) activity. (Wolfinsohn 1980: 38, 44):

While TDU grew in terms of membership and strengthened its organization in the period 1976–1979, it also experienced a decline in the levels of action it was able to initiate—or participate in—against the employers. The employers' offensive intensified. But, in the face of the total capitulation of the Teamster officials at every level, the rank and file did not, in general, succeed in generating sufficient self-organization to launch a counterattack. Militancy had declined.

. . . building the kind of base we have in mind (not just passive voting support) is difficult in the absence of powerful struggles against the employers. It is in the context of the fight against the bosses that rank and filers come up most sharply against the inadequacies of the union and therefore see the need to break the bureaucracy and transform the organization. It is only in this context, moreover, that it seems, to most workers, worthwhile to make the necessary effort.

Wolfinsohn argues that this problem stems from the serious economic decline and from the weakening of the union's power in freight caused by the growth in nonunion trucking and the unwillingness and inability of the union officialdom to stand up to employer attacks. These create fear among the workers, along with a cynical disbelief in their own power.

The 208 experience shows that such downturns in militancy can be resisted. Small-scale direct actions in the barns can win successes even in difficult periods, if their time and nature are chosen carefully. And these successes build confidence for further action. Furthermore, TDU, as a national organization of activists, could pull these efforts together in ways that would greatly increase their effectiveness. Thus, if such actions led to reprisals, TDU could coordinate defense efforts for the victims—such as a general slowdown (or trucks that "break down") in other barns of the same company around the country. Successful actions, on the other hand, could be given wide publicity, whether publicly through *Convoy-Dispatch* or via word of mouth.

These small-scale direct actions may have to be very small indeed. In some barns in which TDU members work, it may be an unusual and brave act to file a grievance. This is particularly likely in "down" periods such as those Wolfinsohn describes because employers are more likely to retaliate against those who file grievances in such periods. In a barn of this sort, a group grievance by a sizable portion of the workers might be a *collective* act that makes further action possible. In one New Jersey warehouse, the TDU members' first step was to organize to replace an appointed do-nothing steward. Collective action can also start with a group hassling their supervisor over a deeply felt slur; with a sabotage campaign and safety work-to-rule (as with PIE in 208 in the 1950s); or with a spontaneous work stoppage (as with Eddie Dietrich at PMT.)

My analysis of the solution for downturns in militancy goes against the grain of some socialist analyses, which have argued that downturns and upturns in the "spontaneous struggle" are beyond the capacity of organized effort to cope with. At best, traditional socialists argue, a general program should be proposed and discussed in the hope that workers educated in such a broader perspective will spark off renewed struggle. This analysis seems to me to misconstrue the nature of a rank-and-file group of the size of TDU. An organization that includes several thousand activists in its membership and periphery—even in a union as large as the IBT—is large enough to have an impact upon the "spontaneous struggle." If it orients exclusively toward electoralism and legalism, then thousands of activists will reduce their activism. If it orients towards building small-scale struggles in the barns, then its efforts can reduce the downturn in militancy, and perhaps reverse it.

Thus, the solution to the downturn in militancy rests in part with TDU. Workers are not helpless pawns of larger forces, but have some room to maneuver—although their ability and willingness to take risks are weakened in periods like those Wolfinsohn describes. Groups like TDU can considerably increase their scope for maneuvers. However, the path taken by TDU is not at all determined. It is a matter for internal discussion and struggle within the rank-and-file organization itself. Here, the nature of TDU's membership is a factor. Although it contains many barn activists, it also contains Teamsters who see union elections as the key to success, and others who orient primarily toward court cases and a more honest use of the grievance procedure. That is, like the 208 movement, it contains a mixture of legalists, electoralists, and activists. A period of downturn shapes the discussion by making activism seem less effective. On the other hand, a concerted campaign of small-scale direct action by the activists in the barns could begin to generate the successes and recruit enough new activists to restore the necessary balance between electoralism and activism.

REACHING OUT

Local 208 ran into trouble in 1970 because it had not helped rank-and-file movements in other locals. TDU is only partially protected against this same fate. Although it is obviously much broader in scope than 208, TDU could still be boxed into the trucking sections of IBT. It has had some success in organizing TDU among the host of factory, brewery, food, and nontrucking warehouse workers in the union, but its base is still primarily among the higher-pay, whiter, and maler trucking part of the Teamsters.

Furthermore, TDU could find itself boxed in even if it organizes a massive rank-and-file movement throughout the union. Its enemies are many and powerful, including every company that depends on Teamster workers and every company whose management fears that TDU might set a dangerous example for its own workers. Similarly, government at all levels will support the owners of industry against workers, justifying this in terms of battling inflation, increasing productivity, and maintaining U.S. competitiveness against foreign producers. Thus, as was true for 208 during the 1970 wildcat, TDU can find itself in a confrontation with enormously powerful enemies. The only defense is to reach out beyond the Teamsters Union toward a broader solidarity with other workers and with activist community groups who share the same enemies. Many TDU members will resist such a strategy, particularly to the extent that it involves risks (as in refusing to drive across picket lines) or politically difficult issues (such as supporting black activism). The feasibility of such a strategy is directly dependent on political events on a wide level. If other rank-and-file movements grow up and develop strength, and if community activism increases, such reaching out will appear natural to all concerned. If quietude reigns, TDU will be boxed in.

PREVENTING THE BUREAUCRATIZATION OF TDU

The fate of the union-building upsurge of the 1930s alerts us to the dangers of bureaucratization. TDU is not "outside of history," but is subject to social and political forces that push toward accommodation and bureaucratization. Michels' (1962) analysis points to the defense of a group's own institutional strength as a conservatizing and routinizing force, so that the very growth of TDU's power can produce tendencies towards bureaucratization. This could occur in either of two ways—directly, or via TDU's becoming an institutionalized "loyal opposition."

The direct bureaucratization of TDU seems unlikely. That would involve the development of a central staff in TDU that could exert power over the membership and that could erode the rank-and-file democracy that characterizes the organization. However, how could this occur? The members of TDU would become aware of this—and they are highly skilled in opposing oligarchy and proceduralism because of their efforts in the IBT and at their workplaces. In addition, their efforts would be aided by the lack of a material base for bureaucracy in TDU. This is primarily because TDU staff are not engaged in activities that give them power over the membership. Thus, unlike union officials, they do not have legal or financial control over negotiations or grievance procedures; and, unlike managers, they do not have the power to hire and fire.

Bureaucratization of TDU is more likely to occur in a less direct way. If TDU becomes an institutionalized union opposition, creating a *de facto* two-party system within the IBT, it might well become bureaucratic. The restriction of TDU activities to electoralism alone would weaken the ability of its membership to recognize and to combat bureaucratization; and the creation of a sizable stratum of TDU officers who are full-time union officials with direct control over grievances and negotiations might give TDU's leadership power over the rank and file by becoming part of the union machine.

Although such an institutionalized opposition would entail an improvement of the Teamsters Union, it would hardly solve the members' problems with their employers. Instead, it would be a step toward a more typical business unionism with a degree of democratic competition for office.

The growth of electoralism* in TDU, and the associated approach of looking toward lower-level union officers to carry out the battle in place of the active struggle of the rank-and-file might well lead to this bureaucratization via "loyal opposition." If Local officials get elected by TDU, and stay in the organization, they will become an influential leadership grouping within TDU. They will, however, be subject to all the conservatizing forces discussed elsewhere, such as no longer working on the job, pressures from the legal system and the International against direct action, and the grievance process. In addition, electoral campaigns have a dynamic of their own towards elitism (they promote the special virtue of the candidate) and professionalism in the conduct of campaigns. One can readily imagine the development of a bureaucratic cadre in the TDU national office around staff members who become experts at running elections.

The tendency toward electoralism is not simply a "natural" one. Conscious choices by business, media, government, and union officials can encourage it. They can mount campaigns

---

* By electoralism, I mean seeing electoral success (and perhaps legal suits) as the be-all and end-all of TDU to the exclusion of direct action on the job.

differentiating between the "irresponsible activists" and the "responsible, statesmanlike electoralists" in the organization. The power of the courts can also be brought to bear. TDU cases that aim to protect its democratic rights in elections can succeed, whereas lawsuits against TDU for encouraging wildcats can lead to fines and imprisonments. After a few such cases, a movement within TDU to control the activists in order to protect the organization so it can "get on with its business" in elections would be inevitable.

Finally, as we have discussed above, a low level of direct action among Teamsters will strengthen the tendency toward electoralism, as will a low level of activism in the United States as a whole.

However, forces exist that may prevent TDU from becoming an institutionalized electoralist opposition. There is first of all the refusal by the International and by many employers to recognize TDU as legitimate. Their attacks undercut the credibility of the view that electoral victories alone can make much difference. Similarly, the continued opposition by the union bureaucracy to rank-and-file attempts to use the union's power against employer demands and attacks means that the day-to-day struggle in the barns remains illegitimate. Thus, the mobilization of workers in these struggles—if, and as, they occur—strengthens both TDU and its direct-action wing. Neither the International nor the employers are likely to change these policies except under extreme duress. Furthermore, the continuing economic hard times, exacerbated in freight by the impact of trucking deregulation, make their acceptance of any form of rank-and-file power or influence even less likely.

Electoralism seems less credible a solution when the rank and file understand the deep-seated nature of union bureaucracy. Thus, the very nature of TDU, and of many of its members, militates against a purely electoralist approach. Since people join TDU in order to fight bureaucratization and proceduralism, and to organize their battles against the companies more effectively, it is not easy to restrict such desires to the strait-jackets of electoral campaigning and court suits. Furthermore, their experiences in TDU deepen their understanding of the bureaucracy. And, once again, the demands that trucking companies make during economic hard times and deregulation will tend to increase the wish to fight back directly rather than to rely on a dubious and time-consuming electoralism.

What lies ahead? A continuing discussion within TDU about the correct balance between the electoral activity and job actions seems inevitable. In the long run, TDU will come up against the dynamic discussed earlier in this book: that workers' struggles and power have to expand and deepen if they are not to die. For TDU, the "cause of death" can be destruction from without, schism from within, or transformation into a "loyal opposition" that accepts the bureaucratic ineffectiveness of mainstream unionism.

THE PROBLEMS IN TAKING OFFICE

Electoral activity has been extremely useful in building TDU. Many Teamsters are willing to get involved in elections who are not willing to get involved in direct action at their workplace, in local bylaws campaigns, or in contract campaigns. Elections seem to offer more hope for change, since they can oust ineffective or corrupt officials. Thus, TDU has found that people become motivated by election campaigns, and that some of them, once active, become involved in other activities as well.

Ken Paff, the national TDU Organizer, tells me that election campaigns spark Teamsters to get involved in barn struggles. Furthermore, electoral victories will be needed if the Teamsters Union is to be changed. My discussions of the pitfalls of electoralism are not meant to deny this, but aim to show that electoral activity *alone* will not do the job. Both winning office and a movement of wildcat strikes and other direct action will be needed.

The issue of electoral campaigns needs further discussion, however. In many cases, TDU candidates have won. Paradoxically, TDU victories have occurred mainly in Locals where the organization is new rather than where it is well-established. Usually, oppositionists decide to run a slate for office, affiliate with TDU, and elect candidates. The Teamsters who vote for them do not support them as the organizers and leaders of rank-and-file struggles, but rather back them as "good, honest bureaucrats" who will do their best to act *for* the rank-and-file. In cases where the TDU slate wins control of the local Executive Board, or the top spot in the Local, the contradictions of office in a bureaucratic union rapidly overwhelm the moral commitment of well-meaning new officers who find that they cannot cope with official business without making their peace with the bureaucracy. For, to be an opposition union official, yet have to deal with the bureaucracy in grievance processing, in obtaining sanction for strikes, and in the course of meetings involving changes of operations or mergers (where the bureaucracy can retaliate by destroying Local members' jobs) imposes an extremely heavy burden. In circumstances where office is won before the rank-and-file has organized itself, the situation can be hopeless. Thus, if the members elect a slate of reformers to fight in their behalf, without organizing to fight on their own account as well, then the new officers cannot call upon the organized activism of the rank-and-file when needed. The result has been that officers have been elected on TDU slates in Flint, Boston, Oklahoma City, and St. Louis, only to drop out of TDU and make their peace with the bureaucracy (Wolfinsohn 1980:41). The dynamics of this process are familiar from 208's experience with the Maheras regime.

Such results should be contrasted to what we might, from the experience of Local 208, predict would happen should TDU elect a slate of officers in areas like Detroit where the rank and file has already used TDU to organize itself for action (but where the understanding that TDU intends to help the ranks fight for themselves has meant that TDU candidates have not yet gained a majority on any Local Executive Board.) In such circumstances, the rank and file would most likely see its electoral victory as making possible stronger action against the employers and within the union. Thus, victory would lead to increased activism within the Local. The newly elected officers could meet the threats and realities of unfavorable decisions in grievances and changes of operations by leading direct action against the employers, and by mobilizing the Local's rank and file to help other Teamsters in the area organize to transform their own Locals.

PREVENTING REBUREAUCRATIZATION

The powerful forces that push unions toward bureaucratization act upon Locals that the rank-and-file movement takes over, and they will act upon the IBT if a rank-and-file movement led by TDU takes over the International. Can such forces be resisted?

In large part, these forces act through the mechanisms of the grievance procedure, contract bargaining, and the legal enforcement of clauses banning strikes between negotiations. These create the internal need within the union to repress rank-and-file direct action, and thus stifle the creativity and the democratic self-defense of the workers. Thus, they elevate the officials above the ranks, and create the need among the officialdom for bureaucratic forms both to control the ranks and to develop maneuvers and strategies with which to deal with the employers (since the strongest weapon, the workers' own potential initiative and strength, must be stifled). However, in a union under rank-and-file control, it is possible to destroy this pattern—if the ranks understand the need and the way to do so, and if the union is able to use the ranks' enthusiasm at running their own union to organize the power needed to win a long and hard battle. This may be possible if TDU leads a takeover of the IBT. The prerequisite for winning the ensuing battles is that TDU activities have already sparked the self-organization among a large part of the membership of the union.

What is needed is a change in the contracts so that strikes would be allowed between negotiations, and a change in the union constitution so that the rank and file would be allowed to call its own strikes. Of course, this is easier said than done. Employers will resist the end of the no-strike clause with all their power, and will receive support from the media and the government. This is clear from the powerful opposition that has been brought against less far-reaching attempts by the United Mineworkers to regain the right to strike between negotiations (Hume 1971; Nyden 1974; Dix et al. 1971; Green 1978; Marschall 1978; Moody and Woodward 1978). Thus, TDU can hope to win its goals only through a long struggle—and only through such struggles before taking over the union can the rank-and-file movement hope to build the strength either to take over the IBT or to be strong enough to win the right to strike between negotiations (at the barn or wider levels) after taking over. However, such strength and such a victory are needed in order to shortcircuit the forces that would lead to rebureaucratization.

The thorough democratization of union forms is another part of the fight against rebureaucratization. Our discussion of 208's bylaws gives some indication of how this might work. In addition, the efforts of the Miners to rewrite their constitution after the overthrow of the Boyle regime are helpful (Nyden 1974). Furthermore, many TDU members want to go beyond these documents and to set up mechanisms (such as the right to recall officers, together with the continued existence of TDU as a rank-and-file led, rather than TDU-official led, organization) through which the membership can keep officials in line.

The most important barrier to rebureaucratization is the creation and strengthening of large numbers of activists whose power and consciousness is rooted in struggles at the workplace and also in struggles to transform the union (and keep it trans-formed). With such a grouping, organized through TDU but also organized at a barn level, the contractual right to strike and the democratization of union forms can be powerful obstacles to rebureaucratization, and these in turn can strengthen the exis-tence of such a grouping. Without these activists, the words of a contract or a union constitution mean little. Thus, the question of rebureaucratization ultimately becomes a question of power: can the rank and file find ways to develop enough of an offen-sive thrust, and a widening and deepening of their movement, sufficiently strong to defeat the efforts of the employers to wear out or disperse the unions' activists?

It is very hard to say much about the form of the needed widening and deepening. From the 208 experience, it is probable that one form of such struggle would be the spreading of the rank-and-file movement to those parts of the Teamsters that had not yet been touched by it, and helping the movement to grow in weaker Locals. This could be done by a combination of en-couragement and assistance from union officials and by the ac-tive aid of rank and filers from already activist Locals in the area or industry. Beyond that, little can be said, except to reiterate the theme that reaching out is necessary to prevent being boxed in, contained, and then pushed back. Ultimately, of course, this raises questions of overarching political and social significance: if reaching out leads to the organization of a rank-and-file, self-organizing movement of workers in a broad range of industries, tied to groups who struggle over the community issues of the working class (including those of racial minorities and women), then the question of what class dominates life and politics in the United States becomes the burning issue of politics. If the workers win such a struggle—what Eugene Debs or Karl Marx would have called the socialist revolution—then the ultimate question about rebureaucratization would be posed: Is participatory, democratic, activist socialism possible, or are there forces that necessarily crush or bureaucratize such a social order? I believe it can be done, and that bureaucratization can be resisted once the forces discussed in chapter 1 have been abolished. Furthermore, the experiences of Local 208 and TDU show the need for the rank and file to be involved in workplace issues in an active and democratic way for this to work. However, further discussion of this goes too far afield. Let us return to Local 208.

The Meaning of TDU for Local 208

During the heyday of rank-and-file activism in 208, the isolation of the Local in a Teamsters Union in which virtually every other Local was dominated by the bureaucracy was rightly seen as its major problem. Thus, one might expect that TDU would be greeted with applause by the members and officers of 208, and that 208 would rapidly become a pillar of TDU strength. Unfortunately, this is not at all what has happened—nor is it what the analysis presented in this book would imply.

Maheras has not welcomed TDU, because he feels that 208 needs to make its peace with the IBT bureaucracy. His whole strategy has been to walk a tightrope between members' desires to fight the companies and the bureaucracy and the insistence by the bureaucracy that 208 members neither wildcat nor take part in opposition movements. The existence of TDU threatens to push him off the tightrope. To the extent that the rank and file organize, Maheras must deal with their demands; he must either back or oppose them. John T. Williams, the activist 208 Business Agent, described the reaction of Maheras and his officers to the TDC contract campaign as follows:

I think they see it as a thing they don't know what to do with or about. They're concerned but don't know how to relate to it. They'd prefer it didn't exist but don't want to antagonize its support.

They were against having the Local endorse the TDC contract

demands. It crossed up the wires they're walking, since the national leaders are repressing it. So endorsements would lead to trouble. Alex and Archie are clean to the National and Western Conference leaderships.

Maheras' approach is feasible because much of 208's rank-and-file membership, while approving of TDU's desire to change the Teamsters, do not want to get involved. They fear a repetition of the long strike of 1970 or of the trusteeship. Additionally even those members of 208 most involved in TDU respect Maheras rather than seeing him, as most Locals' members see their officers, as the enemy. They may disagree with his strategy, and think the idea of working to reform the bureaucracy mistaken or even foolish—but they do not see Maheras as the sort of officer who consciously sells out the interests of the rank and file. This gives Maheras a powerful resource with which to prevent the rank-and-file from mobilizing—their trust in his regime.[5]

He has used this resource to defend what he believes in—namely, making peace with the bureaucracy. His strategy is simple. When TDU makes a proposal, he opposes it openly and above board, arguing that it will not work and that its passage would hurt his efforts to reform the union from within. If he loses, and the members vote to support a TDU initiative, he loyally carries out their decision—while continuing to argue that it was a mistake.

For example, in 1978, Doug Allan of TDU proposed that 208 send two delegates to a meeting called to set up a Majority Contract Coalition (a TDU initiative to build a broad coalition to fight for a strong Master Freight Agreement in 1979). Maheras opposed this motion, but it nevertheless passed. At that point, he made sure the delegates received airplane tickets, and in other ways helped carry out the decision. Similarly, during the strike discussed above (in which a corporation fired its drivers and used a leasing company), he arranged financial aid for the strikers, but refused to give the strike Local sanction, defending his refusal by pointing to the dangers of lawsuits or even trusteeship for sanctioning a wildcat. This argument seemed honest and plausible even to those who disagreed with him. The result, so far, has been that Maheras has maintained the trust of the rank and file; and even the most determined TDU opponents of Maheras' strategy have seen no way in which to win the ranks away from their trust in him.

Such examples confirm the analysis presented earlier of the Maheras regime. Maheras's very integrity has made it more difficult to build the kind of movement now needed by 208's members. The existence of TDU means that the isolation that once led to ambush, wildcat, and trusteeship for 208 need no longer be the fate of rank-and-file Locals in the Teamsters. A Local run by the rank and file would now receive support from the entire membership of TDU. Any trusteeship can now become a national issue in the Teamsters; the most brazen trusteeships might become the focus of a petition campaign and demonstrations throughout the country. Thus, the bureaucracy must be cautious about imposing trusteeships now that TDU exists. Indeed, it is noteworthy that there has been only a single case (and this case involved financial dishonesty) of a trusteeship being imposed in the Teamsters Union against the will of Local officers since TDU began—in spite of TDU members' taking office in numerous Locals and in spite of wildcats among carhaulers, steelhaulers, and others that have received protection from Local officers.* And so, Maheras' view is mistaken; even if it ever were true that 208 had to go along with the bureaucracy, the risks in fighting have now declined considerably. Further, Maheras' belief in the possibility of reforming the union through channels has deeper meaning since the formation of TDU: It now stands in the way of building a fighting movement, of joining in the national effort to build TDU into a movement strong enough to transform the IBT and defend Teamsters against the attacks of their employers.

TDU has nevertheless made some progress in 208. In the December 1979 election, Doug Allan, a national co-chairman of TDU, was elected a Trustee. Furthermore, TDU has led some changes within the Local. Most notably, Allan began a successful effort to have the agendas at Stewards' Council meetings be set by a committee of five stewards and the Local president.

---

* Trusteeships *have* been imposed in cases where the officers have become hopelessly divided such that the local was paralyzed and the rank-and-file members were thus willing to accept trusteeship as a way out. However, there have been no trusteeships imposed against the will of an organized membership nor against the wishes of a unified executive board.

TDU:
The Achievement
and Potential

In 1975, many Teamsters and scholars thought that the creation of a lasting national rank-and-file organization was impossible in any major union—much less the Teamsters. TDU has shown that it is possible. It has now existed for many years. It has won concrete victories in contract fights and in battles within the union.

At a time when economic difficulties and the deregulation of the trucking industry have led to a powerful offensive by employers in the union's central jurisdiction, it may well be that TDU offers the only chance to prevent the collapse of unionism in driving and warehousing. Employers in freight have been demanding—and getting—"givebacks" from the union in most areas of the United States. Thus, the Master Freight Agreement may well be on the verge of collapse as a national contract. Employers' attacks threaten the central integrating core of the union, established by Hoffa as the only way to survive the growth of national trucking companies. The bureaucratic leadership of the union has been unable to organize a defense. Indeed, it seems very unlikely that they can do anything, since successful resistance requires a large-scale mobilization of rank-and-file Teamsters to fight back. The bureaucracy almost certainly is unwilling to lead such a fight, since to do so would train the ranks in how to use their power. Furthermore, even if they wanted to, the bureaucracy could not lead such a fight, since it has lost contact with the ranks and since the bureaucracy itself is organized only to prevent action and not to lead it. An officialdom of hangers-on and corruption cannot transform itself into a fighting leadership. Thus, in the absence of TDU, we would expect a decline of Teamster unionism in the trucking trades that would be reminiscent of the collapse of the American Federation of Labor in the early years of the Great Depression. TDU may prevent this. It may happen directly, by TDU's leading struggles and through TDU leaders' winning elections and becoming the new leadership of Locals and then of the IBT as a whole—or at least of those sections of the union that are involved with freight. Conceivably, it could happen indirectly, if officials who are not fully comfortable with the bureaucracy take fright and lead a less drastic renewal of the union. I do not think this likely. Even Alex Maheras, who would be one of the most likely officers to do this, remains cautious.

Most likely, renewal will not happen. Most likely, the next five to ten years will see the destruction of the Master Freight Agreement and the gross weakening of the Teamsters Union in freight, carhauling, and related trucking jurisdictions. The forces lined up against these workers hold enormous power, and most likely TDU will not be able to organize a powerful enough resistance to defeat them in the immediate future. What then?

At the worst, TDU could collapse. If the employers become too dominant, they can fire militants or close down activist barns. Other activists might be intimidated, or simply see TDU as ineffective and thus drop out. Even then, TDU would leave behind an enormously significant heritage. The thousands of workers who have built TDU, and have learned how to organize and how to lead struggles in the process, would still be around. Some might be forced to leave the union and even the industries in which the Teamsters have jurisdictions (they might well become leaders of struggles in other industries) but a core would remain to lead an increased struggle when this becomes possible. Indeed, a national network of activists in freight, carhauling, and other Teamster industries would continue. Thus, even in the worst case, the rank-and-file movement would come out of these hard times better organized than it was in 1975.

More likely, TDU will continue—and even grow. It will remain, and it will try to organize Teamsters to defend themselves. In the words of Robert Fram, the editor of *CONVOY*, it will be a group of "activists waiting for the breaks." Even now, this is a good description of the situation of most TDU chapters. They consist of a core of committed activists who struggle to get support from less active Teamsters and to recruit and train new members of the core group. In each barn and in each Local, they try to build a rank-and-file machine that is powerful enough to win struggles. In Fram's words, once again, "You need more supporters, more active union members, more stewards—and more of a machine than they have—if you want to win an election." They try to build solidarity in the barns and among the barns, in each Local and among the Locals. And they wait for the breaks. Sometimes the breaks take the form of an upsurge of worker militancy—as in the 1976 carhaulers' strike in Detroit or the 1979 steelhaulers' strike.* Sometimes it is less dramatic, as in the slow but solid growth of rank-and-file organization among Roadway drivers and dock workers in many parts of the country, which TDU is encouraging, leading, and growing from. And sometimes it takes the form of a coalescence of barn activism with Local reform efforts, which can create a rank-and-file takeover like that in 208.

If TDU remains as a group of activists waiting for the breaks, and if the prognosis for the trucking trades over the next few years is as gloomy as it now appears, what then? For the Teamsters in TDU, even with a strategy that combines barn and union struggles, several years of hard work with relatively little reward seem likely—although even in slow times there will be occasional successes, just as the movement in 208 took place in the social desert of the late 1950s. However, the dynamics of economic hard times imply that such effort will reap rich rewards. Whether because hard times lead to an upturn in which worker confidence and combativity are nourished by increasing employment, or because several years of depression breed a willingness to take risks in order to reverse hellish working conditions, the current downturn in militancy will come to an end—perhaps explosively. When this happens, TDU will get the breaks. Its members will have years of self-training in how to organize and how to struggle; they will have gone beyond the parochialism that restrained the activists in 208; they will have developed political sophistication through years of discussion with each other and through years of testing their ideas in practice; and they will have become established in the eyes of Teamsters throughout the United States and Canada as the people who lead struggles. Thus, when conditions change so that mass struggle again becomes possible, TDU (if it survives—or the network it has produced if it does not) will be able to lead it and to help it to formulate new goals for the labor movement and to win them.

* The steelhaulers strike shows the need to "build a machine." No core of organizers emerged—or was developed—in this strike. As a result, the organization set up during the strike fell apart soon thereafter, and the companies were able to impose their desires, reversing the gains won by the strike.

Chapter 11

Conclusion: The Many Meanings of Local 208

IN CONCLUDING this book I first summarize some of what I learned about how workers can organize themselves. Then I consider what the matters discussed in this book can tell us about social theory. I look at a number of different theories, focusing on theories of bureaucracy and theories about social movements and working-class mobilization. Finally, I consider the implications of 208 and TDU for the political situation in which we find ourselves.

How Workers Can Organize

Many cynical workers will tell you that "nothing ever succeeds, and even if it seems to, it will just go back to the way it was." One meaning of the study of 208 is that this cynicism is mistaken. Workers *can* take over a Local union and use it to defend themselves at their workplace.

What does 208's experience suggest about strategies for successful worker organization? First, consider the problem of getting "boxed in." When workers achieve a voice in their unions and therefore can thwart employers' wishes, the employers (and higher union officials) often try to limit the workers' power. Since the employers are often part of larger firms with many workplaces, and part of industries with many companies, they have considerable leverage. For instance, they can let workers shut down one workplace, and then starve them into submission.

Usually top international union officials help employers curb the militancy of a Local. The only counterstrategy that workers have is to reach out to workers in other workplaces, other Locals, and perhaps other cities, and to develop ways to work together to prevent any one group of workers from becoming isolated, boxed in, and crushed.

This usually requires that activists who do take over any one Local help activists elsewhere to organize their own movements. The history of Local 208, and the results, in the 1970 lockout/wildcat, of its failure to reach out during the 1960s, points to the importance of this lesson. Teamsters for a Democratic Union now provides a vehicle for strategic outreach in the IBT.

The history of 208 also demonstrates the strategic danger of ignoring splits among workers. Local 208 has done far more than most unions to combat racism and defend the rights of black members; however, it has been far from perfect. Thus, during the 1970 strike, employers' attempts to hire black strikebreakers for jobs they had previously given primarily to whites nearly disrupted the strikers' unity. Only the presence of militant blacks respected both as union activists and black activists, and their ability to testify that 208 had taken steps against the racism of the employers over many years, prevented disaster.

Workers need to use direct action as well as grievances or the courts in conflicts with employers. In many situations, it is possible to use either approach, and legalism is chosen time after time because it seems safer. However, in the long run, reliance on legalism destroys workers' capability to take direct action, and even weakens workers' ability to use legalism effectively.

The organization and activism that workers develop in workplace struggles are more effective over the long run when tied together with efforts to make the union both democratic and able to fight the employers. Similarly, attempts to reform the union become more meaningful to many workers, and thus gain both in numbers and in dynamism, when the reform efforts are actively tied into struggles with the employers.

Also, working out accurate definitions of workers' problems and developing long-term plans to solve them is a collective process. Thus, it is important to develop ways in which the rank and file can discuss problems and strategies in depth. The absence of such collective strategic discussion weakened 208 during the late 1960s and during the 1970 wildcat. One of the contributions of TDU has been to initiate such nationwide discussions.

Workers must have an accurate picture of union officialdom. Misconceptions lead to disastrous mistakes. Indeed, one point that stands out in the history of 208 is that many of its activists erred because they viewed the problem of union bureaucracy as being a problem of individual corruption. This led them to see the problem only as one of individual "bad apples," so they mistakenly relied on the assistance of "unspoiled" higher officials during the wildcat—and hundreds of workers suffered as a result. But there is a more important consequence of this error. If "bad apples" are the problem, the obvious solution is to kick out the corrupt individuals. Unfortunately, as argued at length in chapter 1, the officials are *not* just a collection of spoiled (and unspoiled) individuals; they are an institutionalized bureaucracy. Worse, the interests of this bureaucracy, and the experiences of the officials who compose it, bind the officials to modes of operation that aid the companies in keeping the workers under their control. In particular, the officialdom is under extremely strong pressure to force rank-and-file workers to use grievance procedures and other legalistic means of defense, and to squash rank-and-file direct action whenever it appears. Thus, the officialdom is forced to keep the union firmly under its own control—which means that the lack of democracy in the Teamsters (and other unions) isn't accidental, or even a result of the greed of the officials in office: it's a necessary result of the social nature of the bureaucracy. This is something a good deal more than theorizing. It has important implications for anyone who would try to change a union. In particular, it implies that: If a rank-and-file movement elects "good" officers, they will come under strong pressure to accommodate to pressures from above, and thus to rely only upon legalism. In the long run, this means they have to erode Local democracy and participation. Local 208 since the Trusteeship is the obvious example. Thus, after electing new officers, even from among its own leaders, a rank-and-file movement cannot dissolve. It must continue—both to pressure the new officers and to support them when they support rank-and-file interests. Further, even under the best of officials, successful unionism depends on the direct action of the rank-

and-file. Officers can (at most) lead the workers, but the workers must do the fighting; to rely on the officers to do the fighting is to leave those very officers helpless.

Theoretical Meanings

Our general understanding of how society operates can be enriched by seeing how preexisting ideas (theories) are illuminated by new knowledge about particular social conflicts. This study of 208 and TDU has implications for theories about bureaucracy, about work and the working class, and about the ways workers build social movements.

BUREAUCRACY AND ORGANIZATION

Bureaucracy.   Our study supports the argument of chapter 1. The Teamsters Union is indeed run by an officialdom whose interests are opposed to those of the rank-and-file worker, and this officialdom has been institutionalized into a bureaucracy that acts in ways that harm workers while benefiting employers. Essentially, this bureaucratization demobilizes the rank and file. To a large extent, this results from the joint insistence by union officials, employers, and government that workers rely on grievance procedures rather than upon direct action.

The forces toward union bureaucratization are strong, but they can be rolled back—at least for a time. 208 and coal miners both did it, and TDU may be in the process of doing it. Thus, the forces described in chapter 1 should not be seen as deterministic.

The Effectiveness of Autocracy and the Iron Law of Oligarchy.   One of the most famous ideas of sociology is the idea that bureaucratic organization is efficient, and that the most effective form of organization for a group engaged in conflict is centralized bureaucracy of a military sort. Michels expressed this idea in his classic study of European social democracy; he coined the term "iron law of oligarchy" to describe his findings that even the socialist working-class parties of Europe, much as they stood for democratic ideals, had become internally autocratic. He theorized that organization inevitably becomes oligarchy (Michels [1911] 1962).

The experience of Local 208—like that of the social movements of the 1960s—is evidence that his view of bureaucracy as being effective is mistaken. The strength of Local 208 came from the active and democratic involvement of the membership, and from their participation in struggles with both employers and IBT officialdom. Indeed, every time the members of the Local accepted bureaucratic fetters upon their actions, their power declined. During the long wildcat in 1970, a strike committee that kept too much power and information in its own hands was the strikers' greatest weakness. Further, on more routine matters, the contrast between the theory of the efficiency of autocracy and the experience of Local 208 is startling. For example, the theory would hold that bureaucratic organization allows the union to bring its full weight against the employers, and thus to obtain the best possible settlements in grievances and in contracts. The reality, however, is that the active involvement of the rank and file in negotiations produces much more favorable settlements of grievances—and national contracts in freight that do less damage to workers. Thus, the 1970 negotiations, where the wildcat disrupted the bargain between the bureaucracy and the employers, and the 1976 negotiations, where the organization of Teamsters for a Decent Contract threatened the bureaucracy with a possible national wildcat coordinated by a militant leadership, turned out far better for freight workers than did the 1967 or 1973 negotiations, where the "efficient" bureaucracy negotiated in the absence of rank-and-file activism.

Activist democracy is more effective than bureaucratic autocracy, in which workers must rely on a social stratum that almost necessarily favors the interests of the companies over those of the workers (see Chapter 1). The real power of a union lies in the power of the workers—their power not merely to stop work, but also to fight strikebreakers, to disrupt the orderly workings of society should State power be used to break a strike, and, above all, to use their knowledge and intelligence for working out new and effective forms of struggle. The creative activism of rank-and-file workers built the CIO in the 1930s; the creative activism of rank-and-file workers transformed 208 into a militant and democratic local in the 1960s; creative activism prevented the 1970 wildcat from crushing the organization and spirit of the workers in Los Angeles; and creative activism underlies the developing movement in Detroit TDU and, to a lesser degree, in TDU nationally.

Thus, the history of 208 strongly challenges the argument that oligarchy is effective. On the other hand, the history of 208 might at first seem to confirm the more basic form of the "iron law," the argument that the sources of oligarchy are primarily internal and inherent in the nature of organization itself, and thus inescapable. Indeed, since 1970, the Local has been much less democratic and participatory than it was in the 1960s. However, the degeneration of 208 stems not from internal sources, but from powerful external forces. The employers locked out the 1970 wildcat; and then the IBT, the employers, and various levels of state and federal government cooperated to impose a trusteeship and manipulate it against workers' interests. It was only in reaction to these events and in fear of a new trusteeship that the post-trusteeship regime restricted the democratic activism of 208. This fact suggests, indeed, that in its application the "iron law" is limited to those circumstances in which the opponents of the democratic power of workers are strong enough to defeat that power.

UNION BUREAUCRACY AND THE TREND TOWARD A BUREAUCRATIC SOCIETY

Bureaucratic rationalization was held to be the main drift of society by such noted scholars as C. Wright Mills (1948, 1956, 1959) and Max Weber (1957, 1958). Business, government, universities, and even religion have become more bureaucratically organized, and their leaders will tell you that this is necessary and (perhaps) useful. We are thus faced with a question: To what degree is union bureaucratization just another facet of this general principle?

On the surface, there is a striking similarity between the bureaucratization of unions and that of the rest of society. In both, bureaucratization puts decision-making power in small groups of top managers, and renders the members, constituents, employees, and clients of these organizations unable to influence them effectively except through action outside prescribed channels. Bureaucratization breaks issues down into cases and reduces differences of interests and values to discussion of efficient mechanisms to reach undiscussed goals. It depoliticizes the use of power while making it hard to mobilize those outside of the organizational elites (Mills 1959; Domhoff 1967, 1970; Domhoff and Ballard 1968; Parenti 1974). Thus, union and other bureaucracies are similar in that they demobilize and depoliticize the people. Furthermore, bureaucracy allows organizations of all kinds to make long-range plans and to administer programs with a degree of consistency.

Nonetheless, there is a fundamental difference between bureaucracy in business or government and bureaucracy in unions. The demobilization and depoliticization of workers and clients of business and government is essential to their purposes: to use workers' efforts to create goods and services that can be sold for a profit, and to maintain a quiescent populace that is willing to let public affairs be managed by political experts who support the general interests of business (Mills, 1959; Domhoff, 1967, 1970; Domhoff and Ballard, 1968; Parenti, 1974). On the other hand, bureaucratization contradicts the purpose of unions. Unions exist in order to defend workers against employers' demands, and bureaucratization decreases their ability to do this. Indeed, union bureaucracy can be viewed as the product of alien and hostile class interests—those of the employers—which have structured the law and the nature of bargaining so as to bureaucratize unions and thus grossly weaken them.

There is, nevertheless, a way in which bureaucratization is true to one side of unionism. Unions are not institutions set up by workers in order to wage general and unlimited class war against the employers in an effort to replace capitalism with a society run by workers. (I would call this socialism—but this is a word that means many other things to many other people.) They are formed to struggle over the terms of the employment relationship within capitalism. However, the needs of workers tend to overstep the boundaries of capitalist profitability. Workers are particularly likely to use their collective power to force improvements in working conditions that threaten the competitive position of their employer (or the nation they live in). Thus, within a capitalist system, democratic unionism tends to create a situation that destroys workers' jobs and their unions' power, and this means that unions cannot long act as the collective power of the workers in pushing for improvements within the capitalist labor relationship. There are two alternatives. This contradiction must be overcome either by the union's being tamed (by bureaucratization or destruction), or by workers' mounting a direct attack upon capitalism. Usually, this contradiction is resolved by bureaucratization.

My argument, however, is true only in the final analysis—the need for workers' movements to expand, deepen, and radicalize lest they be destroyed, since no stable truce is possible. Over the short run—which may mean ten years or even more—worker activism within the limits of militant trade unionism can sometimes win amazing gains (and it can be fun in the process). Even this success, however, requires a willingness to break the rules and laws that define and protect the current bureaucratic system of labor relations.

The Dynamics and Effects of Worker Mobilization

EXISTENCE OF CLASS CONFLICT

There are different classes in society: workers are one such class, the owners and controllers of businesses are another. The two classes are in fundamental conflict. While this, of course, is much too broad a theory to prove by this study alone, the experiences of Local 208 do strongly support such a viewpoint. In particular, 208's experiences show that major interests of companies and of workers are in direct conflict—and there is struggle over them. Trucking companies want workers to work harder, to drive unsafe trucks, and to ignore "minor" violations of seniority rights if doing so increases efficiency. They would even like workers to ignore "minor errors" in computing their paychecks. Further, companies want to punish workers for "disobedience"—indeed, for any behavior that might go against the will of management—and to increase their profits by paying the lowest possible wages and giving the fewest possible benefits. Workers want higher pay and benefits, security (which means a limit on the disciplinary powers of management), flexibility in the manner of doing assigned work, safe working conditions, and a strict observance of seniority and other rules that protect important worker interests even at some cost in productivity.

Further, there is a struggle over the issue of the time workers actually work—what Karl Marx (1967: Volume 1, Part 3) called the "struggle over the working day" and the "struggle over absolute surplus value" in *Capital*. In truck driving, such struggle is all-pervasive, and takes a form guaranteed to drive trucking management into a frenzy (along with any readers who believe that an employee has a duty to work all of his or her assigned time during working hours). Drivers hang out in coffeeshops and on loading docks; and on occasion even use their trucks as transportation while running family errands or in other ways doing what *they* want. Management, seeing such behavior as "theft of time," organizes spotters and the like to find transgressors, who then are disciplined.

In the quietest times, these differences in interest lead to low-key guerrilla warfare between management and workers. Even this might be called class conflict. However, this conflict does not stay small-scale. Instead, daily conflict on the shop floor generates larger struggles. Further, small-scale struggles train workers in leadership skills and in social analysis, and thus build the forces for broader and more political struggle. It was indeed no accident that not only was 208 an outstanding example of class conflict on "narrow" labor issues, but also that many of its members became labor activists involved in the peace movement, the black struggle, and the efforts of the United Farmworkers. In fact, 208 implies that activist industrial conflict can produce a broader awareness of social injustice and of the potential power of organized workers, and thus leads to attempts to bring workers' power into action against the widest range of social ills.

Even in the 1950s, the relatively small-scale struggles in 208 workplaces developed a limited class consciousness; in less conservative times, with a movement not confined to one Local— and thus with a greater sense of the potential power of workers— such struggles may develop much deeper forms of class consciousness. Already, TDU has sparked socialist consciousness among some activists.

WHY 208 BECAME DIFFERENT

Sociologists are rightly fascinated by the circumstances that allow or precipitate social unrest. The question of what made 208's rank and file different is of considerable theoretical interest (as well as practical importance).

While it may disappoint some readers, there is no single answer to the question of why 208 developed a successful rank-and-file movement during the quiet 1950s. However, a discussion of the several forces that made this movement possible illuminates crucial dynamics in the development of worker movements.

Sociologists agree that a number of preconditions must be met for a social movement to develop.[1] The people involved must have problems that seem to be caused by some feature of the social order. They must be able to establish communication and organization among themselves, and then to develop strategies and leadership that give direction to their activities. Their movement is aided enormously if their potential enemies are disorganized or in other ways unable to stop the movement during its early, weak phase. Finally, their ability to mobilize and to develop enough power to win gains depends on the ways in which their social situation provides them with opportunities, skills, and resources that can be used in organizing themselves or in battling their enemies.

The major problem confronting Local 208 was discussed above: Employers act in ways that harm workers' interests. But, of course, this is true elsewhere: there was nothing special about the attacks on 208 members, so this does not in itself account for the differences between what 208 did and what other workers did. However, the difference between the relatively mild pressures on workers in the 1950s and the greater pressures of the last few years helps explain why the 208 insurgency stayed localized whereas recent Teamster insurgency shows signs of becoming a nationwide social movement. It should be noted that the multiplicity of employers in trucking means that at any given time some employers will be attacking workers harder than others, which not only fuels the movement, but also causes conditions of "relative deprivation" in which the drivers most attacked see their condition not as inevitable but as unjust and actionable.

In addition, the Local's undemocratic nature also led to unrest. Embarrassment at being Teamsters at a time when Teamsters were being portrayed in nationally broadcast hearings as racket-ridden, corrupt, and dictatorial intensified members' resentment against Local dictatorships. Thus, many workers were moved to try to change their Locals.

But this in itself says nothing about why 208 was different from any other Teamsters' Local. The movement in 208 was, as social theory predicts, helped by the disorganization of its enemies. The Teamster bureaucracy in Los Angeles was a weak one, and thus found it difficult to destroy the budding movement. Further, Jimmy Hoffa needed allies in Los Angeles and found 208's rank and file useful as a threat in dealing with the Los Angeles officialdom. Hoffa, in turn, was limited in his ability to demolish the 208 activists by pressure from the United States Senate. Thus, the union machine was disorganized. The employers were also disorganized, chiefly since trucking was even more competitive in the 1950s than in the 1970s.

In the development of the movement in 208, leadership and communication were provided by the milieu of driving (see chapter 3). This milieu is characterized by constant communication among drivers, by a multiplicity of barns that are sources of leadership and laboratories for new strategies, and by relative safety for activists. Thus, it is good soil for a movement; and it was fertile soil for the fortuitous development of a successful strategy—barn activism linked with Local union activism.

Finally, the ability of workers in 208 to mobilize and to win concessions was strengthened by their sense of a shared craft—truck driving. This made it easier for them to organize across barn boundaries. Further, the relative shortage of drivers in the 1950s meant that activists who were fired could find other work, if only because the employers had to rely on the Hiring Hall as a source of skilled labor. Furthermore, the drivers' relatively high pay—which resulted from their union's strength but also from the economic value of skilled labor—meant that they could afford to pay for leaflets and to take occasional days off from work during election campaigns, demonstrations, or other activities of the movement. This has also made it possible for TDU to get the funds it needs and for TDU activists to spend more time on the movement.

Thus, the specific question of why a movement developed in 208, and was able to transform the Local, whereas similar movements elsewhere were either crushed or led to the reinstitution of bureaucratic unionism, finds its answer in the conjunction of two circumstances: A relatively disorganized officialdom, and the discovery by 208's activists of a winning strategy. However, 208's successes were also based on circumstances they shared with other drivers, such as their problems, craft skills, and milieu.

DIALECTICS OF MILIEUS

The implication that their milieu makes it relatively easy for drivers to organize ties in with a great deal of literature about the conditions that affect worker militancy.[2] That is, workers in industries with milieus that provide easy communication, freedom from supervision, multiple employers, and the like, should be more able to organize against their employers.

But a second theoretical context exists in which the question of milieu takes on greater complexity and interest. In Marxist theory, it is argued that capitalism undergoes crisis periods in which employers are forced to take actions that hurt workers; these actions provide workers with extra motivation to fight back. In crisis periods, Marxism argues, the intensification of workers' problems tends to create large-scale working-class social movements like the labor upsurge of the 1930s. This theoretical concept of crisis periods illuminates and is illuminated by the history of Local 208. First, we see that the nature of workers' milieu affects their responsiveness; even in the late 1950s, when there was no crisis, the milieu of 208 was nonetheless sufficient to translate workers' "small-scale" problems into a social movement. Second, we see that milieu alone does not cause a widespread social movement in the absence of crisis: the 208 movement did not spread. Third, consider the pattern during an economic crisis such as that during the 1930s (and the one that may be occurring, more slowly, at present). In those industries with milieus that make it easier for workers to organize, workers should more readily respond to the crisis. Further, there should be similarities in response patterns between the 1930s and today (at least among those industries in which the milieu has not meanwhile been transformed in major ways). Thus, certain industries should be "leading indicators" of class conflict during periods of crises. In the 1930s, both coal mining and truck driving were such leading industries; their workers organized themselves and then aided other workers to organize long before the 1937 upsurge that created the CIO. Similarly, today the rank-and-file movement in the United Mine Workers (and the associated wild-cat strike wave in the mines), and the development of nationwide rank-and-file organization (TDU and PROD) among truck drivers and other freight workers appear to be a first reponse to developing economic crisis. These parallels suggest that the milieus of the mining and freight industries do indeed make their workers the first to respond to a crisis.

Marxists (and others) have developed theories that relate both "objective conditions" (such as the state of the economy) and "subjective factors" (such as the values, beliefs, and degree of organization of a group of workers) to the development of workers' social movements. In particular, if objective conditions are not ripe, little can be done to create a workers' upsurge: thus questions of strategy and tactics are of little import. During crisis periods, on the other hand, workers are so oppressed that they organize spontaneously, and thus strategy, tactics, and political organization are again irrelevant to the question of organizing. The discussion of milieus offers a somewhat different approach. In particular, if milieus like that of Local 208 are relatively ready to organize even in the "poor objective conditions" of the 1950s, then strategy, tactics, and political organization may indeed be of critical importance—since they apparently can affect both the degree of success for such movements in relatively unfavorable circumstances and the readiness of activists in such milieus to support other workers should objective conditions move toward a crisis. Thus, patterns of leadership among workers in industries with milieus that let activists function as sparkplugs for other workers can shape the politics of an entire period of workers' upsurge. More abstractly: the degree to which questions of strategy, tactics, and politics become important in an industry is a structural question.

The example of TDU offers further clarification of this interplay among objective conditions, milieu, and workers' activism. TDU has developed into an important opposition group within the Teamsters at a time of low-level crisis, but in most areas was limited by the absence of any spontaneous rank-and-file upsurge. From this we can see that the absence of ripe objective conditions limits, even in a favorable milieu, the organization of workers' movements. Milieu is nonetheless important, since it has been the favorable milieu in the freight industry that has let TDU maintain itself, spread, and deepen its roots despite strong attacks by both the union bureaucracy and the employers. Additionally, the importance of socialist ideas and leadership in TDU's growth indicates the importance of strategy in circumstances where the milieu is favorable to activism but the objective conditions are not ripe enough to create a spontaneous eruption of worker unrest. The presence, that is, of a (socialist) group who believed that Teamster rank and filers could organize for change allowed a contract campaign to develop into the lasting organization of TDU. However, without a favorable milieu or consciousness, a good strategy is of little use. The same socialist organization that initiated TDC attempted a parallel strategy in auto contract negotiations during the same year; their efforts came to naught because both the consciousness (based in part on economic conditions) and milieu of the auto workers were less inclined toward activism and rank-and-file organization.

SKILLED WORKERS AND THE QUESTION OF LABOR ARISTOCRACY AND CRAFT

The relationship of skilled workers to other workers has been widely discussed. Some argue that skilled workers form an aristocracy of labor that acts as a conservative force within the working class. This view was widely held before the 1930s, when craft unions dominated the AFL and prevented the organizing of less skilled workers into industrial unions. Its modern form focuses on the alleged conservatism of "hard hats" and other skilled workers in such crafts as construction, machinery, and truck driving. Others argue that skilled workers find it easier to organize than other workers, and that their example, and sometimes assistance, can spark other workers to organize.[3]

Local 208 is a craft Local, and TDU has had its greatest success among drivers. Thus, the aristocracy of labor thesis raises questions about the wider significance of the movements studied in this book for the working class as a whole, and the processes we have observed can illuminate the issue of labor aristocracy.

Craft workers clearly do have advantages in organizing. This was true in terms of organizing unions in the first place, which let the crafts dominate the AFL. In recent years, the resources and craft solidarity of the trades have let them organize opposition groups more readily than less skilled workers. This has been true in the auto industry, where opposition groups such as the United National Caucus and the Independent Skilled Trades Council have been based primarily on craft workers such as tool and die makers. These groups have been criticized as elitist and unconcerned with the problems of less skilled workers. Similarly, the 208 movement was a movement of drivers, and TDU has been most successful in organizing among drivers and particularly among carhaulers, who have a strong sense of craft pride.

However, these Teamster movements show that the skilled need not function as an exclusionist, conservative aristocracy. Even though craft pride did lead to some lack of solidarity between drivers and other workers in some barns, there was a strong contrary dynamic at work whereby the victories of 208's skilled drivers strengthened the position of other Teamsters as well. Thus, 208's initial activism and victories spilled over to encourage opposition movements in other Locals. Until stopped by the International, 208 activists aided insurgents in these other trades, including warehousemen as well as oppositionists in other trades in the trucking barns. The example of 208, as well as the initiative of its drivers, was a factor in the wildcat of 1970, which spread to all unionized trades in freight. In terms of TDU in Los Angeles, its areas of strength have included dock and clerical workers in Local 357 as well as drivers in 208 and other locals. In terms of political beliefs, 208 was a source of activists in the social movements of the 1960s, and many TDU members are not at all conservative.

What does this discussion imply about whether skilled workers act as a conservative aristocracy of labor or as an organizer and energizer of worker resistance? It suggests that this should *not* be seen as a question that has a determinate answer in favor of one theory or the other. Instead, we need research that sees both as dynamic tendencies, and studies the conflict processes that influence whether conservative in-groupness or energizing outreach becomes the dominant force in a given situation.

THE WORK PROCESS, THE DIVISION OF LABOR, AND THE DIVISION OF WORKERS

Common sense (and most economic theory) tells us that the nature of what workers do on the job and the way in which tasks are arranged into jobs are a product of technological and organizational rationality. The result is supposed to be efficient and productive. Furthermore, this result is held to be "objectively determined," flowing from the technical requirements of getting the work done rather than from the hierarchical structure of workplace relationships or the associated managerial need to keep workers under control. In short, the division of labor at work and the content of jobs are held to be independent of the conflicts and politics of the workplace. Inherent in this view, of course, is the idea that any attempt by workers to improve their working lives by changing the division of labor (and associated differences in prestige and pay) or by changing the nature of what they do at work will reduce productivity and thus cause their firm to lose business and perhaps to fold.

Recent research has challenged this view, and, in my opinion, discredited it. Kathy Stone (1973) shows that hierarchical job structures can result from company attempts to divide (and thus disorganize) the workers; and Harry Braverman (1974) argues that much of the change in workplace technology and job-task organization is designed to minimize the control workers have over their work and thus strengthen management's hand. Braverman also argues that one result of this job degradation is "de-skilling"—the creation of masses of dull jobs that require little real skill.[4]

The division of labor in the Los Angeles freight industry is complex. Clear differentiation is made among long distance drivers, local drivers, dock workers (who load trucks at the barns, then sort, distribute, and reload it onto other trucks), office workers, and mechanics. These differences parallel divisions within the union: each of these crafts is in a separate Local.

(Dock workers and office workers are both in Local 357; however that Local is divided into separate dock and office sections for many purposes.)

Thus, the division of workers into job categories is institutionalized through the union's assignment of different tasks to different craft Locals. This means, superficially, that it is very hard for companies to erode craft divisions, and appears to go counter to Stone's idea that job divisions are established in order to achieve managerial control. At a deeper level, however, this evidence supports the basic thrust of Stone's argument: the job divisions help management (and the union bureaucracy) to control the workers. In the mid-1940s, the union divided the multicraft Local 208 into the current pattern of several craft Locals in order to establish bureaucratic control over Los Angeles Teamsters by disuniting the workers. There is no record of the companies' having objected, which makes it likely that they approved. And the result has indeed helped management retain control over the workers. Thus, the division into different Locals made it easier to restrict the 208 insurgency of the 1950s to the drivers. Furthermore, within each barn, the divisions among the Locals allow the companies to keep the workers disunited. (We have noted earlier a barn where dock workers and drivers were weakened by hostility based on a jurisdictional dispute.) The result of these divisions is, then, a strengthening of management's power.*

The experience in truck driving tends to confirm the general thrust of Braverman's view that changes in technology and work organization aim at establishing greater control over the workers. Technology has produced trip meters and radios to control drivers, and such organizational devices as spotters and production standards achieve the same end.[5] However, in other ways, the 208 experience suggests difficulties for Braverman's thesis. The

---

* It might be argued that the separation of workers into homogeneous craft locals allows an easier development of solidarity, and that this counter-tendency can counteract the weakening effect of these divisions. This would produce an argument similar in structure to that presented above about the conservatizing and energizing effects of craft skills. However, TDU has not found that homogeneous locals are stronger bases of support than mixed locals. Thus, in homogeneous locals, it seems that the reinforcing of craft divisions by union jurisdictional lines greatly increases the conservatizing and parochializing tendencies without increasing the energizing possibilities.

most important gain in driver productivity during the period studied was probably based around the increased use of tractor-trailer combinations, and later, of double trailers pulled by one tractor. This can give somewhat tighter control over the driver, as one trailer can be dropped off while the driver takes the second one somewhere else, a procedure that reduces the chances for the driver to "goof off" while trailers are loaded or unloaded by senders' or recipients' staff. However, it by no means involves a lessening of skills: indeed, driving doubles requires far more skill than driving a one-piece straight truck ("bobtail").

It should also be noticed that there is a major difference between the ways management tries to control the work of truck drivers and the ways it attempts to control work in factories and offices. Braverman discusses how employers totally restructure the nature of the work process in many industries and occupations. For example, skilled machinists are being "de-skilled" by having the control over machine tools transferred to numerical control programs, leaving the worker as someone who monitors the work rather than performs it. Similarly, word processing is transforming the skilled job of secretary into a much more routine occupation. However, in truck driving the controls that management attempts to impose are *external*, rather than basic changes in the work itself. Indeed, it seems likely that a whole range of occupations that involve being "out and around" are highly resistant to having the nature of their work changed "internally." Such jobs as postal deliverer, airplane pilot, and truck driver seem to require much too heavy a capital investment to transform them in ways that would put direct control of the work process in management's hands.*

* However, it may be possible. Conveyor belts between major freight depots, together with computerized routing mechanisms, may now seem like a science fiction vision—and one far too costly in capital and energy to be feasible. But I am made rather cautious by the degree to which the BART subway system in the San Francisco metropolitan area has put control over a major transportation system into the hands of the "system," and thus of management, and thus been able to eliminate the drivers of trains. The fact that BART has had serious problems with breakdowns and accidents may simply mean that such efforts are difficult. On a general level, it seems that delivery systems can be taken out of a "driver's" control only to the extent that other vehicles that are outside of the system's control can be excluded. Thus, for BART, there is no other traffic. For truck driving to be removed from driver control requires a separate traffic system.

Braverman's book is also rather pessimistic in that it understates the ability of workers to resist work degradation. We have seen, however, that one of the effects of the rank-and-file movement in 208 was to give workers the power to resist management demands. Indeed, the Blackmarr period saw a rolling back of work rules and a reduction in the power of management over the way drivers did their work. In effect, the drivers' power counteracted the employers' ability to degrade the work, and many workers were able to organize their runs in ways that gave them personal satisfaction and that also moved considerable quantities of freight. However, as was discussed in relation to Felix Santoro's description in chapter 3 of how he built up his run, this does not necessarily accord with company desires. Moving lots of freight may be socially desirable, but a run that involves lots of small consignments may be less profitable than a run moving less freight for fewer customers. Thus, the dynamics of capitalism—production and services for profit—and the social good can conflict. In this case, at least, a worker's desire for socially useful work contradicted the company's need for profits.

The companies were not able to get their way on these issues until their attacks during the 1970 wildcat and the trusteeship had weakened drivers' organization and combativity. This suggests an amendment to Braverman's underlying model, which sees the dynamics of capitalist development as producing a force toward work degradation that is irresistible (at least, short of revolution). The balance of class forces is not that uneven. Worker resistance is possible, and can prevent (and even roll back) the tendency toward work degradation.

This argument parallels my similar argument about bureaucratization. Capitalism produces strong tendencies toward both union bureaucracy and work degradation. However, these tendencies need not be absolutely determinant. Workers can resist, and they can win major victories. On the other hand, in neither case is a lasting standoff possible. The forces generated by capitalist competition force the employers to destroy impediments to their competitiveness (on pain of bankruptcy caused by companies that more successfully attack their workers or, internationally, by a nation whose workers are more weakly organized than its competitors.) Thus, all gains by workers are under con-

stant attack, and will eventually be pushed back and eliminated—so long as capitalism exists. However, these gains can
mean a lot to thousands, or even millions of workers, while they
continue, and it is only the constant pushing by workers that has
created current standards of living. Furthermore, it is the organization and experience that workers gain in these struggles
that provides them with the skills and powers needed to replace
capitalism with a better system.

THE STRATEGIC POSITION OF DRIVERS IN THE COMMUNITY AND IN THE INTERNATIONAL DIVISION OF LABOR

The nature of their work gives drivers insight, potential cultural
influence, and power. They are a key part of the working class.
Drivers get insights from their work. They see what goes on in
the streets as they drive through them, and often develop a
considerable knowledge about the communities in which their
routes lie. They also see what goes on where they make pickups
and deliveries, and talk with people at these stops. They each
collect an enormous amount of information about social conditions, and through conversations with each other often develop
considerable understanding of the situation, problems, and
moods of other workers and the community.

Relatedly, drivers talk with many other people. Their knowledge and ideas are spread throughout the community in the
course of their daily work. This means that they have a degree
of cultural influence as a natural grapevine. To the extent that
drivers become insurgents through rank-and-file movements,
and become convinced that general worker activism and solidarity is both a good thing and possible, they will convey this
message to others. On occasion, this could even become a conscious effort, and Teamster activists could take on the role of
propagandists and mobilizers of other workers. This is no pipe-
dream. It has happened: in 1934, Minneapolis Teamsters organized themselves, won some major strikes, and then acted as
a cultural force in mobilizing other workers and the unemployed
to organize themselves in unions and to act as a force in politics
(Dobbs: 1972, 1973, 1975, 1977).

The potential power of drivers is obvious. Most manufacturers depend on trucks to bring supplies and to ship products,

and wholesale, retail, and many service establishments (such as restaurants) also depend on trucking. Indeed, even governments need drivers' work—the masses of paper they process have to be delivered first. Drivers' ability to shut down the economy gives them enormous potential power. For this to be effective, of course, they need to be organized; but the Teamsters Union has let the drivers' organization weaken dreadfully over the past decades. Increasing percentages of drivers are nonunion, and increasing percentages of union drivers are unorganized. If TDU is successful, this disorganization will be reversed as part of a general mobilization by Teamsters and a spreading of their militancy to other drivers.

The power of drivers is becoming more strategically important because of developments in the international division of labor (Bergston et al. 1978; Mukherjee 1978; Fröbel et al. 1980). Increasingly, the production process in manufacturing is being carried out in different countries. Advertisements for the "world car," for example, proclaim that the vehicles contain components produced in many different countries. This internationalization of production includes "multiple sourcing" in which each component is produced in several different locations around the world. Thus, labor conflict or political upheaval in any given country will have little effect upon the global production processes of multinational corporations—and labor unions lose much of their bargaining power.

However, internationalization makes these corporations even more dependent on transportation. Increasingly, long distance transportation is used not only to deliver supplies and to distribute finished goods, but also to carry parts and components among the different plants of multinational corporations. *Ships and trucks are now part of the global assembly lines* of corporations such as Ford, Toyota, and Texas Instruments. Thus, transportation workers in general and Teamster drivers (and other motor freight workers) in particular, have increased power. Teamster strikes, if spread to shut down all trucking, can now disrupt production all over the world. The potential power of cooperative strike action or (illegal) secondary boycotts by transportation workers of different countries—"in the air, on land, and sea"—is mind-boggling.

Of course, this potential power of transportation workers

will never be translated into real power if unions continue to be dominated by bureaucracies in the United States and abroad. Only rank-and-file movements such as TDU can change this, both by building solidarity among transportation workers independent of union officialdom and perhaps by taking over and transforming their unions and thus making union solidarity possible. If this change is to take place, rank-and-file groups that do exist must be in contact, internationally; new rank-and-file movements must be created; and all these groups must be strengthened. This will not be easily accomplished. Furthermore, the potential power of such a unionism is an indicator of the efforts that employers and governments will exert to prevent transportation workers from disrupting the activities of the multinational corporations.

Taken together, this discussion of the place of trucking in the community and in the international division of labor is sobering. It shows the potential role of TDU and similar movements in resisting the anti-union implications of multinational corporate production, and thus the probability of strong opposition to TDU's success. However, our discussion of the driver in the community indicates that transportation workers need not be alone in these struggles. Once mobilized, they can influence and mobilize other workers, and community groups, to support them in a spirit of union solidarity, and develop a politics to restrain adverse governmental action.

THE INDIVIDUAL AND "THE SYSTEM"

Local 208 sheds light on a classic dilemma facing activists: whether to struggle to change the system from within or without. This choice is a fateful one. It not only affects an activist's effectiveness in making change, but can alter his or her personality as well.

Ed Blackmarr and Alex Maheras both faced this dilemma. Having been elected to Local office as reformers, they had some leeway to set their own course—to fight the employers with direct action and to aid rank and filers in other Locals, or to rely solely on the grievance procedure, and try to reform the IBT from within the bureaucracy. We have seen the results. Let us now consider what they tell us about the individual and the system.

First, consider Blackmarr. He, like Maheras, is honest, and a capable leader. In addition, he was lucky, because he came to office in a situation that seemed to offer a third choice between being in the system or out of it. In his day, the Teamsters were a looser union, with less stringent controls, run in a bonapartist fashion by Hoffa rather than dominated by a thoroughgoing bureaucracy. This let Blackmarr act half "out" by encouraging limited wildcatting but also stay half "in" by establishing a personal relationship with Hoffa and by restraining 208 members from helping rank-and-file movements in other Locals. However, this depended on delicate and uncertain circumstances. When they changed, Blackmarr's approach to reform was shown not to have changed the union outside of 208, and not to have developed a base of support in other Locals that could let him lead a movement against Fitzsimmons. Furthermore his style of leadership was an underlying factor behind many of the weaknesses of the ensuing wildcat (see chapter 7). In addition, during the wildcat, Blackmarr was no longer able to remain half "in" and half "out." Blackmarr's decisions—not to sanction the strike in April, to recall the picketers from Oakland in May, and to agree to 500 firings subject to judgment by the "kangaroo court"—both constituted an ultimate decision to work within the system, and indicate the futility of this choice.

Maheras also has had to choose. He has chosen to fight from within, to try to change the system through channels. He has relied on his remarkable decency to let him resist the seductive charms of high office, and he has succeeded remarkably well in preserving his integrity. His democracy has frayed in spots, as in his delay and then refusal to implement the members' decision to impose an overtime ban in February 1975; but Maheras' honest implementation of membership decisions to support various TDU initiatives indicates that he still respects democratic principles. However, his very integrity underscores the fateful nature of the decision to work from inside, since it means that working from within can be observed and evaluated in a (rare) situation where the reformer is not personally corrupted. And the story of 208 indicates that working from within turns even an honest reformer into a roadblock. As discussed in chapter 9, Maheras has not been able to protect 208's members from the worsening economic conditions, and has taken actions that weaken their ability to defend themselves by direct action. Beyond that, Maheras' strategy has led him to oppose efforts to change the union and to fight the employers from outside the Teamster bureaucracy. Indeed, his integrity has let him effectively retard the growth of TDU in 208. Thus, his "inside-the-system" stance, adopted at a time when working outside the system might have fatally isolated 208, rendered him unwilling to change when conditions changed such that working outside the system would no longer mean isolation, but participation in a growing rank-and-file movement.

Thus, working within the system failed for Maheras, and straddling the issue failed for Blackmarr. Neither led to the lasting reform which both sought. This reinforces the argument that the forces behind union bureaucratization are very powerful and can easily digest the reformer-from-within.

I am not able to resolve the question of whether working outside the system can succeed. The evidence presented herein does support this view—since the successes of the rank and filers in taking over 208 were based in large part on action outside the system, and since TDU has led struggles outside the system. However, TDU (or other rank-and-file groups) must face and overcome two tests before we can say action outside the system can work completely: They must take over and transform a large Local, and resist the forces that will attack them, over a number of years. And, as a further difficult but key test, they would have to take over and transform the IBT—and then maintain rank-and-file control of the union without bureaucratizing or being destroyed by the employers.

DAHRENDORF AND MARX IN RANK-AND-FILE MOVEMENTS

The study of 208 has other theoretical implications as well. Ralf Dahrendorf argues in *Class and Class Conflict in Industrial Society* (1959) that Marx's analysis of class was subtly wrong. What is important, as Dahrendorf sees it, is not the full range of relations among social classes. Instead, what matters is only the patterns of authority *within* organizations. He argues that within any given organization there are those with authority, who make the decisions, and those without authority, who obey. Let us consider what this implies for rank-and-file struggles.

Rank-and-file workers, like those in 208, are seen as members of two different organizations: the company and the union. As workers for the company, they have a conflict with the bosses; and as union members, they have a conflict with union authorities. Using Dahrendorf's theory, there is no a priori reason to think that there will be any stable relationship between those conflicts within the company and those within the union. Marxists, on the other hand, argue that the struggle of workers with employers is the major conflict, with the struggle within the union to be understood as a struggle over whether the union sides with the employers or with the workers. Further, Marxists argue that the stance toward the employers of any group attempting to change a union will shape whether its success within the union will lead to lasting change or only to its bureaucratization after coming into office.

The movement to change Local 208 had two wings: One wing felt that the problem in 208 was the dishonesty of the Local's officials (and of the IBT top officials as well) and their resultant failure to enforce labor contracts through the grievance procedure. This wing, in Dahrendorfian fashion, oriented primarily toward change within the organization. The other wing focused on the need to strengthen the fight against the companies, and saw the fight within the Local as important primarily in order to allow more successful class conflict. Thus, this second wing corresponds to the Marxist theory of industrial strife.

Indeed, the situation in 208 suggests a hypothesis about working-class social movements: They will develop both a class-conflict wing in the full sense and a union-reform wing that orients primarily toward the problems within the union. The differences between TDU and PROD before they merged roughly correspond to this.

I should add a note here on the fates of these wings in 208. The union reformers largely discredited themselves once the representatives of both wings came into office in the early 1960s. They did so through urging the rank and file to respect the contract and to rely solely on grievance procedures—even to the extent of supporting workers who crossed picket lines set up by their coworkers. The wing that oriented toward class conflict, on the other hand, was the moving force in merging workplace struggles with struggles to change the union, and thus led in the development of participatory democracy in the Local and in the battles to improve drivers' working conditions.

KINDS OF WORKER OPPOSITION MOVEMENTS

A number of opposition movements have been discussed in this book, including TURF and the electoral campaign by Sid Cohen against Filipoff as well as rank-and-file oppositions such as TDU and the movement in 208. I want to summarize briefly a way of classifying and thinking about these opposition movements that I have found useful (Friedman 1979).

Opposition movements can focus on challenging the authority of employers; or that of union officials; or both. Thus, many barn activists battle only with the company; the "Dahrendorfian" approach described above focused only on reforming the union; and the dominant wing of the 208 movement challenged both types of authority.

Internally, opposition movements can make their decisions in any of several ways. Often, they are led and controlled by a union officer who is discontented with the direction of the union. One example of this was John T. Williams' campaign for the presidency of Joint Council 42, and another was the "Steelworkers Fight Back" campaign of Ed Sadlowski for president of the United Steelworkers in 1977. Alternatively, the members of a movement can control it democratically themselves, through meetings where they make their own decisions. This was the pattern in the 208 movement and in TDU. A third pattern is the absence of any mechanism for central decision making. The 1970 freight and postal wildcats, considered on a national scale, may have been examples of this.

We can make a diagram (table 11.1) that shows how opposition movements can be classified according to what authorities they challenge and how they reach decisions.

Rank-and-file movements, combining rank-and-file control of the movement with opposition to the authority of both employers and union bureaucracy, seem to be the most effective. The advantages inherent in movements that challenge both sets of authorities have been discussed at length above, and I shall not repeat them. Many of the advantages of rank-and-file democracy over a movement led by dissident officials come from the fact that dissident union officers are tied down by their legal

Table 11.1 Typology of Opposition Movements

Authority that is Challenged	Decision-Making		
	Dissident Official	Rank-and-File Democracy	No Centralized Structure
Union bureaucracy (reform movements)	Bureaucratic reform movements: Williams' Joint Council 42 campaign; Sadlowski campaign	Rank-and-file reform movements: PROD; TURF; Maheras slate against Easley; Miners for Democracy	Reform networks: *Rape of a Membership* network; Pre-Sadlowski steel network
Both union bureaucracy and employers	Messianic utopianism: dreams about Hoffa returning	Rank-and-file movements: TDU 208 Movement's dominant wing; Disabled Miners and Widows	Activist networks: Barn opposition/ defense network during 208 trusteeship; Wildcat network in UMWA in 1977
Employers	"Campaign strikes:" 1946 UAW/GM strike	Rank-and-file direct actions: 1970 Los Angeles freight wildcat (although in some ways it was less democratic than this)	"Spontaneous" direct action: 1970 national postal and freight wildcats

and career links to the bureaucracy, and this leads to their weakening the thrust of their campaigns. Williams' Joint Council 42 campaign illustrates this. Movements with no centralized structure are weakened in other ways. They are unable to coordinate activities in different areas, and this can leave part of the movement bereft of allies when they are needed. Similarly, they have no way to discuss strategy or to undergo collective learning. Finally, although the lack of a centralized structure protects a movement against betrayal by its own central leaders (since there are none), this strength is illusory. The amorphousness of such a movement makes it vulnerable to manipulation by dissident union officials. The 1970 freight wildcat exemplifies these weaknesses, whereas the strengths of rank-and-file democracy were presented in the discussion of the wildcat in Los Angeles.

If I am correct in my assessment of these kinds of movements, there are implications for further work. It would seem useful for activists to organize their movements around rank-and-file democracy rather than looking to dissident officials to lead them or avoiding centralized structures, and to campaign around issues that challenge both the employers and the union bureaucracy. In addition, further research would be useful on a number of topics:

Do different industries produce different kinds of movements? There is some evidence that the nature of steel production makes it hard to take direct action against the employer, and thus opposition movements in steel orient toward union reform. Miners and Teamsters movements orient toward both employers and the union; however, the Miners have been unable to cohere a national rank-and-file group whereas the Teamsters have built TDU. On the other hand, the miners have been more militant than the Teamsters, with frequent wildcats occurring in the mines since the late 1960s.

What kinds of transformations occur in opposition movements? Are activist networks the natural breeding grounds for rank-and-file movements? Under what circumstances do large-scale rank-and-file direct actions against employers spark bureaucratic or reform movements? Under what circumstances, and how, do "spontaneous" direct actions spark the formation of democratic decision-making structures, and thus change into rank-and-file direct actions? And when and how do they decide to target the union bureaucracy as well as the employers, and thus become activist networks or rank-and-file movements?

What kinds of interventions—by employers, union officials, or government—cause changes in the type of movement? Does this vary by industry? Or by the skill category of workers? Or by their race or sex?

What kinds of strategies by groups of worker activists cause changes in the type of movement? Does this vary by industry, skill, race, or sex?

How do these types of movements vary in their relationship to politics, and why? And how does this affect intervention strategies? Thus, it appears that bureaucratic reform movements in the Steelworkers Union take up political issues such as protectionism or the use of South African coal by the industry more readily than TDU or the miners' networks. Why is this? And what is its significance? Thus, does the politics of the steel reform movement represent a control strategy whereby the union officials who lead it pacify potential radical opposition by passing meaningless resolutions? Or does it represent a real difference with implications of a more radical future movement in steel?

A CONCEPT OF "POLITICS"

Local 208 activists never developed "politics." What I mean here is this: the workplace and the situation of a local union are very isolated. People see them as private matters, perhaps fighting issues for the people involved but not "big issues" that shape the whole society. Relatedly, the actors at the workplace and in the union are seen only as individuals, rather than as representatives of large social groupings like "capitalists" or "union bureaucracy." "Politics" means modes of thinking and acting that break out of these narrow conceptions.

Marxism seems to me to be the best framework for such a politics. For instance, Marxist analysis shows that the particular idiosyncrasies of a given manager are shaped and directed by his or her need to run a profitable operation—and that these idiosyncrasies are important in workers' lives only because the whole structure of society reinforces that manager's power. Beyond this, Marxist analysis argues that the major social groupings are classes, and that the power and needs of the class of business owners create a potential unity among the workers of the entire society. Thus, for a Marxist, politics becomes a question of turning this potential solidarity into a real and active cooperation among the working class against the employing class and against a governmental structure that supports this class.

However, one does not have to be a Marxist to understand or to agree with the basic concept of politics that I have put forth. In simple language, politics consists of developing strategies (that is, thought-out plans of long-term action) through which isolated groups of workers can link up with other groups of workers—or with other people, such as those wings of the women's movement that are open to cooperation with workers, who might have parallel interests. Thus, politics involves the search for *issues* around which struggles may make such links. An example is the way socialists and other Teamster activists used the 1976 freight contract fight to establish contact among activists and union reformers around the country and, thus, to lay the basis for Teamsters for a Democratic Union. Another example is the way links were forged between the 208 movement and the civil rights movement in the early 1960s through common struggle against discrimination in beer driving. Such a politics involves analysis—particularly of who and what workers' friends and enemies might be. For instance, the surface plausibility of viewing a higher union official who offers support as a friend disappears when analysis shows that this is a way whereby the bureaucracy protects itself from the rank and file by enmeshing activists in the internal politics of the bureaucracy. Thus, reliance upon Jimmy Hoffa helped 208 on some occasions, but ultimately boxed in the 208 movement and prevented it from developing a wider rank-and-file movement in Los Angeles.

Thus, in conclusion, politics involves thoughtful approaches to situations, strategies, and issues, as well as outreach, alliances, and activism aimed at breaking everyday routine and drawing new people into the struggle. The contrast should be explicit: Apolitical approaches involve a pragmatic search for the "fix"—for the commonsense way to a quick solution: without much thought, without having to reach out to new people, and without taking the risks involved in struggles over the dangerous issues that create links and break isolation.

Political Implications

It is my belief that we face hard times, and a social crisis of a magnitude not seen since World War II. In part, this stems from economic difficulties—difficulties, reflected in peoples' lives by the stagnation in real incomes since the mid-1960s, that include the tax revolt and the increasing emphasis by employers on productivity increases and on "givebacks" in bargaining with unions. One effect of this crisis is the erosion of the social idealism with which some whites responded to the black movement of the 1960s; thus we see widespread acceptance of the weakening of affirmative action programs and of the reduction of social welfare programs as ways to save scarce money at the expense, disproportionately, of blacks. In the international realm, economic difficulties confront the world with a new protectionism, increased international rivalries among formerly allied countries, and—if the crisis deepens to the level of the 1930s—the threat of war. Unfortunately, there is not space here to prove any of this; however, I think most readers will agree that the optimism of the early 1960s was mistaken, and that hard times are likely for the next decade or two.

The 208 experience suggests that working-class social movements are possible in America, and that these social movements can greatly improve our society. The liberating potential of working-class struggle is of course an old dream, so old that many people now look upon it as archaic. But consider 208. Its struggles benefited more than the members of the Local; they created, among the activists of 208, a greater awareness of society, and efforts to support the struggles of black people, of Chicanos, of the peace movement, and of Farmworkers. More would have been possible, but the militants of 208 were so alone, so isolated within labor, that they could not go very far without being crushed; more important, they saw no real basis for believing their power sufficient to make the risks worth taking. But now the situation is different. The same crisis that holds all the problems also presents the opportunity for broader movements of workers based on the common problems that the crisis creates. Already, in the Teamsters, a national rank-and-file movement is being built; already, the Miners have fought the first major battles of what could be the next working-class upsurge.* And, internationally, the Polish workers have shown that social crisis can prompt workers to create enormous movements for workers' democracy and social renewal. Thus, we may yet live to see the early promise of the CIO become reality, and be able to take part in the building of a liberating working class movement in America.

However, the only way such a liberating social movement can develop from workers' struggles against employers' policies

* Already, the labor bureaucracy is trying to develop its own response, and in the recent past the Sadlowski campaign in the Steelworkers split the officialdom's unity and Doug Fraser, President of the UAW, has developed a rhetoric about the employers' class war upon workers.

is by overcoming the resistance of the labor bureaucracy to activism and to class struggle. Lane Kirkland, Roy Williams (the successor of Frank Fitzsimmons), and even Doug Fraser have close ties to the business establishment, and are the leaders of officialdoms with little to gain and much to risk in any new working-class movement. It is worth recalling that the leaders of the American Federation of Labor fought viciously to prevent a working-class upsurge in response to the Great Depression, even allowing their unions' memberships to drop drastically (along with dues incomes!) and strikes to be smashed (as was the 1981 air traffic controllers' strike) rather than break with business unionist ways of conducting their affairs. And the interests of labor officialdom are even more tightly tied to the status quo today.

Finally, the essence of Local 208, of TDU, and of Poland's Solidarity have been their activist workers' democracy. And, indeed, it is through such activist workers' democracy, through struggles that create a *democratic* workers' movement in which power is held at the bottom, by rank-and-file workers who have become active through their struggles with employers and with union bureaucracies, that all else can grow. The example of 208 shows that workers' democracy is radicalizing, that it both teaches lessons critical of the prevailing social order and shows workers that they have the power and creativity with which to change society. This, of course, is the core of what was called "socialism" up until the 1920s (when the term came to mean the bureaucratic nationalization of industry): That workers can create a democratic mass movement with which to reshape society in ways that serve human needs and wishes.

Appendix

Dates
in Local 208
History

1903	208 founded.
1907	208 power broken by Merchants' and Manufacturers' Association.
1937	Pacific Freight Lines strike.
1948	John Filipoff appointed by International as 208 Secretary-Treasurer.
mid-1950s	208 insurgency begins.
1958	Jimmy Hoffa elected Teamster President by IBT Convention.
1959	January–July: Sid Cohen defeats Filipoff for Secretary-Treasurer, finally seated.
	December: Rank-and-file candidates win several Executive Board seats.
1961	May: Following dismissal of Mike Singer as 208 "overseer," 6 members seize 208 offices.
	July: Bylaws Convention.
	September: Hoffa booed at 208 meeting when he presents proposed Western Freight Agreement.
	December: First 208 Business Agent elections.
1962	June: Cohen resigns as Secretary-Treasurer.
	December: Blackmarr and other rank and filers sweep Executive Board elections.
1964	First Master Freight Agreement.
1967	April: Hoffa goes to prison.
	May: Master Freight Agreement negotiated; brief wildcat leads to 10¢ per hour improvement in MFA terms.
1970	April 3: Los Angeles wildcat begins in earnest.
	May 11: Strike spread to San Francisco area by Los Angeles pickets.
	May 13: Students join Teamster pickets in Los Angeles.
	May 18: Continental carriers agree to amnesty; pickets withdrawn from San Francisco.
	May 25: 208 sanctions strike.
	June 2: Wildcat ends.
	July: TURF founded in Denver.
	August: "Kangaroo Court" upholds firings.
	October: Trusteeship imposed on 208.

1972	Trusteeship ends. "Maheras regime" elected to office.
1973	April: Master Freight Agreement "peacefully" negotiated.
1975	Teamsters for a Decent Contract founded.
1976	April: Master Freight Agreement strike; brief Detroit wildcat.
	Summer: Carhaulers' wildcats; IBT Las Vegas Convention.
	September: Teamsters for a Democratic Union formed.
1979	April: Master Freight Agreement brief strike; Steelhaulers' wildcat, ending May 4.
1981	May: Frank Fitzsimmons dies
	June: IBT Las Vegas Convention
1982	March: Master Freight Agreement is settled early, full of givebacks.

Notes

Chapter 1
Bureaucratic
Unionism

1. This position is argued best in Bok and Dunlop (1970) and in Sexton and Sexton (1971).

2. See particularly Aronowitz (1973); Brecher (1972, 1976); Piven and Cloward (1977).

3. General works in the union bureaucracy approach include Hall ed. (1972); Hyman (1971, 1975); Mills (1948); Weir (1972).

4. This discussion is based on: Brecher (1976) ch. 6; Glaberman (1980); Howe and Widick (1948), ch. 5; Weir (1973), pp. 169–172; Preis (1964), Part III; Seidman (1953); and *Radical America* (July–August 1975) 9:4–5, an issue devoted to American labor during the 1940s.

5. U.S. Dept. of Labor 1972:334.

6. Aronowitz (1973); Weir (1967:468).

7. My interpretation of labor law is based on Hall (1972), and on Lynd (1978), as well as my observations of how it affects labor practice in 208 and elsewhere. In addition, standard references such as Zepke (1977) support the viewpoint that labor law is aimed at maintaining production, preventing wildcat strikes, and stabilizing the power of employers and labor officials.

8. Further information on the failure of Landrum-Griffin to protect union democracy can be found in Hall (1972).

9. This discussion relies heavily on my observations of 208. In addition, see Aronowitz (1973) ch. 4; and Spencer (1977).

10. See William Serrin (1974) and Beeler and Kurshenbaum (1969). Beeler and Kurshenbaum are long-time labor leaders whose book is a training manual for union officials.

11. Beeler and Kurshenbaum (1969) is an example.

12. The literature on which this section is based is vast. Mills (1948), Serrin (1974), Michels (1962), and Hyman (1975) are among the most important.

13. James and James (1965) is the best written source. Many informants have related supporting personal experience. Hoffa, it should be added, was no paragon—as will be clarified in chapter 6.

14. Beeler and Kurshenbaum (1969) and Golden and Ruttenberg (1942) are books that exemplify business unionism. So do the pages of almost any central labor council or international union newspaper. See also Mills (1948): (particularly chapter 5); Perlman (1928); and Foster (1947).

Chapter 3
Drivers
and Driving

1. Names and places in this quotation have been changed to protect my informant.

2. I have not been able to check the overall impact of this crackdown with management. Given the difficulty of separating out the effects of the crackdown from those of other attempts to increase productivity, management might well have no way of knowing the effects. However, a wide literature, based on many experiments and studies, supports the notion that productivity increases when workers are given a wide degree of control over how they do their work. This was one of the main contentions of the famous report by the U.S. Department of Health, Education, and Welfare, *Work in America* (1973). Goldman and Van Houten (1980) discusses this literature and how management views it.

Chapter 4
Rank-and-File
Rebellion
in the
Late Fifties

1. Garnel (1972).

2. Blackmarr interview January 25, 1974.

3. Dietrich interview, July 5, 1974.

4. Williams interview, March 8, 1974.

5. Henderson interview, November 12, 1973.

6. Source: *208 News*, April 15, 1959. This newsletter was put out by pro-Filipoff forces while his electoral defeat was being contested.

7. The quotation is from a *Local 208 News Bulletin* issued by Filipoff on November 10, 1958, in an attempt to make it seem like these innovations were his own.

Chapter 5
Rank-and-Filers
in Office

1. IBT Hearings into the Trusteeship over Local 208 (December 16, 1970) 21:2395–2404. (This transcript was made available to me by members of Local 208.)

2. See Sheridan (1972) for a prosecution view of the many trials Hoffa faced.

Chapter 6
Changes
in the Trucking
Industry
and the
Teamsters
Union

1. Sections of this chapter appeared in Friedman (1978); James and James (1965) provided essential background information about the Teamsters in the early 1960's and before.

2. U.S. Bureau of the Census (1953, 1972).

3. *Moody's Transportation Manual* (1954, 1960, 1967, 1974).

4. See chapter 1. Also see: Hall (1972), Mills (1948), and Parenti (1974).

5. This analysis of the Mohn regime's possibilities is based primarily on conjecture about the man's potential policies, given his reputation and his history before then and since. However, the analysis of the drawbacks of a "standard bureaucratic regime" flows from the situation of the times.

6. Many readers may be unfamiliar with Marx's concept of bonapartism. Let me here refer to a few of the main sources. By far the best is Hal Draper's (1977) discussion (chs. 15–18), which reviews the discussion in many of Marx's and Engels' works. To quote a few of Draper's summary descriptions (420–26, 408): 1. The historical role of bonapartism is modernization of the society; 2. The bourgeoisie trades its political rights and power in exchange for the ensurance of economic expansion; 3. The Bonapartist state had to enforce the interests of the class even against the opposition of the class itself or its unenlightened sections. The autonomized state provides the conditions for the necessary modernization of society when no extant class is capable of carrying out this imperative under its own political power; 4. Bonapartism as a state form does not depend on the personal qualities of the dictator in charge; 5. The crux of Bonapartism is the autonomization of the state power with respect to all classes, including the ruling classes; 6. Still, the objective historical result is a social transformation, a "revolution from above." The most famous works on bonapartism are probably Marx's *18th Brumaire* ([1852] 1963) and Engels' *The Role of Force in History* ([1896] 1968). I would also recommend that the reader see Samuel Farber's (1976) analysis of the Batista regime and the coming to power of Castro in Cuba in terms of bonapartism.

Chapter 7
Apolitical
Activism
Ambushed:
The 1970
Wildcat

1. Much of this information was given to me in interviews on the condition that I not identify my sources. Throughout the remainder of this chapter I shall often make very strong claims without citation for similar reasons (and to protect brave and impressive fighters).

2. The evidence for this connection rests in statements made to me by the strike committee members and by Maheras. It should be emphasized that this strategic advice, given in phone calls and in meetings at restaurants, was of a broad nature. It did not concern itself with questions of violence or daily tactics.

3. See Dobbs (1972) and Walker (1971).

4. It is very hard to write about such matters without sounding like a Monday morning quarterback (immune from the pressures of the time) and thus like a fool. Also, it is easy to be wrong, since suggestions made after the battle cannot be tested under the guns. Yet it would be irresponsible not to comment on the strike's weaknesses, since it is through considering past mistakes that one learns to do better, and since it is impossible to understand what did happen without noting the untried alternatives.

To minimize the arbitrariness of my criticisms, I have based them on the experience of other strikes, insofar as possible, and on the criticisms of the strike made to me by participants and leaders of the wildcat. In particular, the following sources will be of interest to those who wish to consult written discussions of strikes: Dobbs (1972) Glatter (1975), McBride (1965), Steuben (1950).

Finally, I draw on my own experiences during the New Jersey State College Teachers Strike of 1974, during which I applied, with considerable success, some of the lessons I learned from the 1970 strike.

5. The Women's Brigade was the subject of a film, "With Babies and Banners."

6. The following discussion is based on Blackmarr's testimony at the Trusteeship Hearing. Thus, it may be false in some important details, particularly as regards what he said when he called Oakland. But regardless of what he said, the effect was disastrous to 500 strikers' jobs.

Chapter 8
Trusteeship

1. These descriptions are based on newspaper accounts and on interviews with members of these locals. Carey is described sympathetically in Steven Brill, *The Teamsters* (1978:156–99).

2. These hearings and the various Exhibits entered into the record are a very valuable resource upon which I have drawn heavily in writing this book. However, they must be used with caution. As in so many legal and quasi-legal proceedings, and as in the statements of U.S. Presidents, you never know when someone is lying.

Chapter 10
Teamster
Rank-and-File
Organize
Nationwide

1. *CONVOY* (May 1979) 37:6. This issue of *CONVOY*, the newspaper of TDU, is very valuable, particularly for those interested in the details of how a successful wildcat is organized.

2. The information for this discussion is based on my involvement with many of the people involved in NJ TDU as a friend and as a helper. In addition, I have interviewed several of the participants about their experiences.

3. The information on which I base this discussion comes primarily from interviews with Pete Camarata, a dock steward in Detroit Local 299 who became a national leader of TDU and a socialist. Other sources on Detroit include other TDU members; numerous articles in the national press; in TDU's *CONVOY* newspaper; other materials produced by TDU; materials written by socialists, particularly I.S. writings; and the extensive discussion of Detroit Teamsters in Moldea (1978).

4. The information for Los Angeles is based on numerous interviews and documents, both public and private.

5. This analysis parallels that made by Gamson (1968) of the use of trust as a resource by power-holders.

Chapter 11
The Many
Meanings
of Local 208

1. This literature is reviewed in Tilly (1978).

2. The classic exemplar of this literature is Kerr and Siegel (1954). See also Hyman (1975), for a more recent discussion.

3. See Lipset et al. (1962) for the view that craft workers are more likely to be involved in their unions and thus to build democratic unions. Marxist analyses are given in Draper (1978:105–13); Hobsbawm (1970:47–56); and Nicolaus (1970:91–101). Mackenzie (1973), and Goldthorpe et al. (1968a, 1968b) present survey results. Hamilton (1972) presents data critical of the "hard hat" thesis as it is applied to American workers. Szymanski (1978: ch. 3) reviews a number of studies on how skill, income and other factors affect worker politics.

4. There has been a mountain of further work on this general topic. This includes, notably, Edwards (1979) and Zimbalist (1979).

5. This discussion is a brief summary of my ms. "The Degradation of Work and Class Conflict in the Los Angeles Trucking Industry."

Bibliography

Aronowitz, Stanley. 1973. *False Promises*. New York: McGraw-Hill.

Beeler, Duane and Harry Kurshenbaum. 1969. *Roles of the Labor Leader*. Chicago: Labor Education Division of Roosevelt University.

Bergston, C. Fred, Thomas Horst, and Theodore H. Moran. 1978. *American Multinationals and American Interests*. Washington, D.C.: The Brookings Institution.

Berman, Daniel M. 1978. *Death on the Job: Occupational Health and Safety Struggles in the United States*. New York: Monthly Review Press.

Bok, Derek C. and John T. Dunlop. 1970. *Labor and the American Community*. New York: Simon and Schuster.

Braverman, Harry. 1974. *Labor and Monopoly Capital*. New York: Monthly Review Press.

Brecher, Jeremy. 1972. *Strike!* San Francisco: Straight Arrow Books.

—— 1976. *Common Sense for Hard Times*. New York: Two Continents.

Brill, Steven. 1978. *The Teamsters*. New York: Simon and Schuster.

Business Week. 1965. "Trucking Rolls Into an Age of Giants." June 12, reprinted in Farris and McElhiney (1967).

—— 1975. "The Teamsters Press for a 44% Package," December 15, p. 26.

—— 1976. "The Teamsters pact sets the pattern" April 19, pp. 34–35.

Cohen, Martin A., and Martin Lieberman. 1949. "Collective Bargaining in the Motor Freight Industry." *Industrial and Labor Relations Review* (October).

Dahrendorf, Ralf. 1959. *Class and Class Conflict in Industrial Society*. Stanford: Stanford University Press.

Dix, Keith, Carol Fuller, Judy Linsky, and Craig Robinson. 1971. *Work Stoppages and the Grievance Procedure in the Appalachian Coal Industry*. Morgantown: Institute for Labor Studies, Division of Manpower and Labor Studies, Appalachian Center, West Virginia University.

Dobbs, Farrell. 1972. *Teamster Rebellion*. New York: Monad Press., 410 West Street, New York City, N.Y. 10014

—— 1973. *Teamster Power*. New York: Monad Press.

—— 1975. *Teamster Politics*. New York: Monad Press.

—— 1977. *Teamster Bureaucracy*. New York: Monad Press.

Domhoff, G. William. 1967. *Who Rules America?* Englewood Cliffs, New Jersey: Prentice-Hall.

—— 1970. *The Higher Circles*. New York: Random House.

Domhoff, G. William and Hoyt B. Ballard eds. 1968. *C. Wright Mills and the Power Elite*. Boston: Beacon Press.

Draper, Hal. 1977. *Karl Marx's Theory of Revolution: Volume I: State and Bureaucracy*. New York: Monthly Review Press.

—— 1978. *Karl Marx's Theory of Revolution: Volume II: The Politics of Social Classes*. New York: Monthly Review Press.

Edwards, Richard. 1979. *Contested Terrain*. New York: Basic.

Ellis, Gordon. 1970. "LA Teamsters Rank-and-File Demand: Re-hiring of all the Wildcat Militants." *People's World* (July 18), p. 8.

Engels, Frederick. 1968. *The Role of Force in History: A Study of Bismarck's Policy of Blood and Iron*. New York: International Publishers.

Farber, Samuel. 1976. *Revolution and Reaction in Cuba, 1933–1960: A Political Sociology from Machado to Castro*. Middletown, Connecticut: Wesleyan University Press.

Farris, Martin T., and Paul T. McElhiney eds. 1967. *Modern Transportation: Selected Readings*. Boston: Houghton Mifflin.

Foster, William Z. 1947. *American Trade Unionism*. New York: International Publishers.

Friedman, Samuel R. 1978. "Changes in the Trucking Industry and the Teamsters Union: The Bonapartism of Jimmy Hoffa." *The Insurgent Sociologist* (Fall-Winter), pp. 52–62.

—— 1979. "Rank-and-File Movements." Presented at annual meeting of the Society for the Study of Social Problems.

—— Ms. "The Degradation of Work and Class Conflict in the Los Angeles Trucking Industry."

Fröbel, Folker, Jorgen Heinrichs, and Otto Kreye. 1980. *The New International Division of Labour*. Cambridge: Cambridge University Press and Paris: Editions de la Maison des Sciences de l'Homme.

Gamson, William. 1968. *Power and Discontent*. Homewood, Illinois: The Dorsey Press.

Garnel, Donald. 1972. *The Rise of Teamster Power in the West*. Los Angeles: University of California Press.

Geschwender, James A. 1977. *Class, Race, and Worker Insurgency: The League of Revolutionary Black Workers*. New York: Cambridge University Press.

Glaberman, Martin. 1980. *Wartime Strikes: The Struggle Against the No-Strike Pledge In the UAW During World War II*. Detroit: Bewick Editions.

Glatter, Pete. 1975. "London Busmen: Rise and Fall of a Rank-and-File Movement." *International Socialism* (January) 74:5–11. (Available in many libraries or from 8 Cottons Gardens, London, E2, England.)

Golden, Clinton S. and Harold J. Ruttenberg. 1942. *The Dynamics of Industrial Democracy*. New York: Harper.

Goldman, Paul, and Donald R. Van Houten. 1980. "Uncertainty, Conflict, and Labor Relations in the Modern Firm I: Productivity and Capitalism's 'Human Face,'" *Economic and Industrial Democracy: An International Journal* (February) 1:63–98.

Goldthorpe, John D., David Lockwood, Frank Bechhofer, and Jennifer Platt. 1968a. *The Affluent Worker: Industrial Attitudes and Behavior*. London: Cambridge University Press.

—— 1968b. *The Affluent Worker: Political Attitudes and Behavior*. London: Cambridge University Press.

Green, Jim. 1978. "Holding The Line: Miners' Militancy and the Strike of 1978." *Radical America* (May–June) 12:3–27.

Hall, Burton H. ed. 1972. *Autocracy and Insurgency in Organized Labor*. New Brunswick, New Jersey: Transaction Books.

Hamilton, Richard F. 1972. *Class and Politics in the United States*. New York: Wiley.

Hobsbawm, Eric. 1970. "Lenin and the 'Aristocracy of Labor.'" *Monthly Review* (April) 21:47–56.

Howe, Irving, and B. J. Widick. 1948. *The UAW and Walter Reuther*. New York: Random House.

Hume, Brit. 1971. *Death and the Mines*. New York: Grossman Publishers.

Hyman, Richard. 1971. *Marxism and the Sociology of Trade Unionism*. London: Pluto Press.

—— 1975. *Industrial Relations: A Marxist Introduction*. London: The MacMillan Press, Ltd.

International Teamster. 1970. "National Freight Negotiations (An analysis)," July, p. 10.

James, Ralph C., and Estelle Dinerstein James. 1965. *Hoffa and the Teamsters: A Study of Union Power*. Princeton: Van Nostrand Company.

Johnson, James C. 1973. *Trucking Mergers: A Regulatory Viewpoint*. Lexington, Massachusetts: Lexington Books.

Kerr, Clark, and Abraham Siegel. 1954. "The Interindustry Propensity to Strike—An International Comparison," in Kornhauser et al. (1954), pp. 189–212.

Kornhauser, Arthur, Robert Dubin, and Arthur M. Ross eds. 1954. *Industrial Conflict*. New York: McGraw-Hill.

Leiter, Robert D. 1957. *The Teamsters Union: A Study of Its Economic Impact*. New York: Bookman Associates.

Lipset, Seymour Martin, Martin Trow, and James Coleman. 1962. *Union Democracy*. Garden City, New York: Anchor Books.

Lynd, Staughton. 1973. *American Labor Radicalism: Testimonies and Interpretations*. New York: John Wiley and Sons.

—— 1978. *Labor Law for the Rank & Filer*. San Pedro, California: Singlejack Books.

McBride, John. 1966. "Philadelphia Teamsters Strike: 1965." *American Socialist* (Spring), pp. 5–18.

Mackenzie, Gavin. 1973. *The Aristocracy of Labor: The Position of Skilled Craftsmen in the American Class Structure.* London: Cambridge University Press.

Marschall, Daniel. 1978. "The Miners and the UMW: Crisis in the Reform Process." *Socialist Review* (July–August) 8:65–116.

Marx, Karl. 1963. *The Eighteenth Brumaire of Louis Bonaparte.* New York: International Publishers.

—— 1967. *Capital.* New York: International Publishers.

Michels, Robert. 1962. *Political Parties: A Sociological Study of the Oligarchical Tendencies of Modern Democracy.* New York: The Free Press.

Mills, C. Wright. 1948. *The New Men of Power: America's Labor Leaders.* New York: Harcourt, Brace.

—— 1956. *White Collar: The American Middle Classes.* New York: Oxford University Press.

—— 1959. *The Power Elite.* New York: Oxford University Press.

Moldea, Dan E. 1978. *The Hoffa Wars: Teamsters, Rebels, Politicians, and the Mob.* New York: Paddington Press.

Moody, Kim, and Jim Woodward. 1978. *Battle Line: The Coal Strike of '78.* Detroit: The Sun Press.

Moody's Transportation Manual. 1954. New York: Moody's Investors Service, Inc.

—— 1960.

—— 1967.

—— 1974.

Mukherjee, Santosh. 1978. *Restructuring of Industrial Economies and Trade with Developing Countries.* Geneva: International Labour Office.

Nicolaus, Martin. 1970. "The Theory of the Labor Aristocracy." *Monthly Review* (April) 21:91–101.

Nyden, Paul John. 1974. *Miners for Democracy.* New York: PhD diss. Columbia University. Available from University Microfilms, Ann Arbor, Michigan.

Paff, Ken. 1980. "Rebuilding the Labor Movement at the Grass Roots: Teamsters for a Democratic Union." Detroit: Teamster Rank and File Educational and Legal Defense Foundation.

Parenti, Michael. 1974. *Democracy for the Few.* New York: St. Martin's.

Peck, Sidney M. 1963. *The Rank-and-File Leader.* New Haven: College and University Press.

Perlman, Selig. 1928. *The Theory of the Labor Movement.* New York: MacMillan.

Piven, Frances Fox, and Richard A. Cloward. 1977. *Poor People's Movements.* New York: Pantheon Books.

Preis, Art. 1964. *Labor's Giant Step.* New York: Pathfinder Press.

PROD. 1976. *Teamster Democracy and Financial Responsibility.* Washington, D.C.: PROD, Inc.

Radical America. 1975. Special Issue on Labor during the 1940s (July–August).

Raskin, Abraham H. 1953. "Union Leader—and Big Business Man." *New York Times* November 15.

Robson, R. Thayne. 1959. "The Trucking Industry." *Monthly Labor Review* (May) 82:547–51.

Romer, Sam. 1962. *The International Brotherhood of Teamsters: Its Government and Structures.* New York: Wiley.

Rose, Arnold M. 1952. *Union Solidarity.* Minneapolis: The University of Minnesota Press.

Seidman, Joel. 1953. *American Labor from Defense to Reconversion.* Chicago: The University of Chicago Press.

Selznick, Philip. 1969. *TVA and the Grass Roots.* New York: Harper.

Serrin, William. 1974. *The Company and the Union.* New York: Vintage Books.

Sexton, Patricia Cayo and Brendan Sexton. 1971. *Blue Collars and Hard Hats.* New York: Random House.

Sheridan, Walter. 1972. *The Fall and Rise of Jimmy Hoffa.* New York: Saturday Review Press.

Spencer, Charles. 1977. *Blue Collar: An Internal Examination of the Workplace.* Chicago: Lakeside-Charter Books.

Steuben, John. 1950. *Strike Strategy.* New York: Gaer Associates.

Stone, Kathy. 1973. "The Origins of Job Structures in the Steel Industry." *Radical America* (November–December), pp. 19–64.

Szymanski, Albert. 1978. *The Capitalist State and the Politics of Class.* Cambridge: Winthrop Publishers, Inc.

Teamsters, International Brotherhood of. 1970. *Transcript of Hearings into the Trusteeship over Local 208.* Los Angeles: unpublished document.

Tilly, Charles. 1978. *From Mobilization to Revolution.* Reading, Massachusetts: Addison-Wesley.

U.S. Bureau of the Census. 1953. *County Business Patterns 1951.* Washington, D.C.: Government Printing Office.

—— 1972. *County Business Patterns 1971.* Washington, D.C.: U.S. Government Printing Office.

U.S. Bureau of Labor Statistics. 1977. *Employment and Earnings, United States, 1909–75.* Bulletin 1312–10. Washington, D.C.: U.S. Government Printing Office.

U.S. Department of Health, Education and Welfare. 1973. *Work in America.* Cambridge: MIT Press.

U.S. Department of Labor. 1972. *Handbook of Labor Statistics.*

Walker, Charles Rumford. 1971. *American City: A Rank-and-File History.* New York: Arno Press.

Weber, Max. 1957. *The Theory of Social and Economic Organization* (Edited by Talcott Parsons). New York: Oxford University Press.

—— 1958. *From Max Weber: Essays in Sociology*. (Edited by H. H. Gerth and C. Wright Mills). New York: Oxford University Press.

Weinberg, Jack. n.d. *Detroit Auto Uprising 1973*. Highland Park, Michigan: Network Publishing Group.

Weir, Stanley Lewis. 1967. *U.S.A.—The Labor Revolt*. Boston: New England Free Press.

—— 1972. "Class Forces in the '70's." *Radical America* (May–June), pp. 31–77.

—— 1973. "Rank-and-File Labor Rebellions Break into the Open: The End of an Era." In Lynd ed. (1973), pp. 169–72.

Will, Buck. 1980. "Teamster Reformers Unite, Look Ahead." *Changes* (March) 2:25–33.

Wolfinsohn, Dave. 1980. "TDU: Problems and Prospects." *Against the Current* (Fall) 1:33–43.

Wyckoff, D. Daryl, and David H. Maister. 1977. *The Motor-Carrier Industry*. Lexington, Massachusetts: Lexington Books.

Yarrow, Michael N. 1979. "The Labor Process in Coal Mining: Struggle for Control," in Zimbalist (1979).

Zepke, Brent. 1977. *Labor Law*. Totowa, New Jersey: Littlefield, Adams.

Zimbalist, Andrew ed. 1979. *Case Studies on the Labor Process*. New York: Monthly Review Press.

Index

Abel, I. W., 18
Acme Fast Freight, 147
"Action for Hoffa," 135
Activism, 206–7, 227, 233, 248–49, apolitical, 136–38, 183–84, 189–90, 208, 272, 273; in coal industry, 54–55; resistance of labor bureaucracy to, 275. *See also* Militancy; Rank and file; Teamsters Union Local 208; Unionism, activist
Activists: changing system from within or without, 265–67, 268–69; coopted, 15, 82, 178; effect of legalism on, 199–200; effect of 1970 wildcat on, 167, 168; readiness of, to support other workers, 256 (*see also* Outreach); and rebureaucratization, 237; and TDU, 242–43. *See also* Student activists; Unionism, activist
Activists, Local 208, 5, 6, 37, 42–44, 61–62, 89–91, 255; fighting trusteeship, 182–88; pride of, 97, 100, 102, 105; problems faced by, 100–14; after trusteeship, 189–208. *See also* Teamsters Local 208
AFL–CIO, 87
Airline attendants, 3
Air traffic controllers' strike (1981), 275
Alexander, George, 93
Allan, Doug, 213, 218n, 239, 240
American Federation of Labor (AFL), 241, 257, 258, 275
American Federation of State, County, and Municipal Employees (AFSCME), 7
American Federation of Teachers, 9

Apathy, 96, 135, 227, 228; in Local 208, 239
Authority, patterns of, 267–68
Autocracy, 247–51
Auto industry, 222–23, 258
Automation, 17. *See also* Technology
Autonomy, local, 124–25
Autoworkers, 24–25, 257. *See also* United Auto Workers.

Bargaining, 117–19, 123, 127. *See also* Contract negotiations
Bargaining agencies, 120
Barn organization, 69–70, 90, 96, 97–100, 154, 182, 185–86, 188, 198, 237, 242, 243; election campaigns and, 234; post-trusteeship (208), 208–9; and TDC, 213–14; and TDU, 218, 220–21, 233; and the trusteeship (208), 176–77
Barns: number of, 53–54; term, 10
Barrett, Eddie, 68
BART subway system (San Francisco), 261n
Batista y Zaldivar, Fulgencio, 128
Beck, Dave, 2–3, 31, 32, 60, 125, 130
Beeler, Duane, 26
Bismarck, Otto von, 128
Black Caucus, 61, 77, 114, 153
Blacklisting, 139, 170
Blackmarr, Edwin, 31n, 81, 93, 94, 108, 141, 175, 189, 198, 208; approach to reform, 265–66, 267; in 1970 wildcat, 139, 142, 152, 159n, 161–63; retired, 186; as Secretary-Treasurer, 208, 89, 95, 96, 99, 102, 104, 105, 106, 107, 111, 113, 115; ties of strike leaders to, 162–63

Black movement, 6, 154, 252; weakening of, 273–74. See also Racism
Blacks, 67, 111–13, 144–46. See also Racism
Blue Collar (film), 1
Blue Collars and Hard Hats (Sexton and Sexton), 1
Bonapartism, 128–29, 134–35, 266; historical role of, 281n6; in Hoffa strategy, 126–27, 129–30, 131–32
Boyle, Tony, 237
Braverman, Harry, 259, 260, 261, 262; Labor and Monopoly Capital, 1
Breaks, 46, 48, 50, 53
Brenner, Charles, 94–95
Brightwell, George, 200
Bureaucracy: social theory re, 247–49
Bureaucracy, union, 13–33, 53–54, 235, 246–47; Hoffa and, 110–11, 131–35; interests of, different from those of rank and file, 106, 198, 215; resistance of, to activism and class struggle, 275; response of, to working-class upsurge, 274n; Southern California, 224, 254, 255; and trend toward bureaucratic society, 249–51; unwilling to mobilize rank and file, 241–42; used threat of trusteeship to keep rank and file in line, 171–72, 177. See also Officials
Bureaucratic rationalization, 249–51
Bureaucratization, 124, 267; contractual unionism and, 20–26; ideology of, 30–32; prevention of, in TDU, 226, 231–34; as problem for 208 militants, 100–6. See also Rebureaucratization
Busacca, Sam, 171
Business agents, 53, 92, 200; and grievance procedure, 21–22, 39; Local 208, 35, 36–37, 42, 71, 82, 85–89, 92, 104–5, 178, 186–87; and organization of rank anf file, 204
Business unionism, 14, 30–32, 198, 232, 275
Business Week, 121
Butler, John, 49, 84, 89, 96, 99, 109, 157
Bylaws, 236. See also Teamsters Local 208

California: right-to-work referendum, 70; trucking industry, 5
California Division of Industrial Relations, 5
California Trucking Association (CTA), 145–46, 148, 199
Camarata, Pete, 214–15, 217, 218, 224
Canada: labor law, 20n
Cannery workers, 3
Capitalism, 30, 250–51, 255–56, 262–63
Carey, Ron, 171
Carhaulers, carhauling, 214, 215, 225, 227, 228, 240, 258; 1976 strike, 243
Castro, Fidel, 128
Central States Pension Fund, 134
Change(s), 100; in trucking industry and Teamsters Union, 116–35
Change of operations, 4, 119, 135, 196–97
Chavez, Cesar, 3
Chicago: 1970 wildcat, 137
Chicago Truck Drivers Union, 137
Chicanos, 154, 274
Chrysler: Mack Avenue plant, 17
CIO, 16, 248, 256, 274
Civil rights movement, 84, 273
Class and Class Conflict in Industrial Society (Dahrendorf), 267–68
Class conflict, 33, 237–38, 250, 251–52, 268, 272; in crisis periods, 256; in 1970 wildcat, 160; resistance of labor bureaucracy to, 275
Cleveland Businessmen Against the Teamsters' Strike, 160
Cliquism, 96–97; in leadership of 1970 wildcat, 157, 162–65
Coalition for a Good Contract (CGC), 222–23
Coal miners, mining, 54–55, 247, 256, 274; opposition movements in, 271; strikes, 21, 164, 215. See also United Mine Workers
Cohen, Sid, 70–73, 85, 86n, 105, 175, 186, 269; as Secretary-Treasurer of Local 208, 73–75, 77–81, 82, 84, 88, 90
Collins, Paul, 72
Communication, 53, 54–55, 97; in rank-

and-file organization of Local 208, 68, 254
Communist Party (U.S.), 16, 19
Computers, 121. *See also* Technology
Consciousness, 257; class, 252; and rank-and-file organization, 222–23
Consolidated Freightways (co.), 118, 147, 182
Container: defined, 64
Contract(s), 13, 16, 20–21, 101–2, 117, 193, 268; aggressive policing of, 92–93; area-wide, 130; enforcement of, by stewards and officers, 15–16; national, 6, 42, 100, 110–11, 119, 126, 131–32, 160, 241, 248 (*see also* Master Freight Agreement); need to allow strikes in, 236; Southern California, 63; suit for breach of, 19; UPS, 118–19; weakening of, 40
Contract negotiations, 4, 13, 32, 219–21, 273; and bureaucratization, 22–26, 29, 236. *See also* Master Freight Agreement; Strategic discussion
Contractual unionism, 13, 20–26
Convoy (newspaper), 211, 213
Convoy-Dispatch (newspaper), 215, 229
Cooptation, 15, 82, 178
Corruption, 2–3, 19, 28, 54, 171, 246; lack of, in 208, 104–5; Teamsters Union, 28, 123, 124, 126, 127, 222, 254
Cotrell, Sharon, 212–13
Craft unions, 34, 254, 257–59, 260
Croysdill, William, 88, 89
Culture, working class, 255–57, 259–63; social organizing 65–68. *See also* ch. 3.
Cynicism, 96, 227, 229, 244

Dahrendorf, Ralf: *Class and Class Conflict in Industrial Society*, 267–69
Debs, Eugene, 238
Decision-making, 23–24, 269; in 1970 wildcat, 140–41, 150–52
Democracy, union, 19–20, 28, 224, 269–71; activist workers, 275; bureaucracy and, 246; in Local 208, 5,

6, 36–38, 42–44; in TDC, 214; in TDU, 215. *See also* Unionism, activist
Denver-Chicago (co.), 70
De-skilling, 259, 261
Detroit: TDU in, 216, 217–19, 224, 225–26, 235, 249
Dietrich, Eddie, 61, 65, 66, 67, 88, 89, 93, 229
Diplomacy: problem-solving through, 191, 193, 198
Direct action, 63, 69, 183, 189, 245, 265; balance of, with electoral activity, 234; Local 208, 42–43, 93–94, 102, 106; organization for, 208; power of, given up in grievance procedure, 101; and rank-and-file movement, 271; repression of, 236, 246; small-scale, 229, 230
Discipline, 15–16, 251–52
Discussion, informal, 41, 53, 70, 98, 182. *See also* Communication; Strategic discussion
Dissidents: punishment of, 22. *See also* Activists
Division of labor, 259–63; international, 264–65; strategic position of truck drivers in, 263–65
Drivers. *See* Truck drivers
Dynamics of Industrial Democracy, The (Golden and Ruttenberg), 15

Easley, James, 170–71, 174, 175, 176, 178–83, 187, 189
Economic conditions, 115, 130, 135, 169; and activist unionism, 196–97; and creation of social movements, 255–56; and labor militancy, 16–17; and legalism, 198–99; and rank-and-file organization, 221–22, 223, 224, 228, 233, 241, 243; and social crisis, 29, 273–74
Economy, the, 100, 117
Elections, 224. *See also* Teamsters Local 208, elections
Electoralism, 230, 232–34

Employees of trucking companies, 116–17, 118T. *See also* Activists; Rank and file; Workers

Employers, 2, 6, 30, 59, 62, 63, 105, 120–23; change of operations by, 4, 119, 135, 196–97; in class conflict with workers, 251–52; collusion of union leaders with, 15–16, 17–18, 29, 69, 197, 221, 246, 247; as enemy in 1970 wildcat, 159–61; retaliation by, 229; union bureaucracy product of, 250. *See also* Management

England: labor law, 20*n*

Ferrell, Cam, 88

Fifth Wheel (newspaper), 211

Filipoff, John, 81, 90, 186, 269; Local 208 under, 60–62, 63, 67, 68–69, 70, 71–72, 73

Firings, 95–96, 176, 223; in 1970 wildcat, 6, 54, 138, 139, 151–52, 154, 157, 158, 161, 163, 165, 168, 169, 189–90

Fitzsimmons, Frank, 3, 17, 23, 107, 126*n*, 130, 132*n*, 171, 266, 275; and attacks on corruption, 222; elected IBT president, 110*n*; feud with Hoffa, 224, 225; handling of MFA, 108, 212; as head of Teamsters, 134, 135, 165; and Local 208, 32; in 1970 wildcat, 137–38, 139, 149, 159, 161, 162, 169; policy of encouraging employer profits, 181; prestige as statesman, 27*n*; sold out Teamsters, 198; in steelhaulers' strike, 209; and 208 trusteeship, 6, 166, 170–71, 172, 173, 174, 182

Flint (Michigan) strike, 156

Fontaine, Bill, 82

Foster, William Z., 157–58

Fram, Robert, 242

Franklin, John, 49–50, 103, 175

Fraser, Doug, 274*n*, 275

Fraternal Association of Steelhaulers (FASH), 209*n*

Freight industry, 10; Los Angeles, 60, 259–60

Freight, movement of, 3. *See also* Trucking industry

From the Horse's Mouth (newspaper), 211

Garrett (co.), 221

General Motors, 24, 134, 156; 1937 strike, 164

Gibbons, Harold, 152, 161

G. I. Trucking, 82

"Givebacks," 241, 273

Golden, Clinton S., and Harold J. Ruttenberg: *The Dynamics of Industrial Democracy*, 15

Grapevine (newspaper), 9, 213, 219

Great Depression, 14, 241, 275

Great Lakes Express, 18

Greyhound, 77

Grievance: defined, 38

Grievance panels, 110, 132; in 1970 wildcat, 139, 152, 161, 163, 165, 169–70; used to undercut Local 208, 107

Grievance procedure, 13, 40, 177, 230, 246; and bureaucratization, 21–23, 236; Local 208, 38–39, 42, 92–93; power of direct action lost to, 101–2; reliance on, 246, 247, 265, 268; reliance on, post-trusteeship (Local 208), 190, 191–92, 193, 196, 197, 198, 199–200; as tool to prevent activism, 192

Grievances, 35, 69, 229, 248; under national contract, 131, 132

Harding, Jim, 89, 149

Harassment, 50, 115, 176, 184

Health and welfare benefits, 21, 94–95

Henderson, Jim, 62

Hiring hall, 54, 64, 88, 90, 207, 208, 254; as center of rank-and-file militancy, 67–69, 70; racism in, 111–12

Hoffa, Jimmy, 28, 31–32, 52, 71, 72, 73, 74, 106, 159, 163, 266; built bureaucratic power in Teamsters Union, 128, 131–35; disappearance of, 134, 222; feud with Fitzsimmons, 224, 225; and Local 208, 32, 81–89, 90, 107–10, 127–28, 130–31, 133, 198, 254, 273; poor press of, 27*n*; as president of Teamsters, 126–31; in prison, 2–3,

108, 110, 134, 198; reorganization of
   Teamsters Union under, 116, 124, 127,
   128, 131, 134, 241; smothered activism,
   128
Hoffa Defense Breakfast, 108
Holmes, Bobby, 218

Independent Skilled Trades Council, 258
Industrial Relations Act (England), 20n
Inflation, 4, 135, 198, 231
Information, 148, 180–81; lack of, 1970
   wildcat, 144, 151. *See also*
   Communication
Injury(ies), 4, 5, 17, 49–50
International Brotherhood of Teamsters,
   Chauffeurs, Warehousemen, and
   Helpers of America (IBT). *See*
   Teamsters Union
International Socialists (IS), 211, 216n
International Teamster, 160
Isolation, 9–10, 228, 244–45, 272; of
   Local 208, 110, 198, 238, 240, 274. *See
   also* Outreach
Issues: in membership meetings, 41; in
   1970 wildcat, 138, 168; in politics, 273

Job security, 251–52; Local 208, 37; of
   officials, 27–28. *See also* Firings;
   Layoffs
Joint Western grievance hearings (San
   Francisco), 39

Kennedy, Robert, 72, 124, 128
Kirkland, Lane, 275
Kroger Connection, The (newsletter), 216
Kroger grocery chain, 215–16
Kurbatoff, Pete, 170
Kurshenbaum, Harry, 26

Labastida, Mannie, 199
Labor and Monopoly Capital
   (Braverman), 1, 259–62
Labor aristocracy, 257–59
Labor laws, U.S., 13, 18–20, 101, 123
Labor movement (U.S.), 14–18, 19, 29;
   opposition of business to, 124. *See
   also* Rank and file organization;
   Unionism

Labor relations, 121–23, 251
Landrum-Griffin Act, 19–20, 123, 147,
   171
Layoffs, 4, 18, 29, 120, 169, 176, 196;
   auto industry, 223; and rank-and-file
   organization, 228
Leadership, 2, 199, 226–27, 256; Local
   208, 254
Leaseway (co.), 218
Legalism, 13, 20, 22, 43, 132, 207–8, 230,
   245, 246; in fight against trusteeship
   (208), 186–88, 198–200; in grievance
   procedures, 39, 101; in Maheras
   regime, 190–95
Leiter, Robert D., 125
Local(s): and rank-and-file organization,
   69–71, 89–91
Lockouts, 23, 122–23
Long Beach grievance hearings, 39
Long Beach Local 692, 152, 224
Los Angeles (area): freight carrying in,
   34; TDC in, 213, 214; TDU in, 216,
   219–21, 224, 258
Los Angeles Dock and Office Workers,
   Local 357, 68–69
Lying, 22–23. *See also* Trust

McCarthy, Bill, 152
McClellan, John, 72
McKiernan, Eddie, 143, 151, 153, 156
Maheras, Alex, 89, 93, 106, 113–14, 135,
   141, 173, 242; joined TURF, 185; in
   1970 wildcat, 142, 161; as Secretary-
   Treasurer, Local 208, 187–88, 189,
   190–99, 204, 208, 235; reform of
   system from within, 238–40, 265,
   266–67; and trusteeship, 175–76, 178,
   186–87
Majority Contract Coalition, 239
Management, 50, 92–96, 252; power of,
   through division of labor, 259, 260–62;
   sophisticated, 116, 120–21, 199. *See
   also* Employers; Trucking companies
Management-union (grievance)
   committees, 131–32
Manufacturing, 264
Marx, Karl, 238; *Capital*, 252
Marxism, 1–2, 255–56, 267–69, 272–73

Master Freight Agreement (MFA), 4, 9, 20–21, 25, 110, 115, 122, 128, 131, 184, 190, 209; in danger of collapse, 241, 242; first, 107, 108; and 1970 wildcat, 137–38; *1976*, 210–12, 214, 222; *1979*, 215, 220, 239; weakening of, 135
Matula, Frank, Jr., 81
Membership meetings, 41, 97, 205–7
Merchants' and Manufacturers' Association (M & M), 59, 160
Mergers, 65–66, 116, 119–20, 121, 196
MFA. *See* Master Freight Agreement
Michels, Robert, 231, 247
Milieu(s): dialectics of, 255–57; of driving, 51–52, 53–55, 254; and rank-and-file organization, 222, 223, 224
Militancy, 17, 67–69, 96, 101, 243; downturns in, 228–30; milieu and, 51–52, 255. *See also* Activism
Mills, C. Wright, 249
Minneapolis Teamsters, 18; strike of *1934*, 14, 147, 156, 164, 263
Mohn, Einar, 74, 126
Moody's Transportation Manual, 117
Morale, 187, 190, 198, 223; activism and, 42–43, 199; in 1970 wildcat, 143, 144, 151–52, 157, 158, 163–64, 168, 169, 170; and the trusteeship, 177–78
Motor Trucking Association of Southern California, 82
Multinational corporations, 264, 265
Murrietta, Archie, 93–94, 96, 98, 146–47, 189, 190, 206; conservatism of, 191, 194, 195; in 1970 wildcat, 140, 141; on 1970 wildcat, 146, 147, 148, 150–51, 152, 153, 155, 157, 161, 162, 163; and trusteeship, 173, 174, 178, 179, 186

Nader, Ralph, 211
Napoleon I, 128
National Labor Relations Board (NLRB), 19, 69
Networks, 44, 54. *See also* Communication
New Jersey, 48, 158; TDU in, 216–17, 224
Newspapers, union, 42, 151, 183, 185, 194, 195, 205, 211, 215

New York Joint Council, 126
Nixon, Richard, 6, 17, 27*n*
No-strike clause, 13, 18, 19, 20–21, 236
No-strike pledge, 16. *See also* Strikes
Numerical control programs, 261

Oakland (Calif.) Teamsters, 153
Office, lure of, 79, 83, 168
Officials, 6, 13–14, 15, 18, 35–36, 37, 124; are anti-worker, 4, 5, 100; baronial power of, 125–27, 128, 130, 131; benefits of bureaucracy to, 100–1, 106, 132, 236; collusion with management, 15–16, 17–18, 29, 69, 197, 221, 246, 247; contempt for rank and file, 26–27; failed to protect membership, 138; and grievance procedure, 21–22, 63; interests of, different from those of workers, 27–30, 246, 247; limited ability to affect what goes on in barns, 53–54; limited initiative and power of members (208), 103–4; in 1970 wildcat, 149–50, 159–60, 161, 165, 168; pension fund, 132, 134; police their members, 21; power of, 13, 20, 21, 23–26, 210; selling out rank and file, 29, 32, 52, 100, 115, 134, 135; and union bureaucracy, 26–30; workers' concept of, 246
Ohio National Guard, 137
Oligarchy, iron law of, 247–51
On the Waterfront (film), 1
Opportunism, 83, 97, 104, 182, 185
Organization: and bureaucracy, 247–51; by large companies, 122–23; social context of, 221–26
Organizing drive(s), 97, 126–27, 133. *See also* Rank and file
Organized crime, 3, 124
Outreach, 106–7, 245; lack of, Local 208, 108–10, 152–53, 166, 173–74, 184, 190, 198, 245; in 1970 wildcat, 152–54, 166; strategies of, 272–73; by TDU, 226, 230–31, 237–38

Pacific Freight Lines (PFL), 59–60, 65–66

Pacific Intermountain Express (PIE), 63
Pacific Motor Transport (PMT), 61,
    64–67, 70, 88, 90, 93, 107, 140, 147,
    165; division among workers at, 167;
    organization of, 98, 99; under
    trusteeship, 177
Paff, Ken, 234
Patronage, 85, 133
Patton, Pat, 75–76, 84–85, 88, 89, 95,
    109, 159n
Peace movement, 6, 252, 274
Pension funds, 3, 28, 94–95, 184n, 215;
    for Teamster officials, 132, 134
Picketing, 19, 170, 183; 1970 wildcat,
    142–47, 164
Picket Line (newspaper), 7, 167, 183n
Piggybacking, 64, 65, 66
Pig-yard, 64, 66
Plans, planning, 53, 245–46. See also
    Strategy; Tactics
PMT. See Pacific Motor Transport
PMT Club, 65
Politics, 168; class issue in, 237–38;
    concept of, 272–75; and rank-and-file
    organization, 231, 256; of trucking
    industry, 117; union, 41, 89, 90. (see
    also Activism, apolitical; Unionism,
    activist); and worker opposition
    movements, 265, 271–72; of
    workplace, 259
Postal workers, 154, 160
Power, 2, 55, 90, 129, 210, 275;
    monopolized by officials, 13, 20, 21; of
    rank and file, 18, 19, 26, 83; of
    Teamsters Union, 3–4, 115, 117; of
    union, is in power of workers, 248,
    250–51; use of, in bureaucracy, 250
Pride, 97, 100, 102, 105
PROD, 210n, 211, 212, 215, 217, 256, 268
Production: breaks and, 48; control over
    speed of, 55; power to disrupt, 18, 21
Productivity, 17, 18, 32, 55, 115, 121,
    196, 221, 231, 252, 273; and division of
    labor, 259
Profits, 16, 30, 32, 50, 117, 130, 181; and
    social good, 262
Protectionism, 274
Provenzano, Tony, 216n

Provenzano [crime] family, 216
Public opinion, 123, 127, 254

Quintero, Al, 89

Racism, 67, 71, 77, 100; and activist
    unionism, 111–14; in auto industry,
    222; in Local 208, 176, 245; in 1970
    wildcat, 144–46
Radical workers movement, 33, 270–75
Rank and file, 15, 21, 44, and business
    unionism, 30, 32; during Cohen period,
    73–74, 77–81; disorganized by Hoffa,
    133; instruments to keep in line,
    171–72, 181; labor aristocracy and,
    257–59; national organization of, 166,
    197, 209–43; in office (208), 92–115;
    support for Hoffa, 127, 130; and union
    bureaucracy, 33; unrest, 135; value of,
    in contract negotiations, 25–26. See
    also Democracy; Unionism, activist
Rank-and-file committees: in fight against
    trusteeship (208), 182–84, 186
Rank-and-file local: study of, 7–10
Rank-and-file organization, 2, 244–47,
    265; advantages of, 269–71; influence
    of truck drivers on, 262, 263–64;
    patterns of authority and, 267–69;
    social context of, 221–26; threat of, in
    Teamsters crisis, 123, 125, 127. See
    also Rank and file, national
    organization of; Teamsters for a
    Democratic Union
Rank & File News (newsletter), 79–80
Rank and File Speaks, The (newspaper),
    218, 226n
Rape of the Membership (leaflet
    campaign), 179–81, 183
Raskin, A. H., 125
Rebureaucratization, 43, 100; preventing
    of, by TDU, 226, 235–38
Recession(s), 135, 196, 198
Redbaiting, 16, 19, 146, 212
Right-to-Work referendum (California),
    70
Risk(s), 54, 101, 183; in rank-and-file
    organization, 221–22, 231; willingness
    to take, 95–96, 230, 243

Roadway (co.), 215, 243
Romer, Sam, 31
Roosevelt, Franklin D., 15
Ruttenberg, Harold J., Clinton S. Golden
    and: *The Dynamics of Industrial
    Democracy*, 15

Sabotage, 69, 93–94, 101, 183, 190; 1970
    wildcat, 144, 169–70. *See also* Direct
    action
Sadlowski, Ed, 269, 274*n*
Safety, 5, 66. *See also* Injury(ies)
Safeway (co.), 226
Salinger, Pierre, 72
San Francisco Bay Area, 138, 149–50,
    153, 158, 160, 161
San Francisco (Teamsters) Local *85*, 87
Santoro, Felix, 50–51, 262
Savage, Red, 72
Scabs, 158, 208; 1970 wildcat, 142–46,
    147, 164
Scott, Vance, 144–45, 146, 150, 155, 163,
    174–75
Secondary boycott, 19, 20, 60, 264
Seniority, 50, 65, 251–52; in mergers,
    65–66, 120, 196–97
Sexton, Patricia Cayo, and Brendan
    Sexton: *Blue Collars and Hard Hats*, 1
Shagging, 49
Sheridan, Walter, 87*n*
Singer, Mike, 72, 82–85
Sitdowns, 16
Slowdowns, 48, 69, 101, 147, 183, 190,
    229
Smith, Ray, 49, 113, 144; in 1970
    wildcat, 145, 163–64
Social clubs, 44, 65, 90
Social conflict: theory re, 247–51. *See
    also* Activism, Class conflict,
    Militancy, Social movements,
    Strategy, Worker mobilization
Social legislation, 31
Social movement(s), 3, 5, 6, 253, 258;
    working-class, 255–56, 268, 274–75
Socialism, 247, 250, 275; in TDU, 257
Socialist revolution, 238
Socialists, 9–10, 15, 229

Solidarity, 22, 23, 43, 53, 187–88, 231,
    265; craft unions and, 260*n*; effect of
    legalism on, 199; Local 208, 100; in
    1970 wildcat, 146–47; in TDC, 214.
    See also Trust
Solidarity (Poland), 275
Southern California, 130
Southern California Teamster
    (newspaper), 5, 9, 146
Southern California Teamster Joint
    Council *42*, 32, 72–73, 87, 107, 198;
    civil rights board, 77; in 1970 wildcat,
    138, 149; opposed Local 208's militant
    unionism, 106, 107; opposition to
    legalism in, 200–5; supported Hoffa,
    81, 108; Williams's candidacy for
    presidency of, 193–95, 201–5, 207,
    214, 269, 270
Speedup, 4, 16, 17, 222
Spotters, 252, 260
Standoff(s), 197–98, 262–63
Stealing, 112
Steelhaulers, steelhauling, 141*n*, 215,
    226, 227, 228, 240; wildcat, 1979,
    209–10, 243
Steel industry, 271
"Steelworkers Fight Back," 269
Steelworkers Union, 7, 14, 272
Steuben, John: *Strike Strategy*, 156–58
Stewards, 34–35, 53, 70, 71, 72, 92, 199,
    223; black, 114; as disciplinarians,
    15–16; elected, 69, 70, 71; fight over
    (Local 208), 62–63; and grievance
    handling, 21, 39; in 1970 wildcat, 154,
    162–65; as organizers (Local 208),
    97–98; training of, 98; under
    trusteeship (Local 208), 179, 182
Stewards' Council, 41–42, 70, 71, 74, 80,
    82–83, 92, 97, 103–4, 240; opposition
    to legalism in, 205, 206; watered down,
    195
Steward system (Local 208), 74–75, 90,
    102–3, 190
Stone, Kathy, 259, 260
Strategic discussion, 51, 55, 141*n*,
    194–95, 199, 245–46, 270; failure to
    develop, 103–4; Local 208, 40–42

Strategic planning: by large companies, 122–23
Strategy, 2, 54, 59, 97, 255, 256, 257; lack of, for winning 1970 wildcat, 157–58, 159–60, 164–65; of outreach, 272–73; and rank-and-file organization, 222, 223–24, 244–47
Strike benefits, 19
Strike committee, 1970 wildcat, 140–42, 144, 146, 148, 149, 150–52, 153, 157, 183; and weaknesses of strike, 162–65
Strike, right to, 4, 236, 237
Strikers, 143; 1970 wildcat, 148–49, 155, 166–67
Strikes, 14, 17, 19, 23, 29, 93–94, 101, 192, 275; Detroit, 218; and growth of large companies, 118; and labor law, 18–19; Los Angeles TDU and, 220; during MFA negotiations, 123; national, 135, 212; potential disruptive power of, 264; sanctioned, 95, 132, 142; secondary, 123, 147; Teamsters, 59–60, 126–27; TDC and, 214; WesCar, 99; World War II, 16. *See also* Twenty-four-hour wildcat
Strike Strategy (Steuben), 156–58
Student activists, 6, 7, 154; in 1970 wildcat, 138–39, 140, 153–54, 158, 160, 161, 167, 169
Supervision, 4, 48; drivers' freedom from, 50, 51, 53, 105
Sweetheart deals, 104–5, 127, 128
System, individual and, 265–67, 268–69

Tactics, 2, 83, 85–88, 190, 256; in fighting 208 trusteeship, 178–88; in 1970 wildcat, 147–50. *See also* Strategy
Taft-Hartley Act, 16, 19, 69, 147
TDC. *See* Teamsters for a Decent Contract
TDU. *See* Teamsters for a Democratic Union
Teachers, 3
Teamsters for a Decent Contract (TDC), 9, 70, 86*n*, 88, 211–15, 216, 222, 223,

224, 225, 248, 257; Maheras's reaction to, 238–39
Teamsters for a Democratic Union (TDU), 2, 6, 9, 10, 14, 43, 197, 209, 246, 249, 254, 256, 264, 268, 269, 271; achievement and potential of, 241–43; basis for, 273; building support for, 226, 227–30; comparison of three regions of, 216–21; and craft unions, 260*n*; electoral victories, 226, 234–35; essence of, 275; formed, 214, 215; growth of, in 208, 267; history of, 210–16; in Los Angeles, 216, 219–21, 224, 258; meaning of, for Local 208, 238–40; membership, 215, 230; milieu and, 256–57; potential role of, 265; problems faced by, 226–38; social context of, 221–26; and socialist consciousness, 252; Steel Haulers Organizing Committee, 209*n*; as vehicle of outreach, 245
Teamsters International Committee for *500 at 50*, 184, 185
Teamsters' Opportunity Program, 144
Teamsters Union (International Brotherhood of Teamsters, Chauffeurs, Warehousemen, and Helpers of America [IBT]), 2–5, 59–60, 90, 222; attempts to democratize, 184, 226 (*see also* Teamsters for a Democratic Union); autonomy in, 124–25; changes in, 10, 116–35; constitution, 4, 31–32, 85, 132–33, 236; efforts to reform from within, 234, 238, 239, 240; Executive Board, 172; government attacks on, 71–72, 123–24; intervention in Local 208's organization, 81–89, 100, 106–11; metropolitan joint councils, 127; opposition movements in, 271; pro-employer actions, 4–5, 40; refusal to recognize TDU, 233; reorganization of, into centralized bureaucracy, 17, 116, 128–29, 241; reshaped after 1934 strikes, 14–15; secession threats, 87, 130; Special Convention, 85, 87; structural crisis in, 124–27; TDU as loyal opposition in, 231, 232–34;

Teamsters Union (*Cont.*)
threatened by growth of large
companies, 117–18, 120, 124;
weakening of, 241–42, 264. *See also*
Bureaucracy; Corruption; Officials
Teamsters Union Convention, 32, 110*n*,
132–33, 172; *1966*, 114; *1976*, 214–15,
225; *1981*, 218; Special, 85, 87
Teamsters Local *70*, 87, 153
Teamsters Local *85*, 87
Teamsters Local *208*, 2, 14, 17, 21, 25,
32, 34–44, 119, 224–25; business
agents, 28 (*see also* Business agents);
bylaws, 41, 71, 74–76, 80–81, 85, 86,
88, 102–3, 104, 105, 236; in context of
Teamsters Union, 2–5; democracy in,
13; and disappearance of Hoffa,
134–35; elections, 37, 71–73, 78–80,
85, 86–89, 99, 174; Executive Board,
72, 80, 88–89, 99, 109, 187; failure of,
to defend workers, 60–62; fighting
trusteeship, 172–74, 177–88; under
Filipoff, 60–69; history of, 5–6;
Hoffa's alliance with, 32, 81–89, 90,
107–10, 127–28, 130–31, 133, 198, 254,
273; isolation of, 110, 198, 238, 240,
274; lack of outreach by, 108–10,
152–53, 166, 173–74, 184, 190, 198,
245; meaning of TDU for, 238–40;
meanings of, 43–44, 244–45;
membership, 5, 8, 34, 59; in 1970
wildcat, 139, 140, 141, 158–59; officers
of, 41, 42, 161–65 (*see also* Stewards;
Strike committee); opposition to
Maheras, 200–8; post trusteeship,
189–208, 246; rank-and-file rebellion,
59–91; reasons for difference of,
253–55; sanctioned 1970 wildcat, 139,
142, 158–59, 162; Secretary-Treasurer,
35, 37; in trusteeship, 6, 10, 32, 36, 43,
165–66, 168, 169–88, 198, 249; strikes,
83, 93–94, 197. *See also* Wildcat
strike, 1970
Teamsters Union Local *224*, 34
Teamsters Union Local *299*, 217, 218
Teamsters Union Local *337*, 217–18
Teamsters Union Local *357*, 34, 260
Teamsters Union Local *436*, 171

Teamsters Union Local *495*, 34
Teamsters Union Local *598*, 109
Teamsters Union Long Beach Local *692*,
152, 224
Teamsters Union Local *804*, 171–72
Teamsters Union Local *853*, 86*n*
Teamsters United Rank-and-File
(TURF), 174, 182, 183, 184–86, 205,
206, 269; compared with TDU, 223–24
Technology, 120, 259, 260–61
Terminals, 121, 196; numbers of, 117,
118T, 119
Terrazas, Mauricio, 60–61
Tobin, Daniel J., 93, 125
Toledo Auto-Lite, 18
Transportation industries: organized
crime in, 124; strategic importance of,
264–65
Triscaro, "Babe," 171
Truck drivers, 45–55; control of, by
management, 260–62; isolation of,
51–52; nonunion, 228, 264;
personalism of, 52; problems of,
49–51; social relations of, 45; strategic
position of, 263–65; work routine of,
45–48
Truck driving, 3, 44, 45–55; and activist
unionism, 105–6; as leading indicator
of class conflict, 256; as milieu for
organizing militant unionism, 53–55
Trucking companies, 92, 139, 196–97;
employees of, 116–17, 118T; large,
116–20, 124; large/small split, 221–22;
running scab (1970 wildcat), 142–46,
147
Trucking industry, 53–54, 253; change in,
100, 116–35; deregulation of, 135, 222,
233, 241; racism in, 67, 111–14
Trust, 22–23, 52; in TDC, 214
Trusteeship, 4, 101, 240; Local 208 in, 6,
10, 32, 36, 43, 165–66, 168, 169–88,
198, 249; theory and practice of,
170–72; threat of, 107, 110, 142, 159,
190
TURF. *See* Teamsters United Rank-and-
File
Twenty-four-hour strike(s), 21, 83,
93–94, 164, 173, 197; right to, 161

Twenty-four-hour strike clause, 107, 138, 166, 168; loss of, 184, 187, 190
208 News (newsletter), 72

Union forms: democratization of, 236–37
Unionism, activist, 98, 100, 101–2, 105, 106, 115, 132, 188; cynicism re, 96–97; driving as milieu for, 53–55; grievance procedure as tool to punish, 192; racism and, 111–14
Unionism: bureaucratic, 13–33; business, 14, 30–32, 198, 232, 275; contractual, 13, 20–21; democratic, 109; effect of drivers' milieu on, 51–52; honest but nonactivist, 6, 10; rank-and-file, 93–100; workers' approach to, 40–41
Unions, 14–18; become grievance-processing machines, 13, 21; bureaucratic tendency of, 100–2, 124, 250–51; in business unionism, 30–31, 32; defending workers basic responsibility of, 60, 250–51; loss of power in multinational corporations, 264; myths re, 1–2; political role of, 31; view of, in legalism, 199–200; workers' ability to disrupt production is basis of, 21
United Auto Workers (UAW), 14, 17. *See also* Autoworkers.
United Farmworkers Union, 3, 202, 252, 274
United Mine Workers, 171, 236, 237; rank-and-file movement in, 256. *See also* Coal Miners
United National Caucus, 258
United Parcel Service (UPS), 9, 118–19, 126n, 216; strike against, 171–72
United States: labor laws, 13, 18–20, 101, 123; social crisis in, 273–74. *See also* Economic conditions
U.S. Congress: hearings, union corruption, 2, 71–72; labor legislation, 16, 123
U.S. Department of Health, Education, and Welfare: *Work in America*, 1
U.S. Department of Justice, 81, 129–30
U.S. government, 19, 231; attacks on

Hoffa, Teamsters Union, 81, 108, 123–24, 127, 128, 129–30, 133, 134
U.S. Secretary of Labor, 20
Unity, 78–79; need for, 125–26
UPSurge, 9, 86n, 216n

Valdez, Carlos, 187, 202, 203
Violence, 60; in 1970 wildcat, 137, 144, 147–48

Wage Control Board, 17, 27n
Wages, 32, 50, 59, 120–21, 254
Wagner Act, 18–19
Walkouts, 69
Warehousing, 3
Weber, Max, 249
WesCar. *See* Western Carloading (co.)
West Coast Longshoremen, 18, 60
Western Carloading (co.), 107, 140, 153, 177; organization of, 98–100
Western Conference of Teamsters, 32, 81, 107, 108, 125, 138
Western Freight Agreement, 87, 130
Western Gillette, 113, 145, 146
Western Truck (co.), 200
"Whipsawing," 4, 64, 120, 131, 132
Wildcat strike, *1970*, 6, 7, 17, 54, 97, 104, 111, 123, 135, 136–38, 191, 198, 208, 210, 223, 248, 258, 270; amnesty demand, 138, 139, 142, 151–52, 153, 158, 161, 165; Blackmarr and, 266; causes of, 165–66; cliques in, 157, 162–65; companies allowed to operate, 150–51, 163; defeat of, 183; organization in, 140–42 (*see also* Strike committee, 1970 wildcat); success/failure of, 154–65. *See also* Firings
Wildcat strikes, 21, 108, 183, 240, 269; World War II, 16. *See also* Twenty-four-hour strike(s)
Williams, John T., 23, 61–62, 67, 72, 85–86, 107, 108, 109, 110n, 135; appointed Health and Welfare Coordinator, 82; as BA, 187; elected hall steward, 68; leader in Black Caucus, 77; on Local 208 bylaws, 76; on Maheras, 238–39; platform, Secretary-Treasurer candidacy, 71; on

Williams, John T., (*Cont.*)
    racism, 111, 112, 113–14; ran for
    president of Joint Council, 193–95,
    201–5, 207, 214, 269, 270; on
    Steward's Council, 103; on trusteeship,
    173, 174
Williams, Roy, 149–50, 152, 161, 275
Wives, involvement of, 219; in 1970
    wildcat, 155–57
Wolfinsohn, Dave, 228–29, 230
Word processing, 261
Women Teamsters, 146–47, 156
Woodcock, Leonard, 24
Work in America (U.S. Dept. of HEW),
    1
Work degradation, 261–62
Worker mobilization: dynamics and
    effect of, 251–73. *See also* Rank-and-
    file organization; Unionism, activist
Worker opposition movements, 269–72.
    See also Activists; Unionism, activist
Workers: ability of, to resist, 14, 230,
    262; approach to unionism, 40–41;
    control of, through division of labor,
    259, 260; division of, 259–63; interests
    of, conflict with those of management
    and bureaucracy, 28–29, 251–52;

myths, stereotypes re, 1; not protected
    by officials, 4–5; potential of, 2, 236;
    power of union is in, 248, 250–51; role
    of, in business unionism, 31–32;
    skilled, and labor aristocracy, 257–59;
    struggles of, 197, 234, 268; time
    worked, 252. *See also* Activists; Rank
    and file
Working class, 272; social movements
    by, 255–56, 268, 274–75. *See also*
    Class conflict
Working conditions, 5, 17, 28, 29, 250;
    Local 208, 37–38, 47–48, 59, 60–62,
    94, 100; WesCar, 98–99
Working day, 252
Workplace, 245, 268–69, 272; politics of,
    259; rank-and-file organization at,
    64–69, 187–88. *See also* Barn
    organization
Work process, 259–63; *see* ch. 3
Work rules, 15, 92, 105, 135, 252, 262;
    Local *208*, 102; standardized in
    mergers, 120
World War II, 15–16

Yard (term), 10
Yellow Freight (co.), 118